VAMPIRES IN THE NEW WORLD

LOUIS H. PALMER

 PRAEGER

AN IMPRINT OF ABC-CLIO, LLC
Santa Barbara, California • Denver, Colorado • Oxford, England

Library of Congress Cataloging-in-Publication Data

Palmer, Louis H.
  Vampires in the new world / Louis H. Palmer.
      p. cm.
  Includes bibliographical references and index.
  ISBN 978-0-313-39133-0 (hardcopy : alk. paper) —
ISBN 978-0-313-39134-7 (ebook)   1. Vampires—United States—
History.   2. Vampires in literature.   3. Vampires in motion pictures.
4. Vampires in popular culture.   I. Title.
  GR830.V3P35   2013
  398.21—dc23   2012045403

ISBN: 978-0-313-39133-0
EISBN: 978-0-313-39134-7

17 16 15 14 13   1 2 3 4 5

This book is also available on the World Wide Web as an eBook.
Visit www.abc-clio.com for details.

Praeger
An Imprint of ABC-CLIO, LLC

ABC-CLIO, LLC
130 Cremona Drive, P.O. Box 1911
Santa Barbara, California 93116-1911

This book is printed on acid-free paper ∞

Manufactured in the United States of America

Contents

Acknowledgments   v

Introduction: Taking Vampires Seriously   vii

1   Vampire Scholarship   1

2   *Dracula's* American   9

3   Early New World Vampires   17

4   Vamps in Hollywood   27

5   Blood and Pulp   33

6   Class-ic Horror   41

7   Urban Legends   49

8   Hammering It Home   57

9   Countering Vampire Culture   63

10   Black Vampires   69

11   Vampire Celebrities   77

12   Blood Consumers   87

13   Buffy Rules   99

14   Vampires for Children   107

15   White Trash and Teen Melodrama   121

16   Vampire Comedy   131

Afterword: Where Do We Go from Here?	143
Selected Chronological Filmography	149
Bibliography	163
Index	169

Acknowledgments

I would like to thank my colleagues in the English department at Castleton State College, Vermont—Andy Alexander, Chris Boettcher, John Gillen, Flo Keyes, Denny Shramek, Drennan Spitzer, and Joyce Thomas—for their support and encouragement concerning my peculiar interests. I want to acknowledge many years of brilliant presentations in the Gothic area at the annual Popular Culture Association conference, which I have the honor of chairing, and I want especially to acknowledge my fellow chairs in the Welcome to My Nightmare group: Carl Cederholm, Mary Findley, Jim Iaccino, Phil Simpson, and Kristopher Woofter. Thanks to James Sherman at ABC-CLIO for his thorough and patient editing. Finally, for her unflagging and energetic support and advocacy, I would like to thank my partner, Phoebe Jackson.

INTRODUCTION

Taking Vampires Seriously

My first encounter with a vampire scarred me for many years, but I survived. When I was seven years old, I saw *Abbott and Costello Meet Frankenstein*, a comedy from 1948, which marks, for many, the last gasp of Universal's famous run of monster movies. In it, an aging Bela Lugosi appears as Dracula, who, along with the Frankenstein monster (Glenn Strange) and the Wolf Man (Lon Chaney, Jr.) chase Bud Abbott and Lou Costello, shrieking, around an island with a castle on it. Dracula turns into a bat by spreading his cape, initiating a brief cartoon animation as a transition, then flapping off as a very unconvincing rubber puppet bat. It doesn't seem very scary now, but at the time I found it quite alarming. I saw it on a black-and-white TV, in the afternoon on a Saturday, at a relative's house, and I was terrified. Of the various monsters in the film, Lugosi's Dracula was the scariest. I decided that I didn't like monster movies, and I pretty much avoided horror films for 30 years after that. I cannot account rationally for why such a silly film struck fear into my young heart, but my memory of it gives me an insight into the power of such images, even after they have been diluted by overexposure in a media-saturated culture.

All the messages I had received from that culture, it seems to me today, told me not to take vampires seriously, especially the grandfatherly Lugosi. Popular music, TV cartoons, dolls and plastic models, Halloween costumes, eventually even sugar-bomb breakfast cereals—all treated the vampire as harmless. When I was in primary school, we would chase each other around with makeshift capes, intoning, "I vant to suck your blaad!" in imitation of Lugosi's thick Hungarian accent. It was all good fun, yet somehow seeing the film really scared me, causing me to be fearful for years. This isn't a therapy session, so I will leave behind my childhood trauma with the observation that there was something in that figure that, even in a comic film on the small screen, reached deep into my psyche and shocked something there. This is one of the reasons I take vampires seriously.

There are many others. I started my graduate studies in English in the 1990s, at a time when English departments were being accused of colonizing a variety of other disciplines. It was at the point where critical theory, which applied a variety of methodologies to the analysis of "texts," was expanding into cultural studies. I place "texts" in quotation marks to highlight the fact that anything was considered to be fair game for such analysis, not just accepted works from literature. This kind of study applied obviously to film and television, but could also be applied to any kind of cultural products, from popular songs to styles of dress to sports to the behaviors of groups of fans. The application of serious consideration to objects of study that had been considered transitory and unimportant opened up vast new continents of knowledge to explore, as well as a variety of methods to use for such exploration. Cultural studies has allowed scholars to think about aspects of popular culture that have a peculiar historical persistence, figures that change shape and shift in meaning but do not seem to go away, such as the vampire.

This book looks at the history of vampires in America. In it, I trace the vampire as one of those persistent cultural figures, primarily as it appears in books, films, and television shows. I have planned this survey to be representative rather than comprehensive—any one decade could easily fill a much longer book, and I am covering the period from the publication of Stoker's *Dracula* in 1897 to the present time, 2012, a span of more than 11 decades. I have chosen to focus on what I consider to be the major trends in the development of this figure, a development that is not straightforward or unified, but that has many branches and that often turns back to its roots. In the course of writing, I have made decisions and chosen points of focus based on my own background and interests, with which other readers, scholars, and aficionados may very well not agree. I must by necessity have left out many novels, stories, films, and television treatments of this ubiquitous monster. To those who feel that I have slighted significant works in this way, let me apologize in advance, and encourage you to write about what I have not. As the American novelist Cormac McCarthy says, "The ugly fact is books are made out of books" (McCarthy 1993, 31), and I would prefer for this one to spawn a numerous progeny, loving or hostile, rather than to molder away, unread.

Specifically, I have focused on mainstream vampires as represented in fiction and fiction films, excluding a variety of creatures, from the space alien in John Carpenter's *The Thing* (1982) and its progenitors in the science fiction films of the 1950s to the role players and true believers in today's vampire subcultures. I have not been a total purist, and so have included some psychic vampires, especially where there is some question, such as in Leiber's "The Girl with the Hungry Eyes" (which I included to illustrate the figure's appearance in noir fictions), in my treatment of the vamp figure in films, and in my consideration of the New England type of vampire who emerges from curative folklore practices.

In addition to growing up in a vampire-infested popular culture, I developed an interest in vampires through my readings in gothic literature. The gothic is a broad and disputed territory, but most accounts put its origins in 18th-century British literature, starting with a group of authors interested in the antiquarian past. "Gothic" was a term that referred to the medieval period, but with connotations of "barbaric" and "primitive" that reached back, past the historical period we refer to today as Gothic in art and architecture (1100–1400 CE). The term leads us back to the much earlier Germanic tribe, the Goths, who were part of the sacking of Rome. This term, especially as it was used in the 18th century, has connotations that include uncivilized, violent, irrational, and superstitious.

Gothic novels begin with Horace Walpole's odd supernatural story, *The Castle of Otranto* (1764), first published with an introduction that claimed that it was a translation from a medieval Italian manuscript. The story involves an ancestral castle, a prophecy and curse, and a variety of conflicts around the marriage and legitimacy of the real and presumed heirs to the kingdom of Otranto. The action begins with the current (and wrongful) heir being crushed by a huge helmet that appears out of nowhere and falls on him. By the end, the proper heir is revealed and married to the appropriate woman, and rightful succession is assured. According to his preface to a later edition, where he admits authorship, Walpole writes that he had invented the story as,

> an attempt to blend the two kinds of romance, the ancient and the modern. In the former all was imagination and improbability: in the latter, nature is always intended to be, and sometimes has been, copied with success. Invention has not been wanting; but the great resources of fancy have been dammed up, by a strict adherence to common life. (Walpole 1966, 21)

This blending of the past/fantastic and the present/realistic became the basis of gothic fiction, which experienced a heyday from the date of Walpole's publication in the 1820s, and has given its name and some of its characteristics to many subsequent fictions.

Scholars have traditionally divided gothic novels from the Classic period into two groups. One strand, associated with the novels of Ann Radcliffe, is known as the explained or female gothic, where mysterious occurrences are found to have rational explanations. Supernatural or male gothic is associated with the works of Matthew Gregory Lewis, and tends to have plots or events that can only have a supernatural explanation. The female/male distinction is a long-standing tradition, one rendered problematic both by the facts—both genders wrote both kinds—and by changing understanding of the meanings of gender. Explained gothic stories have the gothic machinery of an exotic setting and a mysterious castle or house, where supernatural or magical occurrences seem to happen, and they usually have a young woman protagonist threatened by a sinister older man. There is usually some question of legacy or inheritance. The novels conclude with a rational or naturalistic explanation that accounts for the otherworldly events. For example, in Radcliffe's *The Romance of the Forest* (1791), a young woman, Adeline, hears eerie sounds and voices calling her name at night in an old abbey where she has been trying to decipher an ancient manuscript. She discovers the next day that the sounds were the voice of a concerned servant, distorted by the acoustics of the old structure. Other writers of this type of novel were Regina Maria Roche and Eliza Parsons.

As in Walpole's story, the male or supernatural gothic tale tends to have events that can only be explained as supernatural. Matthew Gregory Lewis's *The Monk* (1797), influenced by European folktales, has a central character who is a brutal rapist and murderer as well as a Catholic monk. After many crimes, he sells his soul to the devil in order to escape the tortures of the Inquisition. Lucifer saves him, and then casts him off a cliff. He lies in pain for six days before suffering eternal damnation. Virulently anti-Catholic, the novel takes for granted the existence of supernatural beings, the effectiveness of witchcraft, and the existence of ghosts. This type of gothic romance owes more to the fantastic that Walpole associated with the past than with the more realistic, present-time treatment of writers like Radcliffe. Other writers in this category were Charles Maturin who wrote *Melmoth the Wanderer* (1820) and Charlotte Dacre, the author of *Zofloya, or, The Moor* (1806).

Regardless of subcategories, gothic fiction puts a special emphasis on the setting, generally in the form of a house or castle, often isolated and often in an exotic place. The past, in the form of a legacy, a curse or a ghostly presence, haunts this central house, often giving it the agency and status of a character. Add to this a young protagonist, usually a woman, and an older antagonist, often a male relative, and you have the basic ingredients. Questions of hidden or multiple identity, insanity, mysterious documents, hints of incest, episodes of prison or confinement, and fears of violence, rape, and murder fill out the mix. These elements provide a lot of room for variety, and many different writers, both popular and literary, have tried their hand at writing them. During the period of the gothic novel's popularity, questions were raised about whether they were corrupting the morals of young people, especially young women, and they were widely criticized and parodied by more sensible writers. Jane Austen, for example, in *Northanger Abbey* (begun in 1798, eventually published 1817), portrays a young woman, Catherine Morey, in the grip of so many gothic novel-inspired fears and fantasies that she misses the obvious social cues by which she must live. The villain, General Tilley, first invites her to stay at his house, Northanger Abbey—which turns out to be a comfortable country house, not a half-ruined castle—then abruptly kicks her out, refusing to let her marry his son. Catherine had imagined that he acted out of guilt and villainy, suspecting that he must have murdered his former wife, but it turns out that his behavior is explained by the fact that he has been receiving contradictory accounts of her family's social and financial status. His worst villainy was that he suspected that she was out to take advantage of his son. As in Jane Austen's other works, all is, eventually, resolved with a suitable marriage.

The decline of the gothic novel in its first iteration saw the birth of the literary vampire. Vampires and similar creatures already existed in many of the world's folklores. In central Europe, they appeared as zombie-like revenants who preyed on family members, a far cry from today's evening-clad aristocrats. Interest on the part of Romantic-era writers and scholars, influenced by German material, brought the vampire into literary stories, most famously in the anecdote of the ghost story contest that led to the writing of *Frankenstein*. During a rainy summer stay on the shore of Lake Geneva in 1816, Mary Shelley, her future husband Percy Shelley, Lord Byron, and his physician and friend John Polidori took to reading German ghost stories to each other for amusement. As Mary Shelley tells it,

> "We will each write a ghost story," said Lord Byron; and his proposition was acceded to. There were four of us. The noble author

began a tale, a fragment of which he printed at the end of his poem of Mazeppa. Shelley, more apt to embody ideas and sentiments in the radiance of brilliant imagery, commenced one founded on the experiences of his early life. Poor Polidori had some terrible idea about a skull-headed lady, who was so punished for peeping through a key-hole—what to see I forget—something very shocking and wrong of course; but when she was reduced to a worse condition than the renowned Tom of Coventry, he did not know what to do with her, and was obliged to despatch her to the tomb of the Capulets, the only place for which she was fitted. The illustrious poets also, annoyed by the platitude of prose, speedily relinquished the uncongenial task. (Shelley 1982, 225)

Seventeen-year-old Mary Shelley began writing *Frankenstein, Or the Modern Prometheus*, which was published anonymously two years later. The stories which Byron and Polidori eventually published were vampire stories, both involving a gentlemanly figure who preyed on his lovers—Polidori's was named Lord Ruthven, which had also been a *nom de clef* for Byron in a novel, *Glenarvon* (1816), written by his former lover, Lady Caroline Lamb.

Polidori's story, *The Vampyre*, was attributed to Byron when it was originally published in 1819, and created a vampire craze in Europe which produced other vampire stories, along with plays and operas. Byron, denying authorship, published what little he had written as "A Fragment" at the end, as Shelley says above, of his poem "Mazeppa." In it, the narrator's traveling companion, Augustus Darvell, dies and is buried in Turkey, but makes Aubry, the narrator, swear that he will tell no one about the death. As in Polidori's version, he was allegedly going to appear later in London, but Byron wrote no more. Polidori's story was so similar to Byron's (including the eastern setting, the death and burial, and the vow) that he has been accused of stealing Byron's idea. In Polidori's story, Aubrey, bound to silence by his vow, suspects and finally confirms that Ruthven, a very Byronic aristocrat, is a threat. He discovers too late that his own sister is dead. The story ends melodramatically: "Lord Ruthven had disappeared, and Aubrey's sister had glutted the thirst of a VAMPYRE!" (Polidori 1966, 283). Both Byron's and Polidori's characters were, apparently, resurrected dead people, and did, apparently, feed on humans, but they were not nocturnal or fanged or sensitive to crucifixes—such attributes would be added later.

The next fictional vampire to appear was in the novel *Varney the Vampyre: Or, The Feast of Blood*, published in 1845–1847. This was an extensive serial (220 chapters, 828 pages), one of those publications known as "penny dreadfuls" because episodes sold for a penny. It is variously attributed to James Malcolm Rhymer or Thomas Prescott Prest. Like later vampires, Varney is an aristocrat, has fangs, has preternatural strength, and sports a cape. He can turn others into vampires, but has no aversions to crosses or garlic or daylight. He is the first sympathetic vampire, conflicted because he hates his condition, and he eventually chooses to end his life without a chance of resurrection by jumping into the crater of Mount Vesuvius. By no means a literary masterpiece, indeed rather inconsistent and self-contradictory, this novel is an interesting record of how vampires were imagined at the time, as well as an important influence on what came later, especially on later vampire stories with ongoing serial plots.

Sheridan LeFanu, an Anglo-Irish writer, published *Carmilla* in 1872. This novella presents the story of a female vampire who is eventually dispatched by means of a stake through the heart. Set in Styria, an Austrian province, *Carmilla* introduces a vaguely lesbian theme, with the vampire appearing as a young woman who focuses her attention on other young women. She also appears as a cat and has the ability to walk through doors, both traits which Bram Stoker will adapt to fit his vampire, Count Dracula.

In some ways, vampires fit well into a gothic paradigm. They exist in a kind of border country between life and death, the real and the supernatural. Their contradictory nature—being both alive and dead, human and supernatural, person and beast, material and immaterial—helps to augment the twists and turns of a gothic plot. An immortal, who preys upon humans, must necessarily assume false identities and live in isolation, and being the owner of an ancient estate makes sense, since the vampire inherits from itself. Most 19th-century vampires are aristocrats and metaphorically reflect modern ideas about feudal aristocracies—that the overlords preyed on the life blood of common folk. Vampires lead especially confined lives, closed in by darkness, by death, by blood-hunger, as well as by coffins and boxes of native soil. This theme of confinement works effectively within the gothic model of the decaying castle, as does the theme of the haunting presence of the past, the return of the repressed. And vampire stories occupy a middle territory between the explained and the supernatural gothic forms—once audiences accept the idea of the vampire's undead nature, the story can take place in a very realistic, modern setting. Stoker's *Dracula* (1897), the first modern vampire novel, takes great pains to highlight its modernity, using an epistolary form created using all of the most up-to-date communications technologies: typewriting, wax cylinder recording, shorthand documentation, and carbon-paper reproduction. These apparatuses serve to document and ground a story about a surviving medieval leader from the Carpathian mountains who walks the streets of contemporary London. And it is with Stoker's use of an American character that literary vampires come into the New World, although, as we shall see, they already had a foothold in New England folklore.

CHAPTER 1

Vampire Scholarship

And, contrary to the old legends that tell us that vampires have no reflection, we do indeed see many diverse reflections—of ourselves—as the vampire stands before us cloaked in metaphor. Indeed, it is the rich metaphorical usefulness of the vampire which, we believe, helps us to explain its continuing "undeath" in contemporary popular culture, its powerful grip on our imaginations.
—Joan Gordon and Veronica Hollinger,
Blood Read (1997, 3)

In this chapter, I want to make a distinction between the varieties of scholarship I will refer to in other parts of the book and what you might call pure vampire scholarship, which focuses on vampires, per se, not as Hollywood effects or folklore revenants, or even literary figures, but as themselves. This is part of taking vampires seriously—being able to write about them and the meanings we give them in a more general sense. You could call these works the beginnings of the vampire theory.

The founding vampire book is *Vampires: Their Kith and Kin* (1928, now in print as *Vampires and Vampirism*), followed by *The Vampire in Europe* (1929), both by British occultist Montague Summers. A controversial figure, Reverend Summers was apparently ordained in the Anglican Church, but later converted to Catholicism and claimed, perhaps illegitimately, to be a Catholic priest. He is the author of several important books on the Gothic tradition, on Restoration drama, and on witches, werewolves, and vampires. He translated the notorious *Malleus Maleficarum* (1487), the guide for hunting witches used by the Inquisition in the 15th century. He preserved an attitude of disapproving belief in the existence of the supernatural creatures that he wrote about, and he wrote in an exaggerated, ornate, somewhat archaic style that has proved to be very influential for later writers of vampire fiction. Summers is remembered from various stints as a teacher and as a jovial, witty man with eccentric habits of dress, such as capes, and a hairstyle that resembled an 18th-century wig.

The book looks at the various European folk beliefs about vampirism, and then surveys world beliefs. The final chapter is on literary vampires. Summers starts by acknowledging that "the very vague definition and indeterminate interpretation one is able to give to vampirism from a purely literary point of view" makes, even in 1928, for a huge field of inquiry, so that "[a] consideration of the vampire theme in literature must of necessity be somewhat eclectic, if not even arbitrary" (Summers 1928, 271). His survey looks at the usual Romantic and Victorian sources, but pays special attention to theatrical versions, even mentioning Bela Lugosi's performance as Count Dracula in the American opening of the British play, *Dracula,* in 1927. His conclusion, in French, suggests that the vampire is most universal of our superstitions, and has the authority of a tradition that surpasses that of philosophy and medicine and is only equal to that of theology. Summers's belief in both the reality and the evil of vampires allows him to make such a claim, one that is echoed by the claims of believers today.

It was many years before someone else would treat vampires as a subject for serious study. Master vampire bibliographer Margaret Carter's seminal (sanguinal?) anthology, *Dracula: The Vampire and the Critics* (1988), brings together some thirty years of work, dating back to a 1956 article by Bacil Kirtley about the folklore sources, but mostly written in the 1970s and 1980s, when new models in gender criticism served to resurrect interest in the novel and in the vampire figure in general. Essays in this collection focus on Eastern European expansionism, female sexuality, the New Woman, and homosexuality as threats associated with Stoker's *Dracula*. Others look at sources that include Stoker's childhood experiences, Vlad Tepes, Countess Elizabeth Bathory, and the criminal theories of Lombroso. The essays include a variety of approaches to interpretation that include psychoanalysis, Marxism, and feminism.

Another anthology of essays, Joan Gordon and Veronica Hollinger's *Blood Read* (1997), provides a rich variety of more recent perspectives on vampires in general. Subtitled *The Vampire as Metaphor in Contemporary Culture*, this collection is divided into four sections, treating, respectively, the history of the figure, a section on specific writers, one specifically on the metaphor of consumption, and one on vampire identity. Its emphasis on culture allows for essays on specific aspects of the vampire, focusing on race and gender, as well as international sources such as Japanese manga dealing with vampires.

Nina Auerbach, who contributed an essay to *Blood Read*, has written what seems to be accepted as the definitive cultural history of vampires for the 1990s. *Our Vampires, Ourselves* (1995) gives us a survey of the vampire figure from Byron to the mid-1990s. Her approach is based on a cultural studies paradigm. As the title suggests, she focuses on vampires as positive, transgressive alternatives to the various forces of conformity and uniformity that mainstream culture presses upon us. She sees the 19th-century vampire as imagined by the Romantics and their heirs as a model for friendship and affinity, affirming both homosocial and suggested homosexual bonds between them and their human prey. Coleridge's "Christabel" and LeFanu's *Carmilla* show similar patterns of attraction between female characters. This model persists through the 19th century, to be broken by Stoker's Dracula, for whom isolation is paramount and whose affinities are more for animals than for other humans. *Dracula*, written in the wake of the Oscar Wilde trial, also initiates a period of compulsory vampire heterosexuality that will not be broken until Anne Rice's bisexual vampires emerge in the 1970s.

Auerbach reads Bela Lugosi's Dracula as an anachronistic throwback to the pre-Stoker homosocial vampire, who seems to be more interested in Dwight Frye's natty Renfield than in the rather dull women he finds in England. The story dramatizes the concerns of the Depression era in its focus on Van Helsing as an expert, who, like the architects of the New Deal, solves the problem of Dracula with the efficiency of a scientist. To Auerbach, the Hammer films demonstrate a weakening of patriarchal structures, which is proven by the increasing relish with which female characters express their desires. By the 1970s, which Auerbach describes as leaderless but "full of promise" (Auerbach 1995, 165), the vampire comes into his own, escaping at the end of Badham's *Dracula* (1979) into a world that is more welcoming than hostile.

In Auerbach's politically tinged perspective, the conservative backlash of the 1980s gives us vampires who are "constricted in their potential, their aspirations, and their effect on mortals" (Auerbach 1995, 165). She sees this as a reaffirmation and reestablishment of patriarchal power after the more open-ended and varied approaches of the 1960s and 1970s. Vampires are weaker and more vulnerable in these depictions, and the focus is more on the family as a threatened unit. Both *Near Dark* (1987) and *The Lost Boys* (1987) have this family focus, contrasting good with bad families, but not looking beyond to the larger realms of national identity or political power. Since Auerbach, no one can claim that vampires have no political affiliation.

Although Franco Moretti's *Signs Taken for Wonders* (1983) is not a book exclusively about vampires, his Marxist approach has been very influential to scholars who wish to argue that vampire stories in particular, and horror literature in general, is not simply a radically conservative way to reinforce bourgeois values through fear of unforeseen threats and consequences. Marx himself famously claimed that "Capital is dead labor, which, vampire-like, only lives by sucking living labor, and lives the more, the more labor it sucks" (Marx 1976, 342). I briefly refer to Moretti in this chapter 2, relating to the way he collapses Quincey Morris into Dracula, accusing the American of vampirism. This is part of a larger argument that envisions the vampire as symbolic of pure, monopoly, capital. Unobstructed by law or custom, Dracula *is* vampire capital, obscenely reproducing itself while feasting on the lifeblood of those who are powerless to affect it. In contrast, the Crew of Light, funded by the old-fashioned landed economy represented by Lord Godalming, freely (and collectively) spends capital in the service of the national good. Their capitalism is impure and nonmonopolistic, and therefore retains some connection, however tenuous, to the world of those who produce wealth. Moretti's reading of the novel as an economic allegory seems to stretch a bit thin in places, but has had a fertile effect on subsequent socially based scholarship.

Ken Gelder's *Reading the Vampire* (1994), which I refer to in Chapter 7, takes a hybrid Marxist and psychoanalytic approach that looks at the figure of the vampire through the lenses of both international relations and identity formation. He pairs vampire texts with specific locales—Dracula and Transylvania, certainly, but also the Greece of Byron's and Polidori's tales, and the effect of the fall of Ceausescu on Romanian vampire narratives. Expanding the contradictory structure of familiar/uncanny (or homelike/unhomelike) from Freud's essay "The Uncanny," Gelder demonstrates the ways in which the vampire is simultaneously in and outside of culture, as foreigner, ethnic other, sexual queer, and rebellious youth. He examines how the stories exhibit a variety of management practices from the Victorian era to the present-day, generational strategies to deal with the familiar threat of the monster that emerges from within to disrupt our ideas of the normal and the accepted.

David Skal has mapped out the terrain of historical inquiry into film vampires, delving into the emergence and development of the horror film in general in *The Monster Show* (1993), tracing the onstage and cinematic forms of Dracula in *Hollywood Gothic* (2004), and, with Elias Savada, documenting the life and career of the director of Universal Studio's 1931 *Dracula*, Tod Browning, in *Dark Carnival* (1995). In *The Monster Show*, Skal uses American culture's fascination with horror to illustrate literary critic Leslie Fiedler's contention that underneath the sunny and optimistic exterior, American culture teems with stories that emphasize the negative, dark fantasies that rely on gothic and melodramatic effects, such as evil twins, sadistic villains, grotesque mutilations, and claustrophobic confinements. Skal focuses on four figures—the vampire, the freak, the double, and the reanimated corpse—to illustrate his thesis. In the early chapters, and in *Dark Carnival*, his emphasis is on the peculiar figure of Tod Browning, an upper middle-class Midwesterner who really did run away to join the carnival, performing as a singer, tap dancer, spieler, blackface minstrel, trick rider, contortionist, and escape artist. His most significant act, according to Skal, was a performance that went on for two years as a living corpse, where he was actually buried for 24 hours—48 on one occasion—in a coffin under six feet of soil. Browning went on to become one of Hollywood's most successful directors of silent melodrama and horror films, working with Lon Chaney on such films as *The Unholy Three* (1925) and *London after Midnight* (1927), in which Chaney played a detective disguised as a vampire. The success of *Dracula* (1931) allowed Browning to make what some consider to be the ultimate horror film, *Freaks* (1932), employing actual circus freaks in a revenge drama. The film shocked audiences to such an extent that it was pulled from the theaters. Because of his emergence from carnival and vaudeville into horror film, as well as his strange obsessions with cruelty, orality, and the grotesque, the mysterious Browning becomes the quintessential horror auteur for Skal, dramatizing the corrupt heart beating in the center of the American corpus.

In *Hollywood Gothic*, Skal focuses on the various staged and screen versions of Stoker's *Dracula*, from a tedious recitation of the novel staged by Stoker to secure dramatic rights, through his widow's legal fight to ban the unauthorized *Nosferatu* (1922), to the successful (and sanctioned) drawing room version by Deane and Balderston that played on Broadway and provided the impetus and the star for Browning's film. Any contemporary treatment of the film, including mine in Chapter 5, is indebted to Skal's careful and wide-ranging scholarship.

Recently, Skal published a scrapbook-style picture book on vampires that provides a rich visual portrait of the creature, especially in the 20th century. *Romancing the Vampire: From Past to Present* (2009) provides not only photographs and movie posters, but also facsimile maps, theater tickets, newspaper clippings, and many other items of interest, all explained by Skal, with an introduction by Auerbach. As I mentioned in the introduction, this is a rich visual supplement to any study of vampires.

James Twitchell, in *The Living Dead* (1981), which is subtitled *A Study of the Vampire in Romantic Literature*, goes beyond the Romantic period as such and displays a preference for highbrow literature, but still gives us a detailed analysis of vampire stories in the 19th century, primarily in England. Much of his focus is, refreshingly, on poetry, and he incorporates some of the insights of feminist criticism in his analysis of differently gendered monsters. Using a broadly inclusive definition of vampire, Twitchell characterizes the vampire as one of the important, indeed defining, mythic figures of the Romantic era. He begins with a cogent summary of the vampire's folkloric and literary antecedents, and concludes with English novelist D. H. Lawrence's early 20th-century versions—Lawrence famously claimed that all love is vampiric. For Twitchell, the vampire myth degenerates until it becomes "gothic stuffing" (Twitchell 1981, 193) for films and "hack" writers. Perhaps, it would be fairer to suggest that the Romantic vampire dies in the 20th century, at least in the earlier part—Twitchell mentions Anne Rice using the vampire to "portray the forces of . . . decadence." But this book is written before the resurgence of Romantic-inflected vampires in Rice's later books and those of many others.

Milly Williamson's *The Lure of the Vampire* (2005) begins where many vampire studies begin, with a defense: "The vampire offers a way of inhabiting difference with pride, for embracing defiantly an identity that the world at large sees as 'other'" (Williamson 2005, 1). She has chosen to examine the sympathetic vampire through the lens of gender, and this focus gives us a revised history, going back to the Byronic sources and tracing the figure to the present day, where she focuses on fan culture, a fascinating outgrowth of the popularity of Rice's books and the *Buffy* series (the study predates *Twilight*). Her examination of fan culture in England and the United States is an important contribution, and provides a way to link vampire fiction, both written and visual, with the performative aspects of the Goth and vampire subcultures, where vampire becomes a temporary or permanent identity. Fans occupy a middle ground here, and Williamson gives us insight into their world, into the distinctions between official fans, whose status comes by way of their participation in organized societies, such as Rice's "Anne Rice Vampire Lestat Fan Club," which is apparently the only fan club endorsed by Rice and unofficial fans who do not participate in such organizations or the events they organize. Rice is fairly unique in that she positions herself both as a recipient of fandom as author—in Chapter 10, I mention her litigious attitude toward fan-generated fiction—and as a fan herself of her own characters. As in any social groups or organizations, fan relationships involve a complex web of hierarchies and relationships, which Williamson gives us access to through interviews with various insiders and outsiders. She also devotes a chapter to the practice of dressing up as a vampire, and explores the meanings that participants give to and derive from such practices. Williamson's study also looks at the other ways in which the various "new media" have affected attitudes toward the vampire figure, such as in slash fiction and online fan stories where characters from the fan source have relationships with each other, usually sexual, and mostly same-sex. Williamson's study takes on the ways in which our literary and cinematic vampires have expanded (bled?) into roles and identities that range far beyond the confines of their textual origins.

In Matthew Beresford's *From Demons to Dracula: The Creation of the Modern Vampire Myth* (2008), we find an emphasis on cultural geography that complements and supplements Williamson's ethnographic approach. Beresford looks at the various sources (pre-Christian and medieval beliefs and practices, the historical figure of Vlad Tepes) and sites (Transylvania, Whitby, Highgate Cemetery) that have developed and taken on lives of their own with the stories of the vampire, especially in the wake of Stoker's *Dracula*.

Margaret Carter is not only an editor (see above), bibliographer and critic, but also a vampire novelist on her own (e.g., *Dark Changeling*, 1999). In *Different Blood: The Vampire as Alien* (2004), she explores an important subset of the vampire world—vampires as aliens. Broadly defined so as to include, for example, the bloodsucking aliens in H. G. Wells's *The War of the Worlds* (1898), Carter's study also includes psychic vampires and others in the realm of science fiction and fantasy that are often neglected in more literary takes on the vampire. This study is an important enhancement to our understanding of the variety of vampiric beings.

With the success of the forensic crime procedural on television, one is not surprised to see some forensic studies of the vampire. In *The Science of Vampires* (2002), Katherine Ramsland explores the various ways in which decaying corpses can be mistaken for the blood-engorged undead—not exactly new information about the various ways in which decay or premature burial could account for various vampire symptoms.

She specifies the connections between consumption and other wasting diseases and various beliefs about vampiric relatives. The study looks at theories about ESP and hypnotism as well, but the most interesting part of the book is where Ramsland demonstrates how vampirism could occur through a viral agent that modifies DNA, creating a new life-form from the inside out. She also investigates the types of psychological disorder that might make someone believe that they need to drink blood or to kill to live.

In a study more focused on forensic findings than speculation, Mark Collins Jenkins's *Vampire Forensics* (2010) looks at findings from all over the world. A very readable introduction to literary vampires leads to a broadening consideration of the folklore and legendary sources all over the world, organized so as to expand out from England, to Europe, to the rest of the world. He demonstrates how various diseases, including consumption, cholera, hydrophobia (rabies), and porphyria, might cause people to exhibit the various physical, sexual, and behavioral symptoms associated with vampirism in its various forms.

Mary Hallab's *The Vampire God* (2010) is an intellectual breath of fresh air. Her lucid no-nonsense writing style reflects her ability to cut to the heart of whatever question she is considering. This perspective works well for her emphasis on religious, philosophical, and metaphysical questions raised by the vampire figure. She covers old ground—folklore, the Romantics, Varney, Stoker, Summers, and the multiplicity of film and fictional vampires we now deal with—but brings a relentless intelligence and curiosity to the task, bringing out new insights that her predecessors seem to have overlooked without resorting to the contortions that some arguments seem to catch themselves up in. Starting with basic questions like "What does it mean to be living dead?" and "What is the significance of blood?," she leads us into the larger questions of good and evil, fate and free will, animal and human, living and dead, and she explores, with reference to a dizzyingly comprehensive field of texts, the implications of those ideas for the strange, contradictory, yet persistent figure of the Western vampire.

Religion, for Hallab, is not the limiting term that it can be, especially in the current political climate, but a lens that allows her to look not only at links with the Christian liturgy, with its vampiric drinking of the blood of the god, its undead savior, and so forth, but also at Old Testament, pagan and classical links to the nature religions that probably hold the original germ from which vampires have developed.

CHAPTER 2

Dracula's American

I heard once of an American who so defined faith; "that which enables us to believe things which we know to be untrue." For one, I follow that man.

—Professor Van Helsing (Stoker 2002, 202)

The title of this chapter, "*Dracula's* American," could be interpreted two ways. It could be seen as a contraction for "Dracula is American" or it could refer to *Dracula's* American—the American character in *Dracula* the novel. Although I will focus primarily on the second meaning, I wanted to point out the first, because Stoker's *Dracula* has, in many ways, become American. The American film industry is primarily responsible for taking a central European character invented by an Irish novelist writing in England and making out of this international mixture a figure who is now recognized around the world. For many people, the name Dracula and the term vampire are synonyms, referring to a suave, masterful, and predatory creature wearing a cape, who drinks blood, has hypnotic powers, and can transform into animals and mist. He also has the ability to reproduce by transforming human victims into vampires. We all know as well that he is an animated dead person.

Stoker's novel is the source of this present incarnation of a figure from folklore that was originally closer to what we now think of as a zombie, a night-walking corpse who preyed mostly on family members. Today, we remember Bram Stoker as the author of *Dracula*. However, in his day, Abraham Stoker would have been known by his contemporaries, if he were known at all, as the manager and biographer for a much more famous person, Henry Irving. Irving was a celebrity, a London theater owner, who was also one of the most prominent actors of the time. He was the first person from that profession to be honored by knighthood, by the hand of Queen Victoria. It is ironic that, just more than a century later, neither the famous actor nor his amanuensis is as well-known as the fictional character that Stoker created. The undead Count Dracula has truly taken on a life of his own.

Literary criticism has been slow to pick up on the significance of Stoker's *Dracula*, but popular culture has run with it. Much of the earliest critical work was investigation of sources, literary detective work, such as Raymond McNally and Radu Florescu's discovery that the title "Dracula" (literally meaning "son of the dragon") comes from the family of Vlad the Impaler, a Wallachian warrior prince, who fought against the Ottoman Empire in the late 15th century. Recent evidence from Stoker's manuscript indicates that he changed the character's name from Count Wampyr to Count Dracula, and may have had the historical Dracula in mind for his character.

Stoker's group of vampire fighters, referred to as the Band of Light, includes four representative British members—Dr. John Seward, Jonathan Harker, Mina Murray (later Harker), and Arthur Holmwood (later Lord Godalming). The two foreigners in the group are the Dutch Professor Van Helsing and Quincey Morris, an American millionaire cowboy. Of the two non-British members, Van Helsing's continental background makes sense because he provides insider knowledge of both Catholicism and European folklore, and because European universities led the world at this time. But Morris seems an altogether odd choice, as well as an unlikely one—how many cowboys, even fictional ones, are millionaires? I hope to show that Morris serves several purposes in Stoker's novel. Primarily, he provides a strong, positive alternative to the attenuated and overcivilized British characters. Although the novel certainly dramatizes the threat from the outsider that many English people felt during the *fin de siècle* era, it also works with contemporary fears of a threat from within. Mina, who provides much of the narrative glue in the story by organizing the various documentary materials, identifies Dracula with the ". . . criminal type. Nordau and Lombroso would so classify him" (Stoker 2002, 336). Max Nordau was the author of *Degeneration* (in German, *Entartung*, 1892), a widely discussed sociological study that argued that the art and culture of *fin de siècle* European society both reflects and contributes to a continuing social and moral disintegration. Cesare Lombroso was an Italian criminologist who used Social Darwinist theories to link criminal types to racial atavism. In his view, criminals could be identified by physical traits, including cranial measurements, which serve to link them to more primitive human forms—criminals are portrayed as evolutionary throwbacks.

We can assume from Mina's comments that Stoker was familiar with such theories of degeneration-from-within. If the imperial center is rotten, the necessity of incorporating allies outside the traditional male, Protestant, British establishment becomes obvious. As exemplified by Morris, Van Helsing, and Mina herself, these allies represent the strength, knowledge, courage, organizing skill, and perseverance needed to track down and defeat the menace—qualities that are not exactly lacking, but seem to be insufficient in the English members of the group. Morris can be seen as embodying a balancing principle, a strong man from the new lands to the West whose presence serves to balance the forces in the fight against the ancient warrior figure from the old, degenerate East.

If scholars were slow to pick up on the significance of this novel at first, they have made up for it by a huge volume of work in the last 30 years. One recent trend in scholarship has been to look at Stoker's Irishness as an influential factor in a novel that has no Irish character or setting. Gregory Castle has argued that Stoker's position as a member of the Protestant Ascendancy class, at a time when Irish nationalism was on the rise, put him (and his class in general) in a pinched position, between the largely Catholic Irish population, who wanted nothing to do with their former Protestant landlords, and the British, who were increasingly unenthusiastic in support for a formerly English population that they no longer found useful. Ascendancy Protestants were losing place in Ireland to a rising Irish Catholic middle class. Following a centuries-long tradition of being landed gentry, they had a reputation for being at worst exploitative and oppressive and at best incompetent, often absent, landlords. Urbanization, modernization, and the demands of a market economy had not worked in their favor, and British policy was tending toward granting the troublesome colony some sort of autonomy, if not outright independence.

Castle notes that a characteristic of Ascendency writers at the turn of the century was subject matter that tends toward the mystical and the fantastic rather than the realistic. Lady Augusta Gregory and William Butler Yeats are probably the most well-known members of this class, especially in the early Celtic Twilight phase of the Irish cultural revival. This took place in the 1890s, just when Stoker was writing *Dracula*, a fantastic novel, in London. To summarize, we have a member of a declining colonial elite (Stoker) living in the central city of the empire (London) and writing a novel about a threat of invasion to that city by a supernaturally powered and reproductively potent aristocrat from an even older empire.

To look at Irish issues in *Dracula* is necessarily to infer them, since the novel does not use Irish settings or characters. If we imagine the novel's American is a stand-in for the Irish, certain things make sense. Quincey Morris speaks in a dialect (which, like a well-assimilated colonial subject, he can turn on and off), plays the fool, acts impulsively (often with violence), and embodies a popular stereotype—the cowboy. In these ways, he can be seen as a sort of stage American, sharing many qualities with the stage Irishman of the time, a stock character with which Stoker, as an Irish theater manager in England, must have been painfully familiar. Perhaps Morris is a parody of this character. He is of British stock, changed by hundreds of years of living in another country, like the Protestant Irish. However, America seems to have avoided the taint of degeneracy that many saw in both the Irish Ascendancy and the British homeland. Although Morris shares traits and behaviors with the Irish Catholic majority, he is still of English racial stock. Like the pure Irish from the western counties, whom *fin de siècle* Ascendancy writers idealized, he is direct, straightforward, and a man of action; but he has the added advantage of being able to fit into the cosmopolitan culture of the London group. As Mina's friend Lucy describes him,

> He is really well educated and has exquisite manners—but he found out that it amused me to hear him talk American slang, and wherever I was present, and there was no one to be shocked, he said such funny things. I am afraid, my dear, he must have to invent it all. (Stoker 2002, 79)

As an amusement, Morris performs American slang, even invents it, yet he still fits in as a gentleman.

If Stoker is writing a fantastic novel that comments, consciously or unconsciously, on the contemporary world situation, what does America represent? Stoker's class of educated Protestant Irish had never fully integrated into their adopted country; yet, in the same historical period, Americans had no such problem integrating into their new country, possibly because they were more ruthless toward the native population. As a British colony, and then as an independent nation, the United States managed to thrive by assimilation—granted, with a few glitches, such as chattel slavery. By the 1890s, when Stoker was writing *Dracula*, the United States was beginning to flex its own imperial muscles.

To someone in Stoker's position, the United States would have been perceived as both an imitator of and a competitor for British imperial power.

Stoker's travels, his previous writing and his international circle of acquaintances provided him with some specific models for a character like Morris. In the course of several American tours with Irving's acting company, Stoker had time to observe the United States first hand. In *A Glimpse of America* (1886), he published an expanded version of a lecture he had given on his impressions of the country, to which he added more material in *Personal Reminiscences of Henry Irving* (1906), a biography of his former employer, and *Snowbound: The Record of a Theatrical Touring Party* (1908). Before *Dracula*, he had published a romance novel set in the American West, *Shoulder of Shasta* (1885), in which a British heiress, Esee, falls in love with an American frontier guide, Grizzly Dick, but is disappointed and eventually ends up with another British tourist. We see then that Stoker had prototypes in previous writings for a character such as Quincey Morris. He also had real-life models. During his tours and in London, he had occasion to meet many prominent Americans of the period, including three men who could be described as millionaire cowboys.

Although Theodore Roosevelt would not participate in the storming of San Juan Hill until the year after *Dracula* was published, he had coined the term "Rough Riders" in 1886. This is the term he would use for his cowboy-themed volunteer cavalry unit (Roosevelt 1970, 23). More than a decade before *Dracula's* publication, in 1885, Stoker had met Roosevelt when the future U.S. President was president of the board of police commissioners for New York City. At Roosevelt's invitation, Stoker had attended a judicial review with him, and had been so impressed that he noted in his diary, "Must be President some day. A man you can't cajole, can't frighten, can't buy" (*Irving II* 2007, 236). Roosevelt's famous emphasis on the strenuous life, and his reputation as a man of action as well as conscience, would have appealed to Stoker, who was a fitness aficionado.

Clive Leatherdale suggests another possible, earlier, model for Morris— the famous Texan Jim Bowie, for whom Morris's weapon of choice, the Bowie knife, is named.

> Both Morris and Bowie were adventurers. Both were hunters who relished entertaining massive odds. Despite their frontier ethos both were urbane, polished, and rich. (Leatherdale 2001, 127)

Bowie can account for the fact that Morris is a Texan, rather than from another Western state. An early list of characters for *Dracula* from Stoker's notes show us "A Texan—Brutus M. Matrix" as one of the original characters; so Quincey Morris was a Texan before Stoker settled on his name. As Leatherdale points out, post-Confederate, pre-oil Texas would not have been seen as an obvious choice for Morris's origin without its association with folk heroes, such as Bowie and Davy Crockett.

Perhaps the most obvious model for the Morris character was the man who became a worldwide celebrity by promoting stories and figures from the frontier West, William "Buffalo Bill" Cody, who had brought his Wild West Show to London in 1887. While in London, Cody had formed a mutually advantageous friendship with Henry Irving, Stoker's employer. Louis Warren has examined this relationship and its influence on Stoker's writing in some detail. He concludes that both Quincey Morris and the earlier Grizzly Dick have telling resemblances to Cody, and that Stoker's attitude, gleaned from a reading of the *Shoulder of Shasta*, seems to be that, despite the frontier's promise of freedom, "the frontier was best left alone and frontiersmen best left out there" (Warren 2002, 1137). Warren looks at the international conflicts dramatized in *Dracula* in terms of the racialist (race-based) conception of history popular at that time, which attributed detailed racial traits to cultural groups (e.g., members of the Anglo-Saxon race were seen as both fierce warriors and competent administrators) and tended to portray history as the process of domination of inferior races by superior ones. This kind of thinking provided justification for the British domination of India—the reclaiming of an Indo-European racial fatherland—as well as for the extermination of Native Americans, as Roosevelt argues in his contemporaneous history, *The Winning of the West* (four volumes, 1889–1896). This kind of racial perspective also obscures possible instances of class conflict by emphasizing racial conflict. As Roosevelt claimed in an angry letter to Denis Donahue, "If you had any conception of the true American spirit, you would know that we do not have 'classes' at all on this side of the water" (Roosevelt 1970, 23). For Roosevelt, character trumps class, and character consists of race, at least in part. This is where Stoker finds common ground, and why *Dracula* needs an American.

If we see *Dracula's* band of vampire fighters as representatives of an Anglo-Saxon race united against the threat that Dracula offers to the blood of England, we can see how they represent a cross section of the

Anglo-Saxon world of the 1890s. Jonathan Harker and Mina Murray/ Harker represent the professional –middle classes, with Mina standing in for the new, more independent women within that group. Professor Abraham Van Helsing represents both the learning and the lore of the mostly Catholic European continent, without the taint of Southern European corruption. Dr. John Seward, asylum director, is a man of science, especially the emerging science of psychology. Arthur Holmwood (later Lord Godalming) represents the British ruling classes. That leaves Quincey Morris, the American, to stand for the new Anglo-Saxon nation, representing the wealth, the bravery, and the innocence of the New World. As Seward opines,

> What a fine fellow Quincey is! I believe in my heart of hearts that he suffered as much about Lucy's death as any of us, but he bore himself through it like a moral Viking. If America can go on breeding men like that she will be a power in the world indeed. (Stoker 2002, 184)

The key word here is "Viking," linking him to the Anglo-Saxon warrior past and breeding, which suggests both hope for a purer racial future and fears about European degeneration and about Dracula's progeny.

Some critics fault Morris for his incompetence—for example, endangering the others by shooting at a bat from outside the room they are in—as well as for being the least-developed character of the band. As the person who introduces the word vampire (Stoker 2002, 164—in reference to the South American bat), and as the final transfusion donor before Lucy dies, Franco Moretti has even suggested that he is himself a vampire (Moretti 1988, 95). I find better evidence to suggest that he is, quite simply, less inhibited and less conflicted than the British characters, a warrior in the old Anglo-Saxon vein, the only one fit to go *mano-a-mano* with the ancient warrior from Transylvania. He is the only one of the young people who shows no weakness or hesitation. Van Helsing describes him as "a brave man . . . and no mistake" (Stoker 2002, 162). We have to remember that Dracula's most deadly foes prove to be Van Helsing for his knowledge, Mina Harker for her organizational skills and later for her telepathic connection and Morris for his bravery. Without these three outsiders, two foreigners and a woman, the Englishmen would be helpless against the threat. Even though the Band of Light's strength comes from their collective skills, the novel emphasizes that the key actors in saving England are not the Englishmen. However, the ones who survive are, significantly, the British core. Morris's pure blood and heroic skills make him valuable, but his American origin makes him expendable.

I want to recap what America, and the American, might have meant to Stoker. The New World could be seen as a more successful Ascendancy, a British settlement uncontaminated by the incompetence and bad blood that characterized the long history of English-Irish relations. It could be a source for fresh blood and old-fashioned heroism untainted by European degeneracy. Morris himself can be seen as a reckless fool who rushes in where the more cautious hold back, or as a Christ-like innocent who sacrifices himself for the good of the group. What he certainly does provide is a third outsider, along with Mina the New Woman and Van Helsing the wise foreigner, to strengthen the ranks and assure the survival of the attenuated British.

CHAPTER 3

Early New World Vampires

Vampire lore, in New England, is a regional variant of a worldwide tradition, with particularly close ties to European practices. Once we remove Dracula's shadow, we can see, lurking in the folkloric countryside, a host of supernatural creatures.
—Michael Bell, *Food for the Dead* (2001, 233)

Oddly, at the same time that Stoker was writing his story about Count Dracula's thwarted invasion of Britain, there was a vampire outbreak of sorts in the tiny New England state of Rhode Island. According to a contemporary account in a Providence newspaper, the bodies of three members of the Brown family, who lived in Exeter and had all died the previous year from consumption, were exhumed and examined for signs of life. This seems to have especially involved an examination of the heart. The heart of the most recently dead, 23-year-old Mercy Brown, was found to contain fresh-looking blood, and so it was burned along with her liver, and quite possibly fed to her brother Edwin Brown, who was suffering from the same disease. Folklorist Michael Bell, who describes his investigations of these stories in his book *Food for the Dead* (2001), found that there were other similar instances nearby and in other parts of New England, going back to the Revolutionary War era.

Another folklorist, Paul Barber, makes a clarification about the collection of vampire stories:

Most of the confusion about the vampire lore came about because it was filtered through the minds of people who had no way of knowing what their unwarranted assumptions were. Told that vampires were dead people who left their graves at night and assailed the living, they didn't ask for clarification. And their sources didn't know that clarification was needed. So although you can certainly find stories in which it is assumed that the vampire attacks as a physical body, whenever outsiders watched corpses being exhumed and listened to the accounts of people who declared these to be vampires, they were never told that the vampire took his body along when he left his grave. The best evidence is clear on this matter: the bodies stayed in the grave. (Barber 2010, vi)

So, when we look at vampires of folklore, we need to be careful not to confuse them with literary vampires, who at the turn of the 20th century have a century-long tradition of their own. The New England vampire did not share many characteristics with the vampire we know today, who is very much the vampire of literature as interpreted through the medium of cinema.

Unlike the Central European vampire, who also could be said to have arrived in the United States through English sources, most notably Stoker's *Dracula*, the New England version is associated with tuberculosis, commonly called consumption, and tends to prey on family members from the grave, using potentially psychic means. The deceased person seems to be able to draw the life force from relatives, without leaving the grave physically, afflicting them in a serial manner, one after another. Once the body is exhumed, this type of vampirism is demonstrated by fresh blood in the corpse's heart. A cure is secured by removing the heart and, in some cases, the liver and/or lungs, and burning the organ or organs. In some cases, the ashes produced would be consumed as a medicine, and in others, the smoke from the burning would be used therapeutically to bathe potential victims. In Mercy Brown's case, the heart was burned on a nearby rock, still pointed out to visitors to this day. In a case reported from Woodstock, Vermont, the suspected vampire's heart was burned in an iron kettle, which was then buried under a seven-ton slab of rock in the town square. Practices such as these seem to be designed to avoid the bodily emergence of the revenant. In some cases, the whole body was burned. The more well-known vampire cure of beheading was also apparently used. A man's grave excavated in Rhode Island, with the initials JB spelled out in nails on the coffin lid, was found to have the skull and the long bones of the legs arranged in a skull and crossbones fashion across the middle of the body, with the grave lined with slabs of rock. These measures were taken some time after the first burial of the body, presumably to impede the corpse from walking out. The clear distinction that we make today between superstition (or magic) and medicine was not at all clear in earlier times. As Bell suggests:

> Both vampires and germs are simultaneously tangible and intangible. The tangible parasite is so small as to be invisible to the naked eye, just as the parasitic vampire moves unseen among its living victims. Did the killer live within, laboring around the clock to destroy its host, consuming the lungs, eating away flesh, leaving behind a rotting mess and bright red blood, all froth and foam? Or did the killer live without, visiting his prey at night to feed on flesh and blood? (Bell 2001, 233)

Both vampires and germs create physical symptoms that seem to be caused invisibly, both in the corpses and in the victims. In his forensic analysis, *Vampires, Burial and Death* (2010), Paul Barber has pointed out that many of the physical attributes of the vampire-corpse—flushing, blood at the mouth, swelling so as to look well-fed—can be traced to the effects of the process of decomposition.

Bell has discovered some 16 separate instances of potentially vampire-related events or practices across New England, dating from the Revolutionary War era to the late 19th century. None of them have the attributes of what he calls "pop-culture" vampires, who are descended from (or at least related to) Stoker's *Dracula* or its predecessors. The New England vampires give us an alternative folk source for some of the vampires we will encounter in the United States in the 20th century and beyond. Bell notes that the primary accounts almost never have the word "vampire" attached to them. It tends to be secondary accounts, mainly newspaper articles, which use the word. These articles also tend to take a civilization versus savagery perspective that looks down on their sources as unsophisticated, isolated, and ignorant people, in much the same way as television shows like *Swamp People* continue to portray Southern rural people in contemporary society. These kinds of sensationalist practices continue in media accounts of the New England vampire material today. As Bell puts it:

> Television interviews and newspaper feature writers seek out individuals . . . who are willing to express a belief in vampires. Although they are usually outsiders who hold fringe views (in relation to expressed convictions of long-time community residents), their interpretations are portrayed by the media as typical or representative

of the community's prevailing beliefs. Based on the examples I've gleaned from recent newspaper and television treatments, as well as my own direct experiences, I can only conclude that the media do not want to hear, indeed will not listen to, perhaps *cannot* hear, views that are not compatible with the popular conception of a vampire as exemplified by the Dracula of film. (Bell 2001, 288)

Bell finds that accounts from community informants tend to emphasize a skeptical perspective. Such a perspective rationalizes unusual actions, such as exhumation and cremation, as attempts to appease distraught family members or to try traditional remedies. Such accounts tend to avoid expressions of wholesale belief on the informant's parts or on that of their forbears. In Bell's view, such behaviors as the choice to exhume a family member are complex in motivation and have been negotiated within the context of family and community relationships. They are the results of reasoned choice and, in some cases, of accepted medical practices, rather than of ignorance and superstition. Media reports, from the newspaper accounts of the 1890s to the documentary television programs of today, tend to run right past such nuances in the service of sensational claims. Literary accounts fill in some middle ground, often using such events, beliefs, and practices for their own purposes, which may be sensational, to create an effect, but which may also have a character-driven, thematic, or symbolic purpose.

New England-style vampires are described in several fictional accounts from the 19th century. The most well-known is Edgar Allan Poe's "Ligeia," the story of a woman with a will so strong that she takes over the body of her husband's second wife. Although it is set in European locales, the story fits in with the idea of the vampire as found in New England, specifically Rhode Island, where Poe lived for part of his adult life. Like Mercy Brown and others, such a vampire is represented here as a psychic agent draining the life from someone, resulting in consumptive symptoms. The story is told by one of Poe's typically unreliable narrators. He introduces Ligeia as his deceased first wife, but claims to not be able to remember where or when they met or what her family name was. He acknowledges also that he has become "a bounden slave in the trammels of opium" (Poe 1991, 7), which gives us further reason to doubt him. He describes Ligeia as superior to him in all ways, including learning and languages: "I was sufficiently aware of her infinite supremacy to resign myself, with a child-like confidence, to her guidance through the chaotic world of metaphysical investigation" (Poe 1991, 4). While she is dying, like many of Poe's heroines, she exhibits the pallor and fever of the victim of consumption: "[t]he wild eyes blazed with a too—too glorious effulgence; the pale fingers became of the transparent waxen hue of the grave, and the blue veins upon the lofty forehead swelled and sank impetuously" (Poe 1991, 5). As she is dying, she quotes Glanvill as to the power of the will: "Man doth not yield him to the angels, nor unto death utterly, save only through the weakness of his feeble will" (Poe 1991, 7). The narrator, apparently enriched by Ligeia's fortune, moves to an abbey in a distant part of England and marries a woman, Rowena, who is blue-eyed and blond, a stark contrast to the raven-haired and dark-eyed Ligeia. True to the pattern, she also sickens and dies, but on her last night the narrator thinks that he sees a shadow in the room, and perceives "three or four large drops of a brilliant and ruby colored fluid" (Poe 1991, 10) to fall out of the air into her goblet of wine. After she dies, he watches as she seems to reanimate several times, finally standing up and unwrapping her hair. It is "blacker than the raven wings of the midnight" (Poe 1991, 13), and the story concludes with the narrator shrieking that he sees her as "the LADY LIGEIA!" (Poe 1991, 13). As the story ends with these words we do not know if this is a drug-induced delusion or not.

Various elements fit this story to both the New England tradition, where a person's influence after death can continue to drain the life from the living, and with the European vampire tradition where an immortal being survives the grave, enthralls or hypnotizes others, and multiplies her kind through blood transmission. The narrator's inability to remember their time and place of meeting, her vast store of knowledge, and the drops of ruby fluid might all point to such an interpretation. Poe, as in many of his stories, leaves such questions open, and the conclusion is ambiguous. The story is designed for the effect.

A New England writer from the generation after Poe, with a very different style, Henry James, insinuated potentially gothic and supernatural themes into some of his tales of manners and social behavior. His short story, "The Friends of the Friends," also incorporates elements of the New England vampire tradition. In this story, told from the point of view of a female narrator, a man and a woman in the same social circle are each known to have experienced the phenomenon known as a "fetch." At the moment of his mother's and her father's death, each had seen the figure of the dying parent in the room with them, although they were many miles away at the time. Because of this curiosity, which is known to their friends, people have wanted the two to meet, but something always seems to come up, and they go for years without meeting. It becomes a kind of a running joke, how they seem to keep missing each other by coincidence, on numerous occasions. In the course of time, the narrator and the man get engaged. Because she is friends with both of them, she sets up a time for the two to meet at her place. Quite suddenly, in a fit of proprietary jealousy, she prevents the meeting by telling her fiancé not to come. Feeling guilty, she goes to apologize to the woman the next day, but finds that she has died during the night. Her husband-to-be tells her that the woman had come to visit him the night before in his room, but that they had not actually spoken and she left as quietly as she appeared. Working out the times, the narrator believes this to have been impossible, because her friend was at home before the time he saw her and she had died there quite suddenly.

The narrator tries to forget the incident and involve herself in her wedding preparations, but finds that she cannot. Finally, she confronts her fiancé:

> Let me then note very simply and briefly that a week before our wedding-day, three weeks after her death, I knew in all my fibres that I had something very serious to look in the face and that if I was to make the effort I must make it on the spot and before another hour should elapse. My unextinguished jealousy—that was the Medusamask. It hadn't died with her death, it had lividly survived, and it was fed by suspicions unspeakable. They would be unspeakable today, that is, if I hadn't felt the sharp need of uttering them at the time. This need took possession of me—to save me, as it seemed from my fate. (James 1922, 319)

She asks him to release her from the marriage, as "another person has come between us" (James 1922, 319). When he points out that that person is dead, she replies, "She's buried, but she's not dead. She's dead for the world—she's dead for me. But she's not dead for you . . . 'She comes to you as she came that evening,' I declared; 'having tried it she found she liked it!' " (James 1922, 321–322). After some further conversation, he asks her, "How on earth do you know such an awfully private thing?" (James 1922, 322). He attempts to convince her that he was just playing along with her delusion. "He challenged my sincerity, my sanity, almost my humanity, and that of course widened our breach and confirmed our rupture" (James 1922, 323). The story concludes:

> He never married, any more than I've done. When six years later, in solitude and silence, I heard of his death I hailed it as a direct contribution to my theory. It was sudden, it was never properly accounted for, it was surrounded by circumstances in which—for

oh I took them to pieces!—I distinctly read an intention, the mark of his own hidden hand. It was the result of a long necessity, of an unquenchable desire. To say exactly what I mean, it was a response to an irresistible call. (James 1922, 323)

James takes a phenomenon from folklore, the idea of the "fetch," and combines it with the concept of the revenant, in a somewhat less corporeal form than Ligeia did, to prey on a living person with whom she shares a kind of psychic sensitivity. In this case, the preying-on seems to be consensual, but the end result is the same as with the New England cases—eventually he goes to join the dead one, having driven the living one away.

Mary E. Wilkins Freeman was one of a number of regionalist writers who became popular in the last decades of the 19th century. During this period of urban and westward expansion, in a country newly connected by networks of railroads and the telegraph, nationally distributed magazines, such as *Colliers* and *The Atlantic*, published tales about the odd and unique customs of people in the remote corners of the country, including the Louisiana Cajuns and the mountain folk of the Appalachian South. These stories often used dialect and tended to stress regional peculiarities, although they were grounded in a realistic worldview. In New England, such writers as Freeman and her contemporaries Sarah Orne Jewett and Rose Terry Cooke wrote stories that emphasized the female-centered lives and communities found in the small towns of the remoter rural areas, where many of the men, especially young ones, had left for the opportunities that manufacturing towns and westward expansion had to offer.

In her 1903 story, "Louella Miller," Freeman manages to combine the psychic vampire figure from folklore with the revenant found in James and Poe. In this case, the vampire figure is not dead, but she causes everyone else to die. She apparently lives off and depletes their energies. The story is told from the perspective of a neighbor who lives across the street in a small New England village. Louella Miller is described as a small, pretty woman with blond hair and blue eyes, as "a beauty of a type rather unusual in New England." According to the neighbor, Lydia Anderson, "She had been a slight, pliant sort of creature, as ready with a strong yielding to fate and pliant as a willow." Mrs. Anderson remembers, "She used to sit in a way nobody else could if they sat up and studied a month of Sundays" and move with a grace that resembled "if one of them willows over there on the edge of the brook could start up and get its roots free of the ground, and move off, it would go just the way Louella Miller used to." (Freeman 2001, 262)

Such vegetative metaphors define Louella as different, but appealing. She is introduced and identified as an outsider, who, although she is not qualified, is brought in to teach the school. Immediately, people start dying around Louella—first, her helper, one of the older girls at school. Her next helper, a boy, took crazy after her marriage, but seems to have survived. She marries Erastus Miller, and he begins to decline "into consumption of the blood" (Freeman 2001, 263) almost immediately. Louella is already displaying her other prominent quality, idleness, which seems to be almost more shocking to the villagers than the deaths. After Erastus dies, his sister Lily moves in, then Aunt Abby Mixter. Both "do for" Louella as their own health declines, followed by death. At the point in the story where her Aunt Abby Mixter is caring for Louella and beginning to show symptoms, Aunt Abby's daughter accuses Louella of killing her and the others: "She told her that she'd killed her husband and anybody that had anythin' to do with her, and she'd thank her to leave her mother alone" (Freeman 2001, 264). Louella responds by going into hysterics, "laughin' and cryin' and goin' on as if she was the centre of all creation" (Freeman 2001, 265). Lydia Anderson sees the hysterics as manipulative, so she gives Louella a strong dose of valerian and puts her to bed. Aunt Abby dies soon after.

Two more deaths, Mariah Brown's and the young doctor's, follow. At this point, no one in town will have anything to do with Louella, who soon begins her own decline. Lydia Anderson does take pity on her on one occasion and brings some packages home for her, to be rewarded with a two-week-long illness. On the night when Louella dies, Mrs. Anderson swears she sees all the deceased ones escorting her out of the house. Years later, on a moonlit night, she suddenly runs across the street and dies in Louella's yard, the final victim. The story ends with the narrator describing the cellar hole where Louella's house used to stand: ". . . in summer a helpless trail of morning glories among the weeds, which might be considered emblematic of Louella herself" (Freeman 2001, 271).

It is an odd ending for a story about someone who has caused the death of at least six people, but Louella is consistently described as a parasite, as a sort of clinging vine that saps the strength of the host. Lydia Anderson seems to be as shocked by the fact that she does nothing for herself as she is by the fact that she is killing people. In a community where self-sufficiency, the Protestant work ethic, and emotional self-control are reigning values, Louella's dependency, laziness, and tendency to hysteria all mark her as monstrous and different. Whereas the vampires of European folklore are often connected with animals, Louella seems positively vegetative.

After the turn of the century, the predatory woman became distinctly sexualized, as we will see in the next chapter. Also, *Dracula's* influence started to be found in the folklore, as Bell points out when recounting a recent version of the Mercy Brown story told by an elderly descendent of the Brown family, Reuben Brown, who claimed in 1984 that all the people who died in his family had "a mark on their throat" (Bell 2001, 291). None of the original newspaper accounts of 1892, sensationalist as they were, happened to mention this detail, so it has probably been added in the century since, either deliberately or inadvertently, to make the story fit more with our perceived version of the vampire as a physical creature who bites necks.

Another example of how the two streams of vampire lore—the folkloric and the literary—have come together, is Edith Wharton's 1927 story, "Bewitched." Wharton set the story, like some of her other works, notably *Ethan Frome* (1911) and *Summer* (1917), in the western Massachusetts hill country near her summer home, The Mount, in Lenox. She also had spent time in Providence, Rhode Island, so it is quite possible she may have used details from the Rhode Island accounts. The story begins, as do some of the folklore accounts, with a meeting of prominent men from the community. The narrator, Orrin Bosworth, has been summoned to meet with Deacon Hibben and Sylvester Brand, a local farmer, at the house of another farmer, Saul Rutledge. They are brought in by Mrs. Rutledge, who is described in terms of her pale whiteness and colorless hair. She informs them that her husband has been meeting Mr. Brand's daughter in an old house by a nearby pond, and that he is bewitched. When Brand denies it, she tells him that it is not his living daughter that her husband is meeting, but his dead daughter, Ora. Saul Rutledge arrives and confirms the story, saying that the meetings had been going on for more than a year and that she had told him before she died that she would come for him. Saul is clearly in poor health, a "haggard wretch" who "looked like a drowned man" (Wharton 2001, 339) to Bosworth. The three men agree to go to the place of meeting at sunset the next day to see her for themselves, as Mrs. Rutledge claims that she has. On the way home, they stop at the abandoned house, seeing bare footprints in the snow. Brand goes in first and fires his pistol:

"They do walk, then," he said, and began to laugh. He bent his head to examine his weapon. "Better here than in the churchyard. They shan't dig her up *now*," he shouted out. The two men got him by the arms and Bosworth got the revolver away from him. (Wharton 2001, 349)

The next day, news comes out that Brand's other daughter is dying of pneumonia. She is buried three days later, and Mrs. Rutledge, at the funeral, tells Bosworth that her husband is better and suggests that Ora, too, will sleep better, "Maybe, now she don't lay there alone any longer" (Wharton 2001, 351).

The folklore vampire of New England who, from the privacy of her (or his) grave, draws the life out of family members, is here combined with a physical revenant who leaves bare footprints in the snow and is "drawing" a man to clandestine meetings, slowly sickening him. The cure, mentioned in relation to a past haunting, is to drive "a stake through her breast" (Wharton 2001, 343). This, like the mark on the neck in the later versions of the Mercy Brown story, seems to come from the type of vampire described in *Dracula*. We don't know to what extent Wharton might have used folklore sources, but we can see the influence of the literary vampire on the story—the traditional vampire stories in New England recommended removing and examining the heart, and if need be burning it, but not staking, which seems to be a practice designed, in part, for keeping the physical corpse in place.

Regardless of the ways in which authors deploy these figures, folklore is the ultimate source for them and will always preserve a tantalizing mystery. The folk record is necessarily incomplete, being made up of the beliefs and practices, over time, of a whole community. Our evidence is based on records that are always partial, and it is from these that we must infer the larger systems they might fit into, which are not only lost, but also dynamic, changing in response to cultural and historical forces.

CHAPTER 4

Vamps in Hollywood

> The sudden blossoming of vampire themes in the popular culture
> of the period after 1870 now reveals its own logical inevitability
> as a transmutation of the economic principles of Social Darwinism
> into the metaphoric realm of gender conflict. Reasonable men
> everywhere had learned to shudder at the realization that woman
> was driven by instinct to go after the "vital fluids" the male needed
> most to survive in the dog-eat-dog economic world . . . widely
> identified as the staging arena for the inevitable imperialist "struggle
> for life" among nations.
>
> —Bram Dijkstra, *Evil Sisters* (1996, 73–74)

Despite his shadowy presence in much of the novel, Stoker's Dracula gave a concrete form to a common metaphor. Most interpreters see the vampire figure's appeal to be related to various cultural anxieties of the late 19th century—fears of invasion, or contamination by lower races by way of sexual degeneracy, or by homosexuality—all cultural declines of one type or another. By the 1910s, with the help of the new entertainment technology associated with the cinema, a new term comes into use, based on the vampire. *The Oxford English Dictionary* identifies the first use of the shortened form "vamp" in the sense of "to behave seductively; to act as a vamp, to be a vamp," as occurring in 1904. By 1911, a vamp is further defined as "a woman who intentionally attracts and exploits men; an adventuress; a jezebel; freq[uently] as a stock character in plays and films."

The early cinema is often seen as developing in two divergent directions. One moves toward increasing realism, "history written by lightning" in President Woodrow Wilson's famous phrase. Wilson, a former professor of history, was describing D. W. Griffith's virulently racist film *Birth of a Nation* (1915), which many saw as an accurate portrayal of Reconstruction (Menand 2001, 387). The other cinematic strand was toward the fantastic, toward portraying things that do not or cannot occur in real life, made possible by illusionistic special effects. Horror films, especially those that portray such monstrous beings as vampires, exist in a middle ground between these two. They present subject matter that is by definition nonrealistic, but if they rely on visual or technological trickery to push too far in the direction of fantasy, they fail to horrify or terrify their audiences. Effective horror must remain anchored in the real world.

Most conventional histories of vampires in early films tend to focus on F. W. Murnau's *Nosferatu*, a German version of the Dracula story that was produced in 1922 and that Stoker's widow sued for copyright infringement. In it, Max Schreck plays Count Orlock, an invader like Dracula, but with a bald head, pointed ears, and huge hands, behaving more like the animated corpse of European folklore than an intelligent predator. In this version, the count is defeated by a woman's sacrifice— she gives herself to him in order so that she can trick him into exposure to daylight, which destroys him. Later tributes to this film include *Nosferatu the Vampyre* (1979) by German director Werner Herzog, which follows the basic plot of the earlier film, and *Shadow of the Vampire* (2000), directed by E. Elias Merhige and starring Willem Dafoe and John Malkovich, which posits that Schreck (Dafoe) was a real vampire and that Murnau (Malkovich) knew it.

The focus on Murnau's film tends to obscure a set of films that focused on female vampires or vamps. In his detailed analysis of the gender politics of the early 20th century, *Evil Sisters* (1996), Bram Dijkstra looks at this phenomenon, focusing on the figure of Theda Bara, the most famous vamp, especially as she appears in the film that made her a star, *A Fool There Was* (1914) directed by Frank Powell. The title is based on a Rudyard Kipling poem, "The Vampire" (1897), which spawned a play and novelization (both 1909) and finally the movie. Bara's character is listed simply as "The Vampire" in the film's credits. The poem reads, in part,

> A fool there was and his goods he spent,
> (Even as you or I!)
> Honour and faith and a sure intent
> (And it wasn't the least what the lady meant),
> But a fool must follow his natural bent
> (Even as you or I!). (Kipling 1897)

The vampire here is not after literal blood, but the economic and moral lifeblood, the vital essence that the male fool provides, "even as you or I" would. Material goods are one thing, but she is also after all the other "goods" that might support him as a person and a successful member of society—his self-respect, and his will, and his worldview. This is the horror of this form of vampirism: the natural bent of the fool (and by implication you and I) subverts him against all that is good, and the woman isn't even capable of understanding the harm she does. The poem continues,

> Oh the toil we lost and the spoil we lost
> And the excellent things we planned,
> Belong to the woman who didn't know why
> (And now we know she never knew why)
> And did not understand. (Kipling 2008, 18)

She, initially introduced as "a rag and a bone and a hank of hair," is apparently also acting on instinct. Her instincts, not her ideas or her will, make her destructive and vampiric. Note that what is lost is both toil and spoil, work and material goods, suggesting that she is out to subvert all that is good, and to take all the goods as well.

Dijkstra's study analyzes medical, biological, sociological, and anthropological texts, as well as cultural ones like *A Fool There Was*, to demonstrate that there was a body of gender-based belief that something very like vampirism is a trait shared by all human females, associated with their atavistic sexuality. As Kipling cogently put it in another poem, where he compares and basically equates female cobras, bears, and squaws: "Her instincts never fail . . . The female of the species is more deadly than the male" (Kipling 1990, 291). Dijkstra's view of the threat of the New Woman of the *fin de siècle* period is that men saw her not merely as a social or cultural threat, but as an expression of an evolutionary biological imperative. A scientific concept of the time, gender dimorphism, describes a developmental process by which males and females progressively diverge from one another as humanity progresses toward civilization. This process results, necessarily, in leaving one gender behind, ensnared in her natural, instinctual need to reproduce. In Dijkstra's terms:

> Evolution, therefore, made an ever-widening gap between the roles of men and women inevitable. The more civilized the male, the more economically aggressive, assertive, and individualized he

would be. A woman proved herself to be part of the crown of creation by being as passive, malleable, and as focused on motherhood as she could possibly be. (Dijkstra 1996, 34)

Her problem—and our problem as a species—proves to be her regressive nature, indeed her regressive connection to nature, which also connects her to all that is red in tooth and claw: animals, primitive people, instinct, sexuality. Of course, this is a scientifically justified version of an old story that blames women, the story of Lilith and Eve and Pandora. Such stories make women responsible for the introduction of evil, or mischief, or original sin. But the new version also connects the social myth of progress with evolutionary biology, and allows opponents to women's rights to label proponents as conservative and regressive. Women are doomed to follow their instincts, but they can be encouraged to channel them into the higher role of motherhood as opposed to the lower role of sexual predator.

The vampire is a perfect metaphor for this kind of degeneration, being associated with death and the past, with the lower orders of animals, with the dark primitive peoples of central Europe, and with instinct and sexuality. The fears of foreign invasion, contamination of pure Anglo-Saxon blood, uncontrolled sexuality, and loss of order that are dramatized in *Dracula*, and that are somewhat mitigated by the presence of an American, are found here to emerge from the evolutionary backwater that lurks in the heart (womb?) of every women, but especially in assertive and sexual ones.

A Fool There Was presents a female sexual predator as a vampire. Bara's character uses her dark, exotic beauty and her overt sexuality to enervate and impoverish John Schuyler, who is, with his Anglo-Dutch name, presumably one of America's racial elite—the opening scene shows him as a yacht captain. Because he gives in to his instincts rather than his higher nature, he is reduced in the course of the film to a mere shell of his former self, broken and discarded as the vampire goes on to her next victim. Kipling's poem was printed in the novel, read at the beginning of the play, and quoted in the film's intertitles. Promotional photos for the film showed Theda Bara (whose stage name is an anagram for Arab Death) crouching triumphantly over a supine human skeleton like a beast of prey.

But female vampirism was more than a metaphor in the age of vital essences and monkey glands—during this time, monkey testicles were actually grafted onto men in order to restore potency. As Dijkstra describes it, the belief was in a seminal economy, where sperm represents a limited reservoir of vital essence or life force that can be spent in positive or negative ways. "Orchitic" means produced by the testicles:

> The orchitic infusion theory thus provided an "organic" explanation for "nymphomania." Ordinarily a civilized woman should promptly ovulate and become pregnant. . . . However, women who diverted man's brain food to nonreproductive uses—women with a masculinized tendency toward primitive bisexuality—would, with each potent seminal infusion, become less motherly and more sexual. This clearly was the sliding scale between the virgin mother and the whore that science had been looking for . . . (Dijkstra 1996, 199)

Good women, once virgins and now mothers, use sperm for reproduction. For bad women, the vital essence is like an addictive (and masculinizing) drug and pulls her back into her natural predatory state. The commonly held connection between sperm and blood as life-giving bodily fluids is explicitly established in the transfusion scenes in *Dracula*—Lucy is transfused not only with the blood of Holmwood, her husband, but also with the blood of Seward, Van Helsing, and Morris. At Van Helsing's behest, all the other transfusions are concealed from Holmwood, and the process results in Van Helsing having a sort of breakdown, bursting into an episode of hysterical laughter where he labels Lucy a polyandrist and himself a bigamist (Stoker 2002, 186). The taking of blood by the vampire (or the transfusionist) is literally understood to be equivalent to the taking of sperm in the sexual act.

The physicians and endocrinologists, who were pushing monkey glands, believed that sexual decline (with age) or too much sexual spending would draw down a man's bank account of life force, causing him to age, become weaker in body and will, and lose his mental capacity. So, there was an actual, scientifically supported connection between wealth and health, which recommended proper spending in both realms. "Spending" was, as well, a popularly used term for the male orgasm. Like the connection between sperm and blood, this is not a simple metaphoric connection, which explains the plot of *A Fool There Was*. The Theda Bara character is not just an adventuress—through her nonreproductive use of sexuality, she is literally sucking the life force out of Schuyler in the form of his precious bodily fluid—all implied; except for the initial kiss, none of this is shown. This strengthens her and at the same time makes her more like a man, even as it makes him more passive and feminine.

The process brings the genders closer together, creating an evolutionary backslide away from the progress that gender difference represents.

The implications of the worldview that Dijkstra describes are alarming. If the vampire is hidden in all females, then there is no escape from gender conflict, or indeed, class and racial conflict. The beleaguered white male is not only opposed by forces of the past, of death and of degeneration, but by nature itself and its relentless push for the reproduction of the species. The threat is everywhere and the only hope is for the (all-male) members of the "evolutionary elite" (Dijkstra 1996, 18) to band together and keep pure against the threats of economic, class, racial, national, and especially biological degeneration, all the time trying to encourage motherhood and discourage independence, especially sexual, in their female counterparts. But even as they find common cause with each other, they must compete with each other as well. The primary threat is from within our own biological or genetic constitution.

The multiple threats that the Crew of Light face in *Dracula* seem tame in comparison, and their binding together of interests—middle class with aristocrat; career woman with professional man; and American and Dutch with British—seem positively socialistic. The paranoid worldview outlined by Dijkstra did lead, arguably, to various dead ends, to eugenics and involuntary sterilization, to support for legalized segregation and the quasi-state terrorism of lynching, to immigration restriction laws in the United States and the Final Solution in German-controlled Europe. Because it was biological rather than supernatural, the threat posed by the vamp was more realistic in the sense that it was based in science, and yet more amorphous and difficult to contain. Later versions of the vampire in film would replace the horror of biological destiny with a more local threat, a less-threatening male vampire, who could be stopped with a stake or a sunbeam. But the biological horror was to be recast into the cosmic horror of the pulp story.

CHAPTER 5

Blood and Pulp

In 1914, when the kindly hand of amateurdom was first extended to me, I was as close to the state of vegetation as any animal well can be . . . With the advent of the United [Amateur Press Association] I obtained a renewal to live; a renewed sense of existence as other than a superfluous weight; and found a sphere in which I could feel that my efforts were not wholly futile. For the first time I could imagine that my clumsy gropings after art were a little more than faint cries lost in the unlistening world.

—H. P. Lovecraft, *Marling* (2009)

Howard Phillips Lovecraft is the most well-known purveyor of pulp stories. He is credited with the invention of cosmic horror, a type of writing characterized by adjective-laden, often purple, prose combined with philosophical speculations on an enormous scale, both in time and in space, which often presents humans as a very small part of an indifferent or even hostile universe dominated by insect-like or reptilian beings, who are themselves ruled by the most basic of instincts. Human intelligence seems to be an evolutionary fluke rather than the crown of creation. Despite its portentous scale, pulp fiction is often leavened by self-deprecating, even self-parodying, humor. It has been traditionally seen as the stuff of adolescent male fantasy, both in style and in subject matter, and many of its writers did begin as adolescents, encouraged by older mentors when they were teenagers. We can see from Lovecraft's account that he tended to stress the amateur nature of such writing, and his cult-like following seems to have developed through fan clubs and personal networks, rather than with the support of the professional publishing establishment. Especially in style, these stories are very different from either literary high modernism or the snappy, colloquial journalistic prose of the time.

"The pulps," inexpensive magazines named for the cheap newsprint on which they were printed, were an outgrowth of earlier mass-marketed sensation literature, the "penny dreadfuls," which gave birth to cheaply printed nickel and then dime novels. These popular outlets not only tended to print the recognizable genre fiction of their given time—horror, romance, mystery—but they also served to provide a spawning matrix for new genre. Cowboy stories had emerged contemporaneously with Buffalo Bill's shows in the 1880s, some of which actually featured him as a character. Vampires were not unknown in the pulp realm. Indeed, the closest precursor to *Dracula* was James Malcolm Rhymer's *Varney the Vampire* (1847), the serial epic published in "penny dreadfuls" that was 868 double-columned pages long and featured a caped gentleman vampire who more closely resembles the later Dracula of stage and screen than the character Stoker gives us in his novel.

Many literary writers were published in the pulps, including Sinclair Lewis, Jack London, and Tennessee Williams. Many well-known writers in the genres, especially detective and science fiction writers, wrote for the pulps. In science fiction, these include Ray Bradbury, Arthur Conan Doyle, Robert Silverberg, Arthur C. Clarke, Isaac Asimov and H. G. Wells. Detective writers for the pulps include James M. Cain, Raymond Chandler, Dashiell Hammett, Chester Himes, and Mickey Spillane.

The heyday of the pulps is generally said to be the 1920s and 1930s, coinciding, interestingly, with the rise and consolidation of the Hollywood studio system. Both provided inexpensive, lowbrow, often sensational, mass entertainment and both depended on genre and genre-blending to catch and keep audiences. Two organizations, the United Amateur Press Association and the American Amateur Press Association supported pulp writing as amateur, in order to contrast it with the established literary and journalistic outlets of the day. Such organizations were crucial in developing and coordinating groups of fans for various types of genre fiction. In Lovecraft's case, ironically, being an amateur allowed him to hold onto an elite persona.

It was during the 1920s that the ideas of Sigmund Freud became popularly known. Everyday discussions might include references to the unconscious or to neuroses and complexes as motivating factors. Freud was and still is of interest to literary scholars because he understood literature to be a form of unconscious expression, akin to dreams, and so often used literary examples to illustrate his models, such as the infamous Oedipus complex, named after the character in a Greek myth. His 1922 essay "The Uncanny" would become very influential, especially for writers and thinkers about horror and the supernatural. The German word that is translated as "uncanny" is *unheimlich*, literally unhomelike, which should be the opposite of *heimlich*, which means domestic, familiar, and homelike. They should be opposites in meaning, but these are two words that have tended to blend their meanings in usage, so that *unheimlich* has qualities of the familiar *and* the creepy. In the essay, Freud points out that *heimlich* not only means intimate and friendly, but also secret or concealed. So, as a working definition, uncanny can suggest "that class of the frightening which leads back to what is known of old and long familiar" (Freud 1955, 218). He connects this to his concept of the return of the repressed, where material that we unconsciously repress finds other ways to reappear and to the feared yet familiar figure of the double. Although he does not mention vampires, several examples that Freud uses of the uncanny—premature burial and the animation of an inanimate object—fit into the vampire tradition. We do not know whether Lovecraft was familiar with this specific essay of Freud's, but scenes of haunted familiarity and the theme of the return of the repressed are very present in many of his stories, as my example will demonstrate.

This period was also the heyday of the Eugenics movement, in terms of its institutionalization into American life. Eugenics, a term based on a Greek root meaning "good seed," applied rudimentary genetic principles to human breeding, with the general goal of improving the race. This goal may sound innocuous enough, but it depends, of course, on how you think about race. For example, if you believe that the Caucasian race is superior, and that Northern European Caucasians are superior to Southern or Central European ones, then the race you are trying to improve becomes a fairly limited group, beset on all sides by ravening hordes of inferiors. We have seen how Stoker presented Dracula as a threat to the British racial imperium and how females were perceived as being evolutionary inferiors to males, but by the 1920s such thinking had the solid backing of science.

Gregor Mendel's genetic experiments had proved that a single genetic variant can create major changes in subsequent generations, and such ideas, when applied to humans, were viewed with alarm by a proportionately diminishing Anglo-Saxon elite. Demographic studies had pointed out that increasing levels of higher education corresponded with declining birth rates. So, people who identified with Anglo-Saxon elite began to be worried that they were on a slippery slope, downward to a kind of amalgamation in the common horde, which might result in a weakening of the vital, superior traits of intelligence, organization, self-control, and thrift that were, theoretically, tied genetically to Anglo-Saxon whiteness. In 1924, to combat the threat of racial swarming, the U.S. Congress passed the most restrictive immigration laws to date, laws that specifically attempted to preserve racial balances from some 30 years earlier, before major waves of Southern European immigrants entered the country. Meanwhile, eugenicists were conducting research into the racial purity of Americans in general. A Eugenics Records Office was established in Cold Spring Harbor, Long Island, New York, where information could be archived, much of it based on the well-known Eugenic Family Studies.

The family studies were sociological scholarly narratives based on interviews, hearsay, and diluted anecdotal evidence that traced degenerate traits, such as alcoholism, imbecility, and promiscuity, through generations of a certain family, who were given a pseudonym, such as the now infamous "Jukes." Other eugenic researchers, most notably in Virginia, attempted to document any and all mixed-blood families so that they could be denied the privileges of white racial membership in the Jim Crow South. Thousands of eugenically unfit people, many of whom were in institutions for the feeble minded, were surgically sterilized so that they would not give birth to new generations of dysgenic (having bad genes) people. Many colleges and universities during this era required a course in eugenics as part of a bachelor's degree.

Eugenics Society president R. Ruggles Gates, writing in the *Eugenics Quarterly* in 1920, outlined the program:

> Eugenic action should be based upon four separate factors; 1, positive selection for desirable qualities, which are frequently dominant; 2, negative selection against undesirable recessive qualities which appear in collateral or ancestral lines and may therefore be carried in the family germplasm; 3, isolation of individuals having undesirable dominant qualities; 4, correlated with this should be an effort to foster marriages between individuals showing the same desirable recessive quality. All of this implies an array of information more elaborate than anyone possesses . . . (Gates 1920, 5)

Gates goes on to suggest "preventation of reproduction" for "undesirables" that is "necessary, not so much for the improvement of the race as for arresting its rapid deterioration through the multiplication of the unfit" (Gates 1920, 11).

In many of the pulp stories, we can see the poisonous effects of this national discourse. The kind of paranoid fear based on gender difference that Dijkstra traces in the portrayal of the vamp has a racial analog in the philosophy of the eugenics movement. The fact that, in the federal immigration restriction legislation, quotas were set to a standard 30 years in the past demonstrates a belief that the current situation has already progressed beyond where it should be, perhaps irretrievably. This pessimistic sense of loss of control, the fear that the situation has proceeded beyond a tipping point, and that the threat is imminent yet mysterious, pervades the cosmic horror of the pulp stories.

H. P. Lovecraft is the writer most closely associated with cosmic horror. He was a reclusive New Englander who spent most of his life living with relatives in Rhode Island. His output included many short stories, some essays and journalism, and somewhere around 100,000 letters, making him one of the most prolific correspondents of the age of letter writing. Although he published only sporadically, mostly in *Weird Tales*, he also did editing and revision for others (including, on one story, the magician Harry Houdini). His influence was remarkable, mainly through his complex of virtual friends and followers. After Lovecraft's death in 1937, two young disciples, August W. Derleth and Donald Wandrei, formed Arkham House Publishers to collect and publish his work, along with that of like-minded writers. These efforts, along with fan clubs and a growing group of scholarly supporters, most prominently Lovecraft bibliographic scholar S. T. Joshi, have resulted in this cult figure's acceptance into the American literary canon, perhaps best demonstrated by his publication in the Modern Library's *Writers of America* series in 2005.

Only a few of Lovecraft's tales deal with vampires, per se, although many have vampire-like beings. "The Hound," from 1923, may be one of the best examples. Its two protagonists, an unnamed narrator and his friend, St. John, are exponentially decadent (superlatives, as well as other adjectives and adverbs, tend to multiply in one's prose after reading Lovecraft). "Only the somber philosophy of the Decadents could hold us, and this we found potent only by increasing gradually the depth and diabolism of our penetrations" (Lovecraft 2005, 81). Their increasingly desperate search for the next thrill leads them into grave robbery and the creation of a private museum: "With the satanic taste of neurotic virtuosi we had assembled an universe of terror and decay to excite our jaded sensibilities" (Lovecraft 2005, 82). They steal an ancient amulet out of a tomb in Holland:

> It was the oddly conventionalized figure of a crouching winged hound, or sphinx with a semi-canine face, and was exquisitely carved in antique Oriental fashion from a small piece of green jade. The expression of its features was repellent in the extreme, savoring at once of death, bestiality and malevolence. Around the base was an inscription in characters which neither St John nor I could identify; and on the bottom, like a maker's seal, was graven a grotesque and formidable skull. (Lovecraft 2005, 84)

The grave robbers recognize the amulet as:

> the thing hinted of in the forbidden *Necronomicon* of the mad Arab Abdul Alhazred; the ghastly soul-symbol of the corpse-eating cult of inaccessible Leng, in Central Asia. All too well did we trace the sinister lineaments described by the old Arab daemonologist; lineaments, he wrote, drawn from some obscure supernatural manifestation of the souls of those who vexed and gnawed at the dead. (Lovecraft 2005, 84)

The story uses imagery to suggest vampirism, such as bats clustering around the grave, a "wide-nebulous shadow sweeping from mound to mound" (Lovecraft 2005, 86) on the moor, and the voice of a hound howling in the distance. It does not actually resort to the mechanisms of the vampire myth. The narrator's companion is "seized by some frightful carnivorous thing and torn to ribbons" (Lovecraft 2005, 86), rather than drained of blood. Now terrified, the narrator decides to return the amulet, but it is stolen from him in Rotterdam. The next day, he hears of an entire family slaughtered "in a squalid thieves' den" (Lovecraft 2005, 87). He proceeds back to the grave and digs up the corpse once again, discovering that the clean skeleton they had originally found was "embraced by a close-packed nightmare retinue of huge, sinewy, sleeping bats" and was covered in blood, "leering sentiently at me with phosphorescent sockets and sharp ensanguined fangs yawning twistedly in mockery," as it clutched the amulet. The narrator "merely screamed and ran away idiotically, my screams soon dissolving into peals of hysterical laughter" (Lovecraft 2005, 88). He now plans to commit suicide.

I quote extensively in order to give examples of Lovecraft's over-written style. In his essay on "Supernatural Horror in Literature," Lovecraft holds Poe up as the most masterful purveyor of supernatural horror and paraphrases Poe's philosophy of writing: "Atmosphere is the all-important thing, for the final criterion of authenticity is not the dovetailing of a plot but the creation of a given sensation" (Lovecraft 2005, 108). Poe's emphasis on the effect of writing over plot and character show in Lovecraft's story. The amulet is stolen; indeed the protagonists' whole collection is motivated out of a kind of world weariness, a continuous, escalating search for the unique and the bizarre. This slim motivation is not augmented by any insight into the narrator's character, beyond his panic at realizing that he has gone too far. The plot is driven by the impetus of this realization, and the characters are crushed or at least shredded by forces they don't understand, even if they can document where they came from.

Lovecraft's cosmic horror, often tinged with racism, seems to be motivated by a feeling of being trapped within our own biology. In 1924, the same year he wrote "The Hound," Lovecraft gives an account of the Lower East Side of New York in a letter to Frank Belknap Long. He described:

> The organic things inhabiting that awful cesspool could not . . . be call'd human. They were monstrous and nebulous adnumbrations of the pithecanthropoid and amoebal . . . slithering and oozing . . . in a fashion suggesting nothing other than infesting worms or deep-sea unamiabilities. . . . I thought of some avenue of Cyclopean and unwholesome vats, crammed to the vomiting point with unwholesome vileness, and about to burst and inundate the world. (Lovecraft 2005, xxiv)

We can see from this that the cosmic horror at the center of Lovecraft's worldview was not only influenced by science's discovery of the vastness of an impersonal universe, but also of another kind of science's fears that mankind was caught in a downward spiral of racial degeneracy. Even though we comfort ourselves by referring to eugenics as a pseudoscience today, its claims were regarded as proven scientific fact in the 1920s.

It may seem odd to link the ideas and prejudices of a marginal literary form, such as the pulps, to a national discourse on race, but I believe that it demonstrates the depth of the racial ideologies of the time that are expressed through the vehicle of such popular outlets as these magazines. For many, the 1920s represents a high point of hope for a modern world, where the new dominates all art and the past and its repressions are left behind. Lovecraft's view of biological decadence, fueled by eugenic fears, is an uncanny reminder of the persistence of the past, of how the horrors repressed would return in an awful future.

CHAPTER 6

Class-ic Horror

Martin: Ain't ya ashamed now! Ain't ya? Spiders now, is it? Flies ain't good enough.
Renfield: Flies! Flies! Poor puny things. Who wants to eat flies?
Martin: You do, you loony!
Renfield: Not when I can get nice fat spiders.
—Tod Browning, *Dracula* (1931)

According to film historian David Skal, horror movies didn't exist as such before Tod Browning's *Dracula* (1931). Or it might be more accurate to say that they didn't exist as a recognized Hollywood genre, like the Western or the gangster movie. There had been models for films that took supernatural monsters seriously. Edison had done a short version of *Frankenstein* in 1910, and European cinema during the silent era produced such films as the German Expressionist classic, *The Cabinet of Dr. Caligari*, by Robert Weine from 1920 and F. W. Murnau's *Nosferatu* in 1922.

"Nosferatu," a term introduced in Stoker's *Dracula* as a Transylvanian word for vampire, gave its title to Murnau's filmed version of the story. In it, a bald and tentacle-fingered vampire, Count Orlock, comes to live in a German town, where he is finally dispatched by a ray of light from the rising sun. The creeping, rat-like Orlock is a far cry from the suave, gentlemanly Dracula that Bela Lugosi's portrayal would make familiar. Orlock connects with Theda Bara's vamp only by way of his predatory intentions. His inhuman features emphasize the film's portrayal of him as an alien invader into an established social structure. Lugosi's portrayal, on the other hand, gave audiences a familiar figure—the aristocrat. This figure developed from the character that he and others performed in a series of stage versions of the novel that played in the 1920s, authorized, unlike Murnau's film, by Stoker's widow. Aware of an injunction that the Stoker estate had prosecuted against *Nosferatu* ordering that all prints of the film be destroyed, Universal Pictures was careful to buy rights to the novel and to the various dramatic versions before proceeding with the film.

Browning's *Dracula* was produced at an interesting juncture in the history of Hollywood cinema. First, it was in the early talkie era, when sound technology was transforming the industry. In addition, Universal Studios was undergoing a change in leadership, with Carl Laemmle, Jr. taking over from his father Carl Laemmle, Sr., a transition that opened the door for the studio to move toward more fantastic subjects and away from adherence to strictly realistic material. Browning himself, who had directed several successful films in the silent era, was said to be less comfortable with sound directing and less enthusiastic about the project, since his first choice for the Dracula character was his friend and collaborator, the famous rubber-faced star Lon Chaney, who had just died of cancer. Added to all this was the financial stress caused by the stock market crash and the advent of the Great Depression, which meant that films in production were expected to do more with less.

Dracula, like many Hollywood adaptations, does not follow the novel. Because the film has become so influential in later films, as well as familiar to us as camp, it is very difficult to imagine how its original audience would have experienced it. The plot was simplified into a series of encounters between Dracula and various characters, with many scenes taken from the stage play. Lugosi's Hungarian accent, slow vocal pacing, and stiff movements provide a distant and reserved, yet uniquely threatening figure that contrasts with most of the other characters, such as the earnest young lovers and the manic Renfield. The opening scenes show Renfield (not Harker as in the novel) arriving in Transylvania to go to Dracula's castle, where he meets Dracula. He returns to England as the familiar insect-eating madman from the novel. The actor playing Renfield, Dwight Frye, who also came from the stage version, provides the character with a wild-haired and wild-eyed freneticism.

The film is alarmingly static by today's standards and, contrary to popular belief, does not show Lugosi's Dracula with fangs or even actually biting his victims. Suspense is developed through tension rather than through dramatic action. According to accounts by the actors, Browning did not take much of an active role in directing his most well-known film, leaving much of the day-to-day business of directing to his cinematographer, Karl Freund, for whose atmospheric compositions the film receives much of its praise today.

Even in recently restored versions, large flaws are evident. At times, transitions are abrupt and editing seems haphazard. Certain plot elements are not resolved—for example, the scene involving vampire brides. It shows three vampire women rising from their crypts and advancing—toward what?—then cuts away. In another scene, Renfield creeps toward an unconscious nurse and we never find out what he does when, or if, he reaches her.

Sound transition is thought of today as just another step in the process of technological improvement, but it was a major transition for the industry and for such silent-film directors as Tod Browning. Browning had been one of the more successful Hollywood directors during the silent era, and had a reputation for bringing in films on time and under budget. He and Lon Chaney, Sr. had paired up to produce some of the best-selling films of the 1920s, including *Outside the Law* (Universal, 1920, remade by Browning as a sound film, 1930), *The Unholy Three* (MGM, 1925), *The Unknown* (MGM, 1927), and *London After Midnight* (MGM, 1927).

According to Robert Spadoni in his *Uncanny Bodies: The Coming of Sound Film and the Origins of the Horror Genre* (2007), the transition to sound replicated, for the audience, the conditions of the original introduction of cinema some 30 years before. The addition of this new element created feelings of the uncanny, marked by discomfort and anxiety, for the audience. Used to the exaggerated acting and frenetic musical scores of silent films, they now experienced talking shadows and unfocused voices coming from differently scaled bodies on the screen. Before sound-cinema conventions were developed and accepted, audiences were often disturbed by the disembodied effects of voices that didn't "locate" in the figures on the screen. Filmmakers and critics debated whether, for example, voices during close-ups should be louder than those during medium or wide shots. Today, we are so used to the conventions developed during those years that we have trouble seeing them as odd. Movie music and clear, isolated vocals are so much the norm that when a film uses realistic sound, with voices fading, overlapping, or competing with background noise, it seems positively odd.

Spadoni claims that this "medium sensitivity"(Spadoni 2007, 14) meaning sensitivity to a new medium, helped to develop the horror genre by breaking through the comforting familiarity of audience expectations and providing a new kind of experience. He refers to Freud's influential essay, "The Uncanny," where Freud suggests that feelings of uncanniness, *unheimlichkeit* in German, evoke both familiarity and strangeness. I cannot reproduce Spadoni's entire interpretation here, but I want to use it as a starting point to suggest that one aspect of the film's effectiveness—its overall uncanniness—emerges from its use of contrasts between comforting and familiar figures against bizarre and disturbing ones. But first, I want to introduce another element, and that is social class.

The film was created in 1930 and released in early 1931. This was the beginning of the Great Depression, the same year when Franklin D. Roosevelt was elected, promising a program of economic reforms. In art and popular culture, what had been a fascination with the rich and the spectacle of their lives—the Jazz Age—was shifting toward interest in and idealization of common people. Outsiders and outlaws, such as John Dillinger and Pretty Boy Floyd, became folk heroes, in contrast to bankers and financiers, who were seen as villains. One of the reasons for worry over censorship in film during this time, which resulted in the eventual establishment of the Motion Picture Code, had to do with the new genre of gangster films that presented outlaws as heroes, such as Mervyn LeRoy's *Little Caesar* (1931) starring Edward G. Robinson. The emergence and popularity of horror films at the same time is often explained as having the appeal of escapism—audiences could spend a small amount of money to forget about their troubles for a while into the worlds of supernatural fantasy. But horror films also represented conflict between social classes, if somewhat more subtly.

Roosevelt's solution to the economic woes of the Great Depression was to bring in the experts. The New Deal agencies that he created were filled with highly educated technocrats, experts in a variety of fields, who were to come together to solve society's ills. Alongside the working class or outlaw hero, the expert stands out as a figure that represents the hopes of the era. Browning's film pits such a man, Van Helsing, a scientific expert representing the future, against Dracula, a brutal aristocrat who represents the past.

Count Dracula is obviously an aristocrat of a kind not found in the United States in 1930, but he is certainly a visual type for the rich man, one who owns large properties and has the means to purchase more. More significantly, he dresses in the evening dress that characterized rich folks during the 1930s (e.g., we might think of another cultural icon from the time, the Monopoly Man, with his top hat, tails, and spats). The familiarity of this image is made unfamiliar as soon as we hear him speak—the slow-paced Hungarian accent is strange and unsettling, not what we expect from the figure we see. In contrast, Professor Van Helsing as played by Edward Van Sloan, first appears as:

> . . . an agent of rational thinking, vision, and action . . . underscored by his goggle-like eyeglasses and white lab coat and by the beakers and test tubes that we see [in his introductory shot]. (Spadoni 2007, 65)

Van Helsing is not portrayed as the semi-comical speaker of broken English that Stoker gives us, but as a working scientist, an expert. He is fluent and well-spoken, someone much like the technocrats leading the agencies of the New Deal. Like them, he leads Dracula's opponents not because of his social position, but by way of his technical expertise. The other members of Van Helsing's team, including Lucy, Mina, Harker, and Seward, seem staggeringly bland and ordinary to an extreme. The most interesting member of the group is the sanatorium worker Martin, whose portrayal is enlivened by a sardonic, working-class humor. After shooting at Dracula in bat form, he confides to a co-worker, "They're all crazy. They're all crazy except you and me. Sometimes I have me doubts about you."

I am not trying to deny that Browning's *Dracula* has elements of escapist fantasy or to claim that it is a masterpiece of social realist propaganda. Dracula is a threatening figure; the uncanniness of the film emerges from contrasts between familiar and unexpected portrayals and conventions. Much of what modern audiences see as theatrical or campy spoke to the original audience in a more disturbing language, both visual and auditory.

Dracula presents the foreign aristocrat as an outsider with supernatural advantages, a master and object of fear in his own realm. But when he enters the modern world, even though he has the power to control his servant (Renfield) and his (potential) lover, Mina, he is defeated by the knowledge of the expert Van Helsing and the collective strength and persistence of a dedicated team of regular people working with him. The corrupt Old Guard, autocratic, isolated and individualistic (not to mention undead), is defeated by an idealistic team with a New Deal in mind. Although the setting is England, none of the characters, especially the workers, seem particularly English. Dracula's defeat seems inevitable, because he belongs to the past. Even where he is most powerful, in a personal confrontation, he is unable to move Van Helsing, the strong-willed, scientific man of the future.

Dracula was successful beyond expectations and became the first in Universal's series of classic horror films, including *Frankenstein* (1931), *The Mummy* (1932), *The Invisible Man* (1933), and many others, eventually including sequels to both *Frankenstein* and *Dracula*. By the end of the decade, the emphasis on horror began to be perceived as an emphasis on monsters per se, and Universal was seen as producing monster movies. To hold onto this franchise during the 1940s, the studio produced a spate of monster mash-ups, such as *Frankenstein Meets the Wolf Man* (1943), *House of Frankenstein* (1944), and *House of Dracula* (1945), all of which provided the monsters in combination. The Universal classic era is generally considered to have come to an end with the self-parody *Abbott and Costello Meet Frankenstein* in 1948, followed by other comic send-ups. But the studio continued to produce horror films in the science fiction style of the 1950s, and served as the American distributor for the Hammer revival of classic horror in the 1950s and 1960s. Browning himself went on to create the truly disturbing *Freaks* (1932), in which he employed—some would claim exploited—a group of actual circus freaks in a bizarre love triangle/revenge drama. The film was pulled from theaters and was banned in England for some 30 more years before being revived in the 1960s. It effectively ended Browning's career. He directed one more vampire film, with Lugosi (the only other time they worked together), entitled *Mark of the Vampire* (1935), before he retired. This was a remake of a silent film that he had directed in the 1920s, *London After Midnight* (1927). In both films, the vampire is fake, an act meant to bring out the real murderer.

In the vampire films that followed *Dracula*, the first thing that a modern viewer notices is that what film historians call production values—a blanket term referring to the level of sophistication of both the narrative and the technical and special-effects details—are much improved. Composition, editing, lighting, depth-of-focus, sound quality, musical accompaniment—all present examples of the art of black-and-white filmmaking at its best, going beyond the almost tentative use of the medium that we see in *Dracula*, and firmly establishing a set of conventions for the sound horror film. The only other Universal vampire film of the 1930s was the Dracula sequel, *Dracula's Daughter* (1936) with Gloria Holden as a conflicted, possibly lesbian, vampire operating in London. Here, again, modern medical expertise, in the form of psychiatrist Jeffrey Garth (Otto Kruger), triumphs over the medieval machinations of the title character, Countess Zaleska (Gloria Holden), who has a Renfield-like flunky, Sandor (Irving Pichel), and an interest in young women as victims. Zaleska's character mimics the attitude of Varney in the penny dreadful *Varney the Vampire* (1847) in that she loathes her undead nature and wishes to be cured. This has, of course, implications for the lesbian interpretation, having been produced at a time when psychiatrists considered homosexuality a mental ailment. In any case, Zaleska kidnaps Dr. Garth's socialite love interest Janet (Marguerite Churchill). A final confrontation results in her being killed by a jealous Sandor. The social message is much less clear than in Browning's film, perhaps because the setting is much more recognizably British, or perhaps because the idealism of the early New Deal was wearing off by 1936, and films were once again emphasizing movie glamour over social content.

CHAPTER 7

Urban Legends

The French word *noir* (which means "black") was first connected to the word *film* in 1946, and it has subsequently become a prodigiously overused term to describe a certain type of film or literary work. Curiously, *noir* is not unlike *pornography* in the sense that it is virtually impossible to define, but everyone thinks they know it when they see it. Like many other certainties, it is often wildly inaccurate.

—Otto Penzler, *The Best American Noir*
of the Century (2010, ix)

Genres, both in literature and film, are fluid categories that tend to change over time. They are defined by a variety of factors—primarily, setting, style, and theme. Westerns, for example, tend to be set in the American West of the late 19th century, tend to have a style that features dialect and description, and tend to feature themes that emphasize moral dilemmas in areas without a firmly established rule of law. Of course, not all Westerns conform to these limits. Vampire films and fiction are both too diffuse to be defined generically; indeed, the objective of this study is to look at some of the ways that the vampire as a fictional figure has changed over time. This chapter will look at the intersection of some genres to give an idea of how film and print interpenetrate in the creation and propagation of these persistent supernatural figures.

This chapter looks at a novel and a short story within the context of generic evolution. They are Fritz Leiber's story, "The Girl with the Hungry Eyes" (1949) and Richard Matheson's novel, *I Am Legend* (1953). Both are fictions written during the time and under the influence of film noir, a style of film that became prominent in the 1940s and grew out of the decline of the horror films of the 1930s.

Film noir is a term that was applied in retrospect to a group of American black-and-white movies, usually crime dramas, which featured urban settings, alienated protagonists, expressionistic lighting and camera effects, and plots that were often neither comic nor tragic in the traditional sense. The French term *film noir* literally means "black film," but the term actually comes from *roman noir*, a literary term referring to a genre of novel. The closest American equivalent would be gothic novel; but the two terms do not correspond exactly, because the *roman noir* includes thrillers, mysteries, and detective fiction as well as supernatural fiction. Film noir is an example of a genre that got its name in retrospect. The *Oxford English Dictionary* lists its first use in English in 1958, yet there was a study published in France three years earlier that used the term, and according to Otto Penzler, quoted above, the term was coined in 1946. In the French study, published in English as *A Panorama of American Film Noir, 1941–1953* (1955), Raymond Borde and Etienne Chaumeton describe the genre as "oneiric, strange, erotic, ambivalent, and cruel" (2), while admitting that this is an oversimplification. Noir has often been linked, like the Universal horror films that preceded it, to the German Expressionist filmmaking style of the silent era. Many of its practitioners, such as directors Fritz Lang, Robert Siodmak, and Michael Curtiz, were European immigrants directly or indirectly linked to Expressionism. Many of the same personnel who worked on the Universal horror pictures of the 1930s brought their talents to film noir. According to Blair Davis, in his study of the intersections between horror film and film noir, "the cinematic techniques and imagery of these same horror films are one of the major unacknowledged contributions to the development of *film noir*" (Davis 2004, 191).

The five terms that Borde and Chaumeton used give us a starting point: "oneiric, strange, erotic, ambivalent, and cruel" (Borde and Chaumeton 2002, 2). Oneiric means dreamlike, and the expressionistic, asymmetrical, high contrast, or foggy and misty cinematography that we find in many films noir lend a dreamlike quality to the style, as the often noncontinuous narration does to the plot. Dreams are associated with the unconscious, and during the 1940s a simpler version of Freudian psychology prevailed, one that tended to see dreams as coded messages that could be decoded for their (usually Oedipal) truths. This carries into hard-boiled or *noirish* fiction through the extensive use of metaphor, with its substitution of one object for another. All the effects of noir can be seen as strange, the second term, with the effect of estrangement or distancing of the audience from the actions of the characters and the story. Alienation, the separation of the person from his life or milieu, the feeling of disconnection, is a major trope in noir narratives. The third term, erotic, is more difficult for us to see in our current cinematic climate where films can show practically anything. This was the era of the Motion Picture Association of America Production Codes, which strongly limited the erotic content, banning words, such as pregnant, along with any explicit demonstration or implication of sexuality. So, erotic was found in the realm of innuendo and metaphor. To viewers from the earlier era, these films teemed with subtle expressions of powerful sexual undercurrents. Ambivalent applies not only to the moral dilemmas raised in these films, but also often to the actual narrative. When the camera follows an individual's point of view, we can no longer be certain of the accuracy of the information it is giving us, and film noir's frequent use of dream sequences and flashbacks, as well, reinforce such uncertainty. Finally, Borde and Chaumeton use the term cruel, which not only applies to how the characters treat each other, but also to how the films often treat the audience. Although these are still commercial narrative films, they play relentlessly with the expectations of moviegoers who want a simple love story or a straightforward action film. Good guys turn out to be corrupt, ingénues morph into femmes fatales, and nothing is what it seems or, more accurately, what we expect. The world of most films noir is gothic, even though it is usually an urban gothic. It is also a relentlessly physical world, in which the physical frailty of the human body is constantly emphasized.

Psychologically, noir presents us with a world of horror that is not supernatural, but moral. Its protagonists tend to be isolated, alienated individuals who are subject to forces that they can't control. It is a world of betrayal, paranoia, sudden violence, and unexpected outcomes. But it is assuredly a modern world, and often is set in an urban environment of shadowy streets and rainy nights. The plot usually involves an investigation, which can lead to revelations about larger conspiracies and further threats. The powerlessness and alienation of the protagonist is often reinforced by an unjust and tragic ending. As J. P. Telotte states in his study of narrative patterns in film noir:

> On the one hand, then, we shall see *noir* in a *reactive* context, as a response to or resistance to the dominations of power in society, and thus as a generic effort at revealing, examining, and, as far as possible, gaining some freedom from the forces that both structure and violate our daily lives. In a sense it is a social myth, one evoked

by the particular conditions of postwar America. On the other hand, we can see it as a symptom, a distortion that cuts across generic lines and that is caused by the same desires and powers that propel our culture and our lives. (Telotte 1989, 12)

So, film noir both serves and reacts against its historical conditions. It not only creates myths of freedom and empowerment, but also demonstrates how one's freedoms and power are limited. Noir films tend to use such narrative techniques as point-of-view camerawork, flashbacks, and voice-over narration to focus the perspective of the audience on the first person.

Fritz Leiber's story, "The Girl with the Hungry Eyes," reinterprets the vampire figure in a new way, much as his early mentor Lovecraft had done. But instead of linking this figure to a vast and cruel cosmos, he brings it into the modern setting of the city, linking it to present-day discourses of self-promotion and advertising, in the style of the film noir. It is a first-person narrative in the form of a flashback, describing a down-at-the heels photographer in a cheap studio in a bad part of town—an appropriate noir setting, even to the four flights of stairs he has to climb. He refers to "The Girl," who is apparently now famous, a national advertising icon, but refers to her as "poisonous," "evil," "unnatural," "morbid," and "unholy" (Leiber 2001, 417). He mentions "murders— if they were murders" and says he isn't quite sure what he knows, except that "There are vampires and vampires, and not all of them suck blood" (Leiber 2001, 417). This introduction serves to make us a little suspicious of the narrator's credibility. Is it a case of sour grapes? Is this the model who could have made him rich, but who got away?

The flashback begins with the isolated narrator in his studio. A woman shows up wanting to be a model. She doesn't impress the narrator much, but he is willing to give her a try. She is thin and cheaply dressed. Her only distinguishing feature is her dark eyes, "looking at you with a hunger that's all sex and something more than sex" (Leiber 2001, 418). After the modeling session, she leaves while he is developing the pictures, leaving no contact information. When his clients all want to hire her, he has no way to find her, but she shows up after a few days and they begin a very profitable partnership, governed by her rules—they only work in his studio, with no one else around, and he must never try to find out where she lives. Eventually, obsessed, he follows her. She goes into the downtown area and waits by a store display featuring her photograph, then goes off with a passer-by who recognizes her from the picture. More such forays correspond with men being found dead from heart attacks in suspicious circumstances—one of whom the narrator recognizes as the man he saw her with. Eventually, she agrees to go out with the narrator, but when he begins to get intimate with her she tells him, "I don't want that . . . I want you. I want . . ." and she catalogs a list of details from his life that he has told her about, ending with "I want your life. Feed me, baby, feed me"(Leiber 2001, 428). He breaks away and runs.

It is a plot from a film noir—ambiguous—with the vampire angle being either a delusion on the unreliable narrator's part, or a true account of a supernatural, psychic vampire. The mysterious girl is a perfect femme fatale, and the underlying theme of sexual obsession fits the genre perfectly. The gritty setting and hard-boiled, slang-laden narration told in retrospect match the voice-over and flashback plotting often found in the genre, and the lonely, isolated, uncertain narrator fits as a noir protagonist/investigator.

The story has been filmed in three different versions, each entitled "The Girl with the Hungry Eyes": a 1972 TV episode of Rod Sterling's *Night Gallery*, directed by John Badham; a 1967 film directed by William Rotsler with a lesbian subplot; and a 1995 film directed by Jon Jacobs. Of these, Badham's follows Leiber's story the closest, but the lush, colorful 1960s setting tends to dilute the story's noir mood.

Matheson's *I Am Legend* is an original take on the vampire, introducing the biological plague model of vampirism into an apocalyptic plot that has been described as a merging of the traditional vampire story with science fiction. What readers miss when they choose to view it through the lens of science fiction is that Matheson is using the apocalyptic scenario as a way of literalizing the world of the film noir. The hallmarks of noir are all over this story—isolation, anomie, and the feeling of being trapped in a paranoid dream. The main character and narrator, Robert Neville, is the last surviving human after a plague has reduced all others to vampire zombies. Matheson uses all the paraphernalia of the classic vampire tale—garlic, mirrors, staking—but puts them in the context of vampirism as a disease which causes people to want each others' blood, to avoid light, and to come out only at night. Neville is a disillusioned, alienated, lonely man, who goes through the motions of survival—growing garlic, scavenging food, sharpening stakes, and fortifying his house—all the while fighting ennui and inertia. The claustrophobic atmosphere and first-person narration place us immediately in a world closer to film noir than to space opera. Neville is depressed and mourning for his lost wife and daughter—we find out in flashbacks that he tried to bury his wife instead of burning her, and she came back. He drinks excessively in the evenings, listening to records so that he won't hear the vampires yelling outside his door.

His thoughts are portrayed in internal dialogs with himself, often when he is drinking. For example:

> Pore vampires, he thought, pore little cusses, pussyfootin' round my house so all forlorn.
>
> A thought. He raised a forefinger that wavered before his eyes.
>
> Friends, I come before you to discuss then vampire; a minority element if there ever was one, and there was one.
>
> But to conclusion: I will sketch out the basis for my thesis, which thesis is this: vampires are prejudiced against.
>
> The keynote of minority prejudice in this: They are loathed because they are feared. Thus . . .
>
> He made himself a drink. A long one.
>
> At one time, the Dark and Middle Ages, to be succinct, the vampire's power was great, the fear of him tremendous. He was anathema and still remains anathema. Society hates him without ration.
>
> But are his needs any more shocking than the needs of other animals and men? Are his deeds more outrageous than the deeds of the parent who drained the spirit from his child? The vampire may foster quickened heartbeats and levitated hair. But is he worse than the parent who gave to society a neurotic child who became a politician? Is he worse than the politician who set up belated foundations with the money he made by handing guns to suicidal nationalists? [. . .]
>
> All he does is drink blood.
>
> Why, then, this unkind prejudice, this thoughtless bias? Why cannot the vampire live where he chooses? Why must he seek out hiding places where none can find him out? Why do you wish him destroyed? Ah, see, you have turned the poor guileless innocent into a hunted animal. He has no means of support, no measures for proper education, he has not the voting franchise. No wonder he is compelled to seek out a predatory nocturnal existence.
>
> Robert Neville grunted a surly grunt. Sure, sure, he thought, but would you let your sister marry one? (Matheson 1954, 32)

Starting out in the slang of a Western movie, this parody of an academic speech certainly puts Neville's prejudices on display. He is joking, but he is also serious. Vampires are the same as any minority element in their difference and their demands. The irony is that it is Neville who is the minority in this situation. This monolog is especially telling given the novel's conclusion.

Neville adopts a dog, which dies. Then, he meets a woman who is apparently healthy. He manages to gain her trust and brings her home. Although a rather reluctant version, she turns out to be a femme fatale, a spy sent by a group of infected survivors who are using a combination of drugs to control the sickness and allow them to be exposed to light. She leaves him with a note that confesses her duplicity and advises him to try to escape before they come for him. In spite of this, he stays in his fortified house, and eventually they storm it, slaughtering the zombie vampires around it.

The woman Ruth, a "ranking officer in the new society" (Matheson 1954, 168), visits a wounded Neville in jail, where he is about to be executed. She gives him suicide pills and tells him he is "the last of the old race" (Matheson 1954, 167). When he looks out of the cell window, he sees a crowd of people who are waiting for his execution:

Then someone saw him.
For a moment there was an increased babbling of voices, a few startled cries.
Then sudden silence, as though a heavy blanket had fallen over their heads. They all stood looking up at him with their white faces. He stared back. And suddenly, he thought, I'm the abnormal one here. Normalcy was a majority concept, the standard of many and not the standard of just one man. (Matheson 1954, 169)

He realizes that he has come full circle. The novel ends with the phrase "I am legend," which signals Neville's acceptance that, despite his moralizing and his rationalization, he *has* become anathema, a legendary horror to the new society.

Despite its science-fiction frame, the story inhabits the world of film noir with its lone, alienated protagonist, its moral ambivalence, its flashbacks, its wasted urban setting—even the short, choppy sentences of the internal dialogues. It presents such a world literally, avoiding the usual use of metaphor and analogy. The paranoia characteristic of film noir is literalized as well—they *are* out to get you, in a world where the definition of humanity has changed.

I Am Legend has been developed into three major films, *The Last Man on Earth* (1964) with Vincent Price, *The Omega Man* (1971) with Charlton Heston, and *I Am Legend* (2007) with Will Smith. Of these, the first is the closest to the novel, but changes the final scene to one where Price, as Neville, is shot and falls on the altar of a church, giving the story religious overtones lacking in Matheson's novel, lacking what Nina Auerbach describes as its "dry, hate-filled pragmatism" (Auerbach 1995, 138), also a good way of describing film noir.

All the film versions fail to capture the style or tone of noir, relying instead on the flashy, fast-moving style of the action film. By the mid-1960s, when the first film version was made, the noir style was out of fashion.

Leiber and Matheson provide us with examples of noir-inflected stories that put the vampire in the middle of the American city at mid-century. Like film noir itself, they deal with the failure of the American Dream and the urban wasteland that has resulted. Instead of places of freedom, wealth, and hope for the future, many migrants to the American cities were finding urban blight, pollution, crime, and corruption. Postwar unemployment, paranoia about Communism, fear of juvenile delinquency, and the continued ghettoization of minorities combined with suburban growth to send the middle classes fleeing from urban areas in the late 1940s and 1950s. The grim, amoral world of the film noir tended to reinforce a view of cities as corrupt and corrupting influences, dead zones that still harbor an underlife, lurking to prey on good people. In such fears, vampires found a new home.

CHAPTER 8

Hammering It Home

The film [*Brides of Dracula*, 1960] solves its family crises through the figure of Dr. Van Helsing. He shows both concern about the growing "cult" and understanding for those who would be drawn to it; that is, his role in the film is paternal, rather than patriarchal. Through him the film rehabilitates the figure of the doctor who carefully and correctly diagnoses what is wrong.

—Ken Gelder (1994, 100)

Although they were British in origin, the Hammer horror films dominated the American horror market from the late 1950s into the late 1960s. They were financed in part and distributed by American studios. Christopher Lee was Hammer's Dracula, starring in seven films. These were: *Dracula* (1958; American title: *Horror of Dracula*), *Dracula: Prince of Darkness* (1966), *Dracula Has Risen from the Grave* (1968), *Scars of Dracula* (1970), *Taste the Blood of Dracula* (1970), *Dracula A.D. 1972* (1972), and *The Satanic Rites of Dracula* (1973; American title: *Dracula and His Vampire Bride*). Hammer also produced other vampire films, notably the Karstein trilogy (*The Vampire Lovers*, 1970; *Lust of a Vampire*, 1971; *Twins of Evil*, 1972). These were based loosely on J. Sheridan LeFanu's *Carmilla*, and featured Danish actress Ingrid Pitt in the first two and twin Playboy playmates Madeleine and Mary Collinson in the third.

The Hammer studio developed a signature style that featured elaborate period settings and costumes, understated acting, bright colors (especially blood), and increasingly explicit violence and sexual content. They were materialistic in a very literal way, eschewing special effects— Lee's vampire does not shape-shift—in favor of a clear focus on physical

materiality. The colorful, detailed sets emphasize this, as do the signature scenes of blood-spurting stakings and the defeated vampire's body
dissolving by stages into ash. Christopher Lee's Dracula is stiff and
poised, imperious, yet manages to convey a fierce, feral predatory sexuality just beneath the surface. His vampire provided a kind of bodice-
ripper sex appeal to the male-oriented members of the audience, while
the pretty, young, buxom, and increasingly undressed victims appealed
to those who prefer women. Lee provided a no-nonsense monster who
is what he is, without Lugosi's unctuousness, and with more explicit,
if problematic, erotic appeal. He was, perhaps, more like a Nazi—at
least a propaganda Nazi—to an audience who still remembered World
War II. But, like World War II by the 1960s, he also displayed certain
remoteness, and I think this accounts for another appeal of the Hammer
films, especially for the American audience.

During a time when nuclear annihilation was a very real and
immediate possibility, and when many American horror films focused
on science-fiction threats directly or indirectly caused by nuclear technology, there was something comforting about monsters who were far
away in some vaguely Central European setting, often in an earlier
time. The opening sequences of many of the Hammer films—a kind
of cinematic signature—features a horse-drawn coach passing through
a forest. This scene served to remind audiences that the cinematic vehicle they were traveling in was just as old-fashioned and would deliver
them to a fairly predictable outcome. This was also true of the conflict in the films, which was often presented as a simplified version of
a Freudian conflict between father figures—as Ken Gelder points out
in the opening quotation—an old-fashioned, authoritarian, patriarch
(Lee's Dracula) against a sympathetic, rational, and paternal figure
(Cushing's Van Helsing). Without the distancing effects of a full-blown
camp, which we will look at in the next chapter, the Hammer films
delivered an encapsulated product in a satisfying way. This is a gener-
alization, and I wish it to apply to the main run of Hammer films. As
we shall see, the studio did adjust to the times in the later work, not
always with success.

Dracula (1958) introduced Lee as the count. Its plot seems to follow
Stoker's novel at first, but we soon find that Harker, in Transylvania as
Dracula's guest, is really there to kill him. The story that develops is a
fairly straightforward struggle between good and evil, as personified by
Lee's Dracula and Peter Cushing's equally imperious Van Helsing, here
portrayed as a vigorous middle-aged man rather than the elderly, semi-
comic character Stoker portrayed or the bespectacled scientist from

Browning's version. In this first film, the Count never comes to England, although he does travel far enough to vampirize Lucy Holmwood, Harker's fiancé, and to threaten Mina, her brother's wife. Vampire Lucy almost gets to her young niece, but is staked by her brother Arthur Holmwood and Van Helsing. When they realize the threat to Mina, they wait outside the house to keep the vampire at bay, but it turns out that he has secreted in his coffin in the basement. He attacks from within the house and then escapes with Mina. The men, then, pursue him to his castle, where he is killed in a final confrontation with Van Helsing, and Mina is saved.

We can see from this summary that the international scale of Stoker's and Browning's versions is scaled down. The Holmwoods live in a middle European country next door to Dracula's—the names of towns given are Klausenberg and Karlstadt, and there is a bit of comedy about a border post where the characters pass back and forth, frustrating a buffoonish border guard. In keeping with Lee's highly sexualized presentation of vampirism, the film presents its horror as a threat to the family, not the nation. Like uncontrolled sexual desire, it comes from within, as suggested both by Lucy's threat to her niece and by the coffin's presence in the cellar of the house. The enemy within is able to turn anyone, even a perfect wife like Mina Holmwood, into a creature of instinct. In this way, Lee's tall, handsome, compelling persona works together with his sudden switches to feral violence. *Dracula* was a hugely successful film, and this success allowed Hammer to develop its signature style in a variety of horror films throughout the 1960s.

By the early 1970s, the conservative, family-oriented messages of these films were failing to attract audiences at the same rate; so we can see attempts to appeal to a new audience. In his analysis of *Dracula A.D. 1972*, Paul Newland sees both a recognition of the new counterculture/ youth culture and a critique of it. Its plot centers around Jessica Van Helsing (Stephanie Beacham), a descendant of the original Dr. Van Helsing, who had died in a struggle with Dracula 100 years before. She is running with a group of bored, disaffiliated youth. In an opening scene, they crash a party full of stuffy upper-class people, leaving just ahead of the police. Looking for more thrills, they break into a ruined church, where Johnny Alucard (spell it backward), a mysterious new member of the group, performs a ritual, mixing his blood with the ashes of Dracula. After Jessica and the others flee, Alucard resurrects Dracula. "I did it. I summoned you!" he exclaims. Dracula replies dismissively, "It was my will." This signals a clear disconnect between the desires of the young and those of the older generation, and suggests that

Alucard doesn't know what he is doing. Fortunately, Jessica Van Helsing isn't too far gone. As she explains to her grandfather, Lorrimer Van Helsing (a direct descendant from *Dracula's* Abraham Van Helsing, played by Peter Cushing), "I've never dropped acid, I'm not shooting up, and I'm not sleeping with anyone just yet. The full extent of my wild ways amounts to a pint of lager now and again." The plot develops, of course, into a confrontation between the old enemies, Cushing's Van Helsing against Lee's Dracula. The film ends with most of Jessica's group dead, along with Dracula, and with Jessica safely enclosed once again in her proper place in the social order. According to Newland, this signals the defeat or incorporation of the counterculture within the greater culture:

> [The film] clearly exploits the countercultural codes and conventions of the 1960s. It presents stereotypical hippie figures that indulge in the type of countercultural practices being inculcated into the discourses of mass culture by 1972. As such in *Dracula A.D. 1972* we see what is left of the transnational counterculture become effectively "un-dead." (Newland 2009, 148)

Like this film, later Hammer films tend to associate both youth culture and vampirism with the broader category of the cult. *Dracula A.D. 1972* and the final film in Lee's Dracula series for Hammer, *The Satanic Rites of Dracula* (American title: *Count Dracula and His Vampire Bride*, 1973), both exploit this cultural anxiety, and feature James Bond–like soundtracks to fit in with their modern London setting. Examples of actual cult-associated activities at the time included the Manson murders of 1969 and the Highgate Cemetery vampire episode of 1970, where crowds of young vampire hunters actually showed up to help eliminate a reported vampire in a Victorian cemetery in North London, recruited by a group called the British Occult Society. (Highgate Cemetery, while not explicitly identified in the novel, is generally supposed to be the site of Lucy's staking in Stoker's *Dracula*.)

Even though these films can be seen to be exploiting contemporary fears, the youth culture/youth cult connection in the Hammer films can be traced back to the early 1960s, as Gelder has pointed out. Hammer's second Dracula film, *The Brides of Dracula* (1960), was often overlooked because it did not feature Christopher Lee; it features a young Baron Meinster (David Peel), described in the film's voice-over introduction as "liv[ing] on to spread the cult and corrupt the world." The film develops a contrast between the patriarchal father figure of

Dr. Tobler, a schoolmaster, and the kinder, more paternal Van Helsing, who *manages* the wayward young rather than commanding and denying them in an authoritarian manner. Other Hammer films feature cults and ritual ceremonies. For example, in the *Kiss of the Vampire* (1963), a professor uses a pentagram invocation to defeat a vampire cult. The invocation brings swarms of demonic vampire bats that attack and kill the vampires. Again, to use Gelder's terms, management succeeds where prohibition fails. *Taste the Blood of Dracula* (1970) reprises the youth cult connection, reviving Dracula through a black magic ceremony which transforms a young occultist, Lord Courtley (Ralph Bates) into a reincarnation of Lee's Dracula, after he drinks a potion of his own blood mixed with Dracula's ashes. There is no Van Helsing character in this film, and Dracula is defeated by being trapped in the church where the Black Mass had been performed, now reconsecrated by Paul (Anthony Corlan), a young man trying to save his girlfriend from the clutches of Dracula. He uses crosses and sacred candles, and Dracula, unable to escape, falls on the altar and is destroyed. The general pattern is to contrast the unsanctioned ritualistic behaviors of the cult with that of an established family or potential familial relationship, which is associated with the triumph of good.

The threat of youth cults develops in the final Hammer films to a focus on cults in general. In *Twins of Evil* (1971), the twins of the title move to Karstein, where we find another young Count who becomes a vampire through human sacrifice and black magic rituals. But the real threat to society is the twins' uncle, Gustav Weil (Cushing), who travels the countryside as the head of a group of night riders, burning young women suspected of being witches. Here, Cushing plays the patriarchal authority figure, a fanatical cult leader who is much scarier than the bored, sensual vampire, Count Karstein. Predictably, one twin survives after the other becomes a vampire and must be beheaded. The film is somewhat unique in that it doesn't feature a contrasting Van Helsing–type older character. Order is restored instead by a young schoolteacher, who ends up romantically involved with the surviving twin.

The final Lee/Cushing vehicle, *The Satanic Rites of Dracula* (1973), features a cult of high government officials working with Dracula to release a biological agent that will kill all humans. Here, Cushing reprises his Van Helsing character and, working with a hip young detective, saves his granddaughter, stakes Dracula, and saves the day. The cult leaders are old men—businessmen and pillars of the community—but they have a cadre of long-haired, motorcycle-riding thugs in sheepskin vests to do their dirty work.

The last Hammer vampire film was a collaboration with a Hong Kong studio, Shaw Brothers, to produce a martial arts/horror mash-up entitled *Legend of the Seven Golden Vampires* in 1974. Much like Universal's late mash-ups, this can be seen as an attempt to shore up a failing dynasty by combining genres.

As I suggested earlier, the appeal of these films lie, despite their explicit gore, in their comfort level. They all predictably end with the destruction of evil and the restoration of order. To use Ken Gelder's terms (1994), management triumphs, whether through Van Helsing's paternal care or the reintegration of a formerly rebellious young person into the familial fold of normality, often coded as either home or as a vaguely Christian religious orthodoxy. For films that stress the physicality and visual solidity of the settings, as well as the physical/sexual nature of the vampire's presence, it seems odd that the objects used in the defeat of the vampire are most often such religious paraphernalia as crosses and holy water. But, this reinforces the comforting theme of clearly delineated good versus evil. Again, the messages are expressed in material terms—crosses and holy water actually burn the evil flesh of the vampire. They serve as tools, good things to oppose the bad things, such as pentagrams, vampire dust, and blood that are associated with evil. The consistency of these contrasting objects, as well as their concreteness, serves to ground the supernatural elements in a way that is comfortable to the audience.

Eventually, the simplicity of the Hammer formula began to lose its appeal. We can see that Hammer did make attempts to change with the times, but they never developed far beyond their basic themes and formulas and never managed to bring in new stars and directors as their central players aged. The great horror films of the 1960s, including Hitchcock's *Psycho* (1960), Romero's *Night of the Living Dead* (1968), and Polanski's *Rosemary's Baby* (1968), all show the influence of the Hammer style, but were able to develop beyond it in ways that the Hammer studios could not, often by presenting moral questions in complex and ambiguous ways. But Hammer had certainly resurrected the vampire and given it a solid, visceral life alongside its campier avatars.

CHAPTER 9

Countering Vampire Culture

Little girl: Mommy, what's a vampire?

Mother: Shut up and drink your tomato juice.

By the 1960s, the vampire was no longer a terrifying foreigner or a violent predator. He was a common visitor to everyone's living room. Television, which had been so heavily sanitized in the 1950s in an attempt to dilute the offensiveness of the stage and vaudeville acts that gave birth to it, began to expand and to produce material for separate audiences. The expansion of available programming time on the airwaves made it necessary for the networks to use already-filmed material as filler. This included short subjects and cartoons for children and older films for adult late-night viewing. In this way, the Universal horror catalog was reintroduced, often in heavily edited form, to new generations of both adults and children. And television, having established itself as squeaky clean, opened itself up for a different kind of viewing, one that ironically acknowledged the sanitized content and made fun of it by exaggeration and imitation. So "camp" was born, and it thrived on—and in reference to—the small screen.

In 1964, Susan Sontag published "Notes on 'Camp,'" in the *Partisan Review*. In it, she labels camp "[a] sensibility (as distinct from an idea)" (Sontag 1999, 53) and gives 58 numbered examples or vignettes that describe this sensibility. She emphasizes artifice, style exaggeration, performance, and irony, and she acknowledges camp's ties to underground gay culture. She distinguishes between naive camp and deliberate camp. She talks about camp as a way of preserving certain aspects of outré style from the past, citing feather boas from the 1920s, Aubrey

Beardsley prints, and Tiffany lamps as examples. These examples point out the instability of camp over time. Today, Tiffany lamps and Beardsley prints have migrated into the category of high art, but feather boas keep their campy allure. Now we not only think of fashions from the 1960s, such as beehive haircuts and go-go boots, as camp, but we also look to other decades, such as the 1980s, for our primary markers—big hair and leopard-print tights, for example. Someone has suggested that it takes 20–30 years for fashion to become camp; but certainly not all fashion achieves the status of camp, only distinctive, theatrical, and spectacular styles.

In discussing the relationship between a mass-media audience and camp as a subcultural phenomena that developed mass appeal, Chuck Kleinhans claims:

> There is a tendency for mass-culture media to take up almost anything which is different and to turn it into an aspect of fashionable change: something different to spice up jaded tastes. The media world's cannibalization of subcultures is a structural feature of the culture industry. It is staffed by people who are predominantly petty bourgeois professionals whose very occupation implies a distance from and an irony towards the personalities, programs and politics they produce—a true dissociation of sensibility. Unable to believe in what they make, to have a naive acceptance of it, mass-culture makers are often drawn to particular subcultures precisely for their difference, their newness, their not-as-yet-commercialized qualities. All of which, incidentally, can be turned back into one's work; a weekend in the subculture inspires Monday morning's new ad campaign. (Kleinhans 1994, 161–162)

Subcultural materials and styles become fashion, and some of those materials get recycled later into camp.

Camp is generally recognized as emerging from gay subcultures into the main culture during the 1960s. An often-cited example is the *Batman* TV series, which ran from 1966–1968 on ABC, with Adam West as Batman and Burt Ward as Robin. The show's cliché-ridden dialogue, stiff acting, and use of comic book intertitles ("Pow!") during fight scenes all seem campy enough, but a variety of over-the-top costars, usually cast as villains, sealed the deal. Guest appearances included Milton Berle, Eartha Kitt, Burgess Meredith, Joan Collins, Vincent Price, Julie Newmar, and Cesar Romero. The show's all-out campiness is now often understood as a response to psychologist Fredric Wertham's paranoid best seller *The Seduction of the Innocent* (1954), a homophobic screed that condemned comic books in general and held up the Batman comic books in particular, as examples of a homosexual agenda designed to corrupt the morals of American youth by normalizing a gay couple as heroes. Ironically, if we are to think of camp as a gay sensibility, the small-screen *Batman* introduced it to children as harmless, funny, and fun, a way of deflecting the anxieties that children often feel during crime dramas or horror films.

The Universal monsters, including Dracula, began to take on aspects of camp in the 1940s, with the Abbott and Costello films. Sontag calls camp "a sensibility of failed seriousness" (Sontag 1999, Note 36, 61), and we can see the serious nature of the early films dissolve into a kind of knowing self-parody. In *Abbott and Costello Meet Frankenstein*, for example, Lugosi's Dracula lines up with the Wolf Man and the Frankenstein monster to provide cheap scares and slapstick humor. By the late 1950s, these films, mixed with formerly serious films, like Browning's *Dracula* and Whale's *Frankenstein*, were being recycled on television. In contrast to the increasingly graphic horror fare available on the big screen (e.g., the Hammer films), such classic horror films were experienced differently by television viewers. They were appreciated as camp. The older figures became funny monsters in contrast to the Hammer films' edgier horror. This led to a marketing bonanza for Universal—Dracula, Frankenstein, and Wolf Man dolls, games, costumes, and models—as well as a growth of such less direct (and copyright-free) cultural references as the popular novelty song "Monster Mash" (1962), the Dracula-like Grandpa character in the campy horror-inspired sitcom "The Munsters" (1964–1966), sugar-filled breakfast cereals for children, Frankenberry and Count Chocula (both introduced in 1971), and eventually the harmless, math-obsessed Count Von Count in the Sesame Street educational program (introduced in 1972).

One aspect of camp is a sort of indirect acknowledgment that, as Karl Marx suggested, what appears first as tragedy comes around again as farce. With the domestication of the vampire figure into a harmless, Hungarian-accented, evening-dressed buffoon, we might have expected to lose the monster completely. But as we have seen with the Hammer films, the monster kept his hold on the film industry by becoming more sexual and violent, and by appealing to an adult or at least late-adolescent sensibility.

An example of the dilemmas faced by the televised vampires of the 1960s can be found in Barnabas Collins, a vampire who appeared in the afternoon soap opera *Dark Shadows*. The show ran from 1966 to 1971. Barnabas was vampirized by way of a curse from a spurned lover and much of his motivation in the show involved trying to become normal again. The transformation from an evil vampire into a conflicted one who dislikes his vampire identity would become commonplace in later treatments. Such vampires are sometimes referred to as sympathetic. Previous to *Dark Shadows*, only Varney from the penny dreadful and Gloria Holden's Countess Valeska in *Dracula's Daughter* had claimed to want to change, and in the case of the Countess, this may have been only a ploy.

In the course of the 1,225 episodes of *Dark Shadows*, Barnabas Collins manages to revert to normal human status more than once, finally achieving it permanently. He had originally been introduced as a short-term character in an attempt to revive flagging ratings, but he quickly became a central protagonist on the show. His vampire traits were fairly standard—he only came out at night, could transform into a bat or a mist, was vulnerable to crucifixes—but he also was a bit of a sorcerer, using spells and, with typical 1960s eclecticism, the Chinese book of oracles, *I Ching*. The vampire character was augmented by other supernatural beings, including ghosts, golems, and witches. The show's writers resorted to most of the plot conventions that have kept serial stories going on television and in comic books, including time travel, amnesia, hypnosis, reincarnation, demonic possession, and a parallel universe. Barnabas's motivational focus remained a soap opera staple— his search for true love, understood to be a desire to find a reincarnated version of his first love. In this way, he is presented as *normal*, just like one of us, with certain specialized eating habits.

This is the first example, as far as I know, of the reincarnation plot, where the vampire finds a resemblance in a contemporary woman to a long-lost love, usually from his human life. Dan Curtis, the producer/ director of *Dark Shadows*, also directed a TV version of *Dracula*, the first to be titled *Bram Stoker's Dracula* (1973), which applied the reincarnation plot to a fairly close version of the Stoker novel's plot, with Jack Palance as a somewhat unconvincing Dracula. The style was serious and melodramatic and very similar in visual and dramatic style to the Hammer films, even down to the red lettering in the title sequence. The reincarnation plot would become a vampire story staple, significantly used again in Coppola's 1992 *Bram Stoker's Dracula*.

The endless plot of soap operas emphasizes the banal, everyday. As *Dark Shadows* appeared every afternoon on one's television—at home, every day, no big deal—so vampires became domesticated in the course of the 1960s. By the early 1970s, vampires were being used to sell breakfast cereal and to teach arithmetic. By filtering their scares through the double screens of television and camp, vampires were given a new life in the 1960s, especially for children. The vampire, especially Lugosi's Dracula, became a stereotypical and even a comforting figure with a long list of conventional attributes. This standardized figure was heavily mediated through television, merchandizing, and advertising by a culture industry that turns everything into saleable products or commodities. The political changes and challenges of the 1960s were prompted by the children who had been raised, more than at any time before, by this industry, but social change was slow to affect the calcified and now camped-out figure of the vampire.

In their study, *The Vampire Film*, Alain Silver and James Ursini suggest that the vampire films of the 1970s "all represent a kind of neo-traditionalism, i.e., a return to Gothic, Expressionistic and Romantic conventions" (Silver and Ursini 1993, 150). If we add camp to the mix (Ursini and Silver use the term serio-comic), we have four different styles, all based on previous incarnations of a fairly tired figure. The camp vampire found a home in a series of comedies throughout the 1970s. David Niven starred in *Old Dracula* (alternate title: *Vampira*, 1975), a title changed in order to capitalize on Mel Brooks's successful Frankenstein spoof, *Young Frankenstein* (1974), which was actually filmed in black-and-white in order to use some of the old Universal sets from the 1930s. *Old Dracula* also attempted to capitalize on the *Blacula* films by having a black vampire's bite change Niven black. (Like much-dated humor, this aspect of the film only seems embarrassing in retrospect.) Other films using forms of camp humor during this period include Paul Morrisey's *Andy Warhol's Dracula* (1974), an over-the-top morality tale that is based on Dracula's decline due to the unavailability of virgin's blood. This film is played straight with very camp-influenced performances, including Udo Kier as an enervated Dracula and Joe Dallesandro as a Marxist farm worker. *Dracula Sucks* (1979) was an attempt to make a campy pornographic spoof of Dracula. Other attempts to exploit the camp vampire included *Dracula's Dog* (also titled *Zoltan: Hound of Dracula*, 1978). In short, by the 1970s, we find vampire stories to be seriously in need of new blood, looking for new ways to reinvigorate that figure.

CHAPTER 10

Black Vampires

Definitions belong to the definers, not the defined.
—Toni Morrison

By the early 1970s, vampires were thoroughly familiar and thoroughly banal. The vampire identity was available as a campy costume role for adults or for children. Everybody knew about vampires—they are yesterday's horror, today's party theme. To judge from Barnabas Collins's attitude, even vampires don't want to be vampires. By this point, the Hammer films were relying more on titillation than on fear to sell their adult vampire films, but they were borrowing heavily from other genres in order to keep it interesting. Politically, the reforms of the 1960s and the decline of the Vietnam War left the United States in an odd stew of complacency on the one hand and extremism on the other. The earnest solidarity of the early Civil Rights movement has split into white liberal reformers versus Black Power nationalists. Legally, African Americans have been granted equal rights and legal protections, and they are entering the professions in greater numbers than before, but the majority of poor black Americans are warehoused in housing projects or isolated in other traditionally poor rural and urban areas. In cinema, as black writers and directors gained more control, films began to appear that exaggerated stereotypical attributes of blackness—virility, athleticism, violence, soul—in a camp-influenced style known as "Blaxploitation." These films feature cool larger-than-life protagonists who triumph over the racism and traditions of an enervated white culture by way of sheer bravado and style, backed by a thumping funk and/or soul soundtrack. Intellectually, such films often feature style over substance, but their campy send-up of racist stereotypes finds broad audiences among whites who imagine themselves to be cool, as well as across class lines in black communities.

Melvin Van Peeble's *Sweet Sweetback's Baadasssss Song* (1971) is usually seen as the first in the Blaxploitation genre, followed closely by Gordon Parks's *Shaft* (1971). Both were basically crime dramas set in inner cities. With the success of these films, directors sought to expand the style into other genres, so we have *Coffy* (1973) with a female protagonist, *Mandingo* (1975), an historical epic, *Boss Nigger* (1975), a Western, *Uptown Saturday Night* (1974), a comedy, and the vampire/horror films, *Blacula* (1972) and *Scream, Blacula, Scream* (1973). We also have the difficult-to-classify *Ganja and Hess (1973)* with a vampire theme.

Recent academic work in whiteness has tended to see it as an invisible standard, a default, an unacknowledged norm against which various shades of otherness are discerned. This is appropriate, perhaps, for the last few decades, but tends to ignore the ways in which being white was an acknowledged and self-conscious identity in earlier times. Such a perspective is also rather white-centered, and does not take into account the fact that others excluded might have their own perspectives on whiteness. Instead of seeing whiteness as ground or background, as negative or neutral in other words, whiteness can manifest as what I call a positive pejorative whiteness—in this case, in the visible ways in which it can be seen as a category of oppression. Whiteness has never been particularly invisible to those oppressed by it. For example, African Americans have a literary tradition of imagining whiteness as vampirism. Coexisting with the vamp craze inspired by *A Fool There Was*, James Weldon Johnson wrote "The White Witch" (1922), a ballad about a woman who preys on men, but here the vampire/witch is a white woman, and she threatens young black men.

The poem opens:

> O brothers mine, take care! Take care!
> The great white witch rides out to-night.
> Trust not your prowess nor your strength,
> Your only safety lies in flight;
> For in her glance there is a snare,
> And in her smile there is a blight.

The traditional mesmerizing gaze of the vampire is combined with imagery from the vigilante terror practices of groups like the Klan. "[R]ides out to-night" suggests the term "night riders," which refers to such groups. In like fashion, if we look at the last word in each line of Johnson's conventional description of the witch's beauty:

> Her lips are like carnations, red,
> Her face like new-born lilies, fair,
> Her eyes like ocean waters, blue,

we see that he substitutes fair for white so as to not make it too obvious that the primary colors described here are red, white, and blue, the national colors of the United States. These are described as a mask for her true nature—ancient, animal, and predatory:

> And underneath the soft caress
> Of hand and voice and purring sighs,
> The shadow of the panther lurks,
> The spirit of the vampire lies. (Johnson 1922, 42)

The poem does not treat race directly except in the designation of the witch/vampire figure as white, and, as in the embedded references above, it is possible to read the poem as a supernatural ballad in the European tradition of such poems as Keats's "La Belle Dame Sans Merci" or Kipling's "The Vampyre," especially if the reader did not know that the author was black.

This poem turns the female vampire or vamp figure in a new direction. Johnson's double-coded language appropriates vampire discourse by connecting it to whiteness, a recognizable and pernicious quality to African Americans, especially regarding white female sexuality, a force that, as the poem emphasizes, could literally kill any black man who even acknowledged its existence.

One of the hallmarks of the Blaxploitation film is reversal of roles, with powerful black characters dominating weak whites, often emphasized by name calling. The vampire films in this genre take this a step further by coding vampirism as a white condition passed on to unsuspecting blacks. In *Blacula*, the main character is an African prince turned into a vampire by the original Dracula in the 18th century while he tries to get help to suppress the European slave trade. Instead, Dracula turns him into a vampire, curses him, and seals him in a casket. In a switch to the present time, the casket is imported to Los Angeles by a couple of white interior decorators who become his first victims. First the decadent, deceptive Dracula, then a couple of stereotypically silly gay men serve to introduce white people in the film in negative ways, as deceptive or incompetent. The Blacula figure, Prince Mamouwalde, is played by the Shakespearian actor William Marshall, who brings dignity and gravitas to what could have been a seriously demeaning role. Marshall reportedly worked with the director to make the character both African in origin and more dignified, and, against the studio's wishes, insisted on the references to the slave trade. The result is an oddly bifurcated film that alternates campy vampirism with moments where Marshall's presence urges us to take him seriously. As motivation, the film uses the reincarnation plot, similar to that used in *Dark Shadows*. The vampire is searching for the reincarnation of his lover from his human incarnation, and believes he has found her in a woman named Tina (Vonetta McGee). He woos her while killing several other people, prompting a police investigation. In the climactic scene in a Los Angeles water works plant, Tina is accidentally shot by the police and Mamouwalde, in despair, seeks out the sun to destroy himself. The film does present a variety of African American characters sympathetically. The makeup for the vampirized black characters is generally whiteface, suggesting by way of a visual metaphor that white racism is vampiric. For some reason, Marshall's makeup is different—when his fangs come out, his face becomes hairy, giving him an almost Wolf Man-like look. Other than forming an animalistic contrast to his usually urbane character, this seems to have no purpose, and further emphasizes the film's two-sidedness.

The troubling doubleness of style that seems to be a flaw in this film might be an attempt on the filmmaker's part to portray in visual terms the concept that the great African American scholar and civil rights leader, W. E. B. Du Bois, posited in his *Souls of Black Folk* (1904):

After the Egyptian and Indian, the Greek and Roman, the Teuton and Mongolian, the Negro is a sort of seventh son, born with a veil, and gifted with second-sight in this American world;—a world which yields him no true self-consciousness, but only lets him see himself through the revelation of the other world. It is a peculiar sensation, this double-consciousness, this sense of always looking at one's self through the eyes of others, of measuring one's soul by the tape of a world that looks on in amused contempt and pity. One ever feels his twoness,—an American, a Negro; two warring souls, two thoughts, two unreconciled strivings; two warring ideals in one dark body, whose dogged strength alone keeps it from being torn asunder.

The history of the American Negro is the history of this strife,—
this longing to attain self-conscious manhood, to merge his double
self into a better and truer self. (Du Bois 1997, 38–39)

Although it is probably a stretch to see *Blacula* as a product of an exclusively African American perspective, it is certainly an example of a
film that attempts to incorporate that perspective. Two other films from
the early 1970s also deal with vampires from this hybrid point-of-view,
Blacula's sequel, the unfortunately named *Scream, Blacula, Scream*
(1973) and *Ganja and Hess* (aka *Blood Couple*, 1973).

Scream, Blacula, Scream finds Marshall's Mamouwalde reanimated
from his bones by way of a voodoo ceremony by Willis (Richard Law-
son), an arrogant and egocentric young man who wants to take over his
mother's voodoo congregation, even though they are more inclined to
vote for his adopted sister Lisa (Pam Grier). Mamouwalde meets Lisa
and her boyfriend Justin Carter (Don Mitchell) at a party at Carter's
house. They discuss Carter's extensive collection of African art and arti-
facts, and Mamouwalde offers some insights. Mamouwalde turns Willis
into a vampire, and Willis turns several others. As the circle of undead
increases and Carter, who is a former policeman, figures out the vampire
angle, Mamouwalde reveals his true nature to Lisa and asks her to return
him to normal life through a voodoo ceremony. The police interrupt the
ceremony and Lisa ends up dispatching Mamouwalde who suddenly
wants to be called Blacula, by staking his voodoo doll likeness. A more
stylistically consistent film than the first one, *Scream, Blacula, Scream*
presents both black intellectuals and voodoo as normal, and has a scene
where Mamouwalde berates a pimp for enslaving his own people. On
the other hand, there is a lot of screaming, and the second-generation
vampires seem rather zombie-like in their whiteface makeup.

Ganja and Hess, because it was released in 1973, is sometimes
included in lists of Blaxploitation films, but it is really misplaced there.
Where the Blacula films, especially the first one, have elements of Blaxploitation, this film is simply an example of an Afrocentric vampire tale,
filmed in a slow, poetic style by its director, Bill Gunn. It was also released as *Blood Couple* in a severely edited version, but the original
has been restored for DVD publication. The vampirism in this story
comes from an ancient African dagger. Archaeologist Dr. Hess Green
(Duane Jones) is stabbed by a troubled assistant, and the infection
not only makes him want blood, but also connects him psychically to
the African tribe from which it came. He infects and marries Ganja

(Marlene Clark), the assistant's widow, and the lovers eventually go in two different directions—she embracing their African forbears and he committing suicide through Christianity (an interesting metaphor). The film represented the United States at the Cannes Film Festival in 1973, and was voted one of the 10 best American films of the decade. When a white reviewer wondered "where was the race problem?," director Bill Gunn replied, "If he looks closely, he will find it in his own review" (Gunn 1973, 7). The vampire angle is only an excuse for Gunn to explore three interesting characters and their psychological conflicts—he is interested in individual motivation rather than representing the race or explaining it to a white audience. Speaking to white critics in general, he stated: "I know this film does not address you" (Gunn 1973, 7).

In stark contrast, we have British comedian David Niven's performance in blackface in *Old Dracula*. Black vampires return in Richard Wenk's 1986 film *Vamp*, starring Grace Jones. It's a story about frat boys looking for a stripper and wandering into a vampire bar. Jones, playing the owner, does a fascinating dance in whiteface, but the film degenerates from there. She turns out to be a vampire queen who sleeps in an Egyptian sarcophagus, but she says nothing in the whole film, instead emitting animal growls or hysterical laughter, as she rips throats and yanks out hearts. She is portrayed as sexual and animalistic, so much so that she grows a whole snout when she feeds. Needless to say, this plays to the worst of racist stereotypes of blacks as animalistic, physical, sexual, and nonverbal. Not much better is the frat boy's Asian sidekick, there to provide constant comic relief until he has to be killed. The film's most interesting and funniest character is Vic, the Italian club owner who dresses in a pink tux and talks constantly of Vegas and class. But he is still a stereotype. Except for an MTV music video-influenced visual style, the film has little to recommend it. In general, films in the 1980s were not taking risks as far as race was concerned, tending to reinforce stereotypes rather than to interrogate them.

By the mid-1990s, things had changed, a bit. Established horror director Wes Craven directed comedian/action hero Eddie Murphy, along with Angela Bassett, in *Vampire in Brooklyn* (1995). In this film, race is another novelty item like the Brooklyn setting or the film's Italian Mafiosi, providing stereotyped comic characters like the nearsighted night watchman/landlord played by John Witherspoon and the vampire's decaying ghoul sidekick (Kadeem Hardison). The story centers on Murphy's character, the last of the vampires, and his quest for a woman with half-vampire blood, who turns out to be Detective Rita

Veder (Bassett). The film keeps our interest by focusing on Veder's quest to understand herself, which turns on her accepting her supernatural heritage. Through his shape-shifting ability, Murphy's vampire gets to become a Mafioso wannabe as well as a showy, drunken preacher, who gives a sermon concluding with, "Evil is good!" As Craven's entry into the vampire genre, it is a stylish, workmanlike horror film with episodes of humor, much like his *Nightmare on Elm Street* and *Scream* series films. Race is simply an attribute of the characters, and is used as a joke when Jerry Hall, doing a cameo as an upper-class Manhattanite, tells Murphy's vampire, "I understand the Negro people. I understand how you've been chained by the oppression of white capitalist society," before he bites her.

Wesley Snipes starred in the *Blade* trilogy (1998, 2002, and 2004). Blade is a Marvel Comics character, introduced in 1973 as an African American semi-vampire (his mother was bitten while giving birth), who becomes a vampire hunter. He was originally conceived by Marv Wolfman and sketched by Gene Colan. Apart from being black, he has, due to his vampire blood, much of a vampire's abilities without their susceptibilities to sun, silver, or garlic. He is a martial arts expert, and especially good with edged weapons. The *Blade* films are basically superhero action films, where vampires provide the enemies and the hero's conflict is to keep himself from becoming too much like them (he takes a serum to counter his bloodlust). Because Blade is the only one of his kind, race does not serve much of a function in these films, except as another mark—along with his semi-vampirism—of the superhero's status as other and unique. Were there other black superheroes, he would hardly seem unique at all. He does represent another direction in vampire figures, one related to the cyborg.

The most interesting recent intervention into questions of vampires and race is Octavia Butler's final novel, *Fledgling* (2005). It is a first-person narrative from the perspective of Shori, an adolescent vampire who awakens in great pain in the dark. She senses another creature nearby and kills and eats it, gradually healing and gaining her sight back, but unable to remember anything about her former life. As the novel develops, she pieces together information about herself and her community, while being pursued by relentless killers. She finds that she belongs to a vampire race, the Ina, who adopt humans as "symbionts." The symbiont derives pleasure and a telepathic bond from being bitten, while the Ina derives nourishment. Shori is unique as an Ina, further-more, because she has dark skin, a genetic variation that makes her more sun tolerant. The people trying to kill her, who had originally left her for dead with head injuries, are a conservative faction of Ina who want to preserve their white racial purity.

As with her other work, Butler combines science fiction (the Ina are an alien race) with racial issues, to raise questions about the best ways for humans to form communities and combat violent and destructive social tendencies. She preserves the sexual appeal, long life, physical strength, fast healing, and bloodsucking aspects of the traditional vampire, but makes them a (mostly) gentle race whose victims are not killed, but choose to live in groups together in symbiotic relationships with vampires. In this way, she presents the most sympathetic vampire type yet—even Stephenie Meyer's vegetarian vampires are killers of animals. Perhaps her form of benevolent dictatorship by vampire is what humans should hope for—the implication is that we humans don't govern ourselves all that well.

Black vampires exist along a broad spectrum. In some cases, they are merely a different-colored variation on a common figure, such as the comic book superhero. In other cases, they reinforce racist stereotypes. African Americans have used the vampire figure as a racial metaphor for the destructive power of whiteness, as well as to represent black identity and the power of African traditions. In our attempts to come to terms with racial difference, Americans seem to want it both ways—we want race to be a defining category and we want it to be insignificant, not to matter.

CHAPTER 11

Vampire Celebrities

After Rice, . . . the vampire was used to provide a vehicle for social commentary, and vampirism itself became a convincing metaphor for such varied topics as drug addiction, homosexuality, AIDS, and the general selfishness and narcissism of the baby boomer generation.

—Candace Benefiel, "Blood Relations: The Gothic Perversion of the Nuclear Family in Anne Rice's *Interview with the Vampire*" (2004, 261)

Although there will always be a harmless, campy side to the vampire now, newer monsters were emerging. Two authors helped to resurrect fictional vampires from the self-referential morass of camp irony. Stephen King's second novel, *'Salem's Lot* (1975), brought vampires back to hometown America, by resituating the mythological vampire into a village in Maine and surrounding him with familiar, almost stereotypical characters. King's novel is in many ways a traditional vampire story, except for its ambiguous ending. Anne Rice is the other author responsible for the emergence of a new, serious vampire literature. Her *Interview with the Vampire* (1976) used the journalistic interview to ground the story in a way similar to the way Stoker used epistolary evidence. More importantly, she deployed the emerging celebrity culture of the entertainment world to create celebrity vampires.

Rice's initial trio of vampires are Louis, Lestat, and Claudia. Louis is the interviewee in *Interview with the Vampire*. In an interview setting in San Francisco, a young man asks Louis questions about his 200-year life. Rice gets the reader's interest immediately by starting *in medias res*: " 'I see . . .'said the vampire thoughtfully" (3). We already know from the book's title that it involved vampires, but the opening line brings the vampire right out into the open and has him being thoughtful, moving slowly around a room in a recognizable contemporary American city. We have left the vampires of the past behind—the hissing, feral Christopher Lee or the remote European aristocrat played by Bela Lugosi. In literary terms, Rice is avoiding the techniques that Stoker used, and that the Hammer films generally followed, and that King imitates so effectively in 'Salem's Lot of hiding the vampire, surrounding the central character with mystery throughout much of the story. Instead, she places him front and center, being interviewed, in the spotlight. In a very immediate sense, the vampire has come to us and is having an intelligent conversation. We are going to get his perspective.

But not without a scare. The interviewer, only described as "the boy," expresses doubt: "I'm really anxious to hear why you believe this" (Rice 1976, 3). The vampire cuts him off and looks at him:

> The vampire was watching him with his back to the window. The boy could make out nothing of his face now, and something about the still figure there distracted him. He started to say something again but he said nothing. And then he sighed with relief when the vampire moved towards the table and reached for the overhead cord . . . The vampire was utterly white and smooth, as if he were sculpted from bleached bone, and his face was as seemingly inanimate as a statue, except for the two brilliant green eyes that looked down at the boy intently like flames in a skull. (Rice 1976, 3–4)

This is the boy's first good look at the vampire, and he is shaken from his journalistic objectivity. It is the reader's first look as well, but our disbelief has already been suspended—we know we're reading a vampire novel, after all. The interviewer's next question, "You weren't always a vampire, were you?" allows Louis to take control of the narrative, saying that he doesn't want to give simple answers. He begins by describing the luxurious and primitive world of the late 18th-century plantation where he grew up.

As Louis tells his story, the basic structures of Rice's vampire universe emerge. It is indeed vampirism from the vampire's perspective. The focus is not, as in the antinomian films of the Hammer series, about a choice between good and evil, although there is a good deal of religious discussion. Rather, becoming a vampire in Rice's world is about a change in consciousness. Louis was disillusioned by his devout, perhaps insane, brother's death for which he blamed himself. "I lived like a man who wanted to die but who had no courage to do it himself" (Rice 1976, 10). At this low point, he is attacked by Lestat, a vampire who wants his plantation. After the attack but before his transformation, he meets the vampire and experiences a moment of insight:

> I think that I knew everything in that instant and all that he told me was only aftermath. What I mean is, the moment I saw him, saw his extraordinary aura and knew him to be no creature I'd ever known, I was reduced to nothing. That ego which could not accept the presence of an extraordinary human being in its midst was crushed. All my conceptions, even my guilt and wish to die, seemed utterly unimportant. I forgot *myself*! [. . .] I saw my real gods . . . the gods of most men. Food, drink, and security in conformity. Cinders. (Rice 1976, 12)

This is a replayed version of the boy reporter's experience in the opening scene. Like an army recruit in boot camp or a libertine before his conversion to sanctity, Louis must be broken down before he can be reborn. The actual turning is also described in terms of a change in consciousness. Louis perceives that:

> all things had changed. It was as if I had only just been able to see colors and shapes for the first time. I was so enthralled by the buttons on Lestat's black coat that I looked at nothing else for a long time. Then Lestat began to laugh and I heard his laughter as I had never heard anything before. (Rice 1976, 19)

This is beginning to sound like a drug experience. The reason I have quoted at length from these passages is to give an idea of what it is that Rice is doing differently here. She is often given credit for bringing back the Romantic vampire, a figure based on the fatal or Byronic hero who had become a common figure in the literature of the 19th century, not necessarily as a vampire. But if we look at cultural trends of the 1970s, we also see that there was a wide cultural interest in consciousness, not all of it based on drugs. Theodore Roszak, who wrote *The Making of a Counter-Culture* (1968), an analysis of the intellectual currents that young people brought to the counterculture of the 1960s, opined in his subsequent study *Where the Wasteland Ends* (1972) that the intellectual focus of the 1970s was characterized by a turn inward, by an imperative to examine consciousness in its various forms, including through drugs and through practices, such as fasting and meditation. Feminists and other social reformers conducted consciousness-raising activities that were designed experientially, with the goal to shock or destabilize the worldview of participants, so that they actually change their perceptions and preconceptions about reality. During this time, the University of California at Santa Cruz founded a History of Consciousness program, with degrees at the doctorate level. Such books as Princeton psychologist Julian Jaynes's *The Origin of Consciousness in the Breakdown of the Bicameral Mind* (1976) sought to reconfigure our understanding of early literatures and mythologies by way of a radical shift in consciousness based on bicameral brain research.

Rice's novel focuses on being a vampire in terms of consciousness. Many of her readers in 1976 would have been people who had experimented with drugs, meditation, yoga, fasting, prayer, chanting, and so forth, with the goal of altering or raising consciousness, a goal that was not necessarily religious, or at least not exclusively so. Although she includes elements from traditional vampire literature—long life, superhuman strength, sensitivity to sunlight, feeding on humans—her focus on vampire *consciousness* made the novel seem fresh to her readers.

Rice provided her audience with familiar territory in terms of contemporary issues. Lestat seems to be a perfect example of the hedonistic "if it feels good, do it" philosophy of many young people from the 1960s youth culture. It is as if the older vampire represents the confident, rebellious spirit of the 1960s, whereas the younger Louis represents the more inward-looking, conflicted point-of-view of young people in the 1970s. The conflict between Louis and Lestat enacts a conflict of consciousness between contrasting philosophical perspectives.

Another pattern that emerges in Rice's work is that, like human relationships, vampire relationships change over time. Vampires have lots of time, which opens the door for much conflict. Many vampires come to hate their makers, but are prevented from destroying them by a prohibition punishable by death. Lestat and Louis remain together for several years, Louis trying to avoid killing humans and instead feeding on animals. Eventually, Lestat turns Claudia, a five-year-old girl, so that they can form a family of sorts. Unlike Louis, Claudia turns out to be a conscienceless killer, and comes to hate Lestat for trapping her in a little girl's body for eternity. She kills Lestat, but he comes back (twice), and she is eventually burned as a punishment for her actions. Louis, who assisted her in her attacks, is put in a coffin to starve to death, but is saved by his lover Armand. Eventually, he leaves Armand, claiming:

I thought you were powerful and beautiful and without regret, and I wanted that desperately. But you were a destroyer just as I was a destroyer, more ruthless and cunning even than I. You showed me the only thing that I could really hope to become, what depth of evil, what degree of coldness I would have to attain. (Rice 1976, 305)

At this point, we are left with a Byronic hero, conflicted yet cruel. At the conclusion of *Interview with the Vampire*, Louis feeds on the boy reporter but refuses to do what the human wants most—turn him into a vampire. He claims, "I have completely failed" (Rice 1976, 308). Rice's vampires are sexually attractive and sexually active, unlike King's, and express a remarkably large range of sexualities, going beyond heterosexuality and homosexuality to sado-masochistic power games and child molestation (in a sense, because the child is a chronological, if not a biological, adult).

Rice followed *Interview with the Vampire* with *The Vampire Lestat* in 1984. By 2012, her Vampire Chronicles series included 12 novels. These trace the vampires back to their Egyptian origins and expand outward to include other supernatural characters, including witches, ghosts, spirits, devils, and angels. Much of the tension that occurs in the stories concerns turning humans; because of immortality, many humans want to be vampires, but many of Rice's vampires are, like Louis, troubled by their need to constantly kill, and bored and isolated by eternal life. Various theological and ethical questions emerge in the later books as well, such as if the true nature of evil works as part of God's plan or counter to it. Unlike some authors, Rice actively and litigiously discourages fan fiction, fiction written by others based on her characters. She has written other, non-vampire series as well, including a trilogy based on the life of Jesus.

One thing that all of Rice's works have in common is the way they seamlessly blend the traditional Romantic idea of an extraordinary heroic (or antiheroic) individual with the modern cult of the celebrity. Whether they are pre-Egyptian queens, Roman senators, medieval lords, or Renaissance aristocrats and artists, her characters are all stars. In the earlier books, Lestat, for example, becomes a rock star after being a performer in the *Théatre des Vampires* in turn-of-the-century Paris. Where King focuses on the ordinary and the quotidian, Rice brings us into the lifestyles of the rich and famous. F. Scott Fitzgerald was certainly right in this case—these rich folk *are* different!

As befits a focus on celebrity, the structure of the sequels that Rice has invented is personality based, not sequential. Each novel tends to focus on a specific figure introduced in a previous work. *Interview* focuses on Louis, *The Vampire Lestat* focuses on its titular character, and so on. One of the ways that the novels work is through the audience's willingness to treat the main characters as celebrities. *Interview* provides us with an example—the boy reporter treats Louis like a famous person, and indeed, who else in the media environment of the 1970s would be the subject of an interview? But the interview itself carries the possibility of making its subject into a celebrity. As the reporter says, "It has to be a good story. That's only fair, isn't it?"(Rice 1976, 3). Louis tells him, "I want this opportunity. It's more important to you than you can realize now" (Rice 1976, 4). Readers assume that the book they are reading *is* the interview.

But what is Louis's motivation for coming out of the shadows? Does he, as a member of a secret underground world that no one believes in, want publicity? Is this an exposé? At the end of the narrative, when the boy asks Louis to make him a vampire, Louis replies angrily, "This is what you want? . . . This . . . after all I've told you . . . is what you ask for?" He concludes with, "I have completely failed." Apparently, he wants his story to be a cautionary tale, a warning against being made to suffer as he believes he has suffered, but the boy sees only the advantages of vampirehood. He complains, "You don't even understand the meaning of your story, what it means to be a human being like me" (Rice 1976, 308). The reader is left with a quandary—whose interpretation to accept? What is the meaning of Louis's story?

This conflict is one that often appears in celebrity biographies. The writer wants to tell us how hard his climb to fame has been, how difficult his life is. But the audience, like the boy in Rice's novel, wants to be the celebrity, to live the lifestyle of the subject, and the cautionary tale is lost on us. We assert: I would handle the situation much better. Make me a star!

As I mentioned, Rice is often credited with bringing back the Romantic vampire, and her closely bonded pairs, often of the same sex, do resemble the sort of close homosocial bonds prized by the Romantics—Wordsworth and Coleridge, Shelley and Byron. According to Lionel Trilling's famous distinction, the Romantics idealized *sincerity*, whereas the Modernists who followed them valued a more individualistic *authenticity*. According to William Deresiewicz, our culture has replaced these values with *celebrity*, being known (even on a Facebook or YouTube scale), and *connectivity*, being able to connect at any time. Rice's vampires do want to be known, do not necessarily want isolation, and, ironically, live the same kind of isolated lives as modern celebrities, mainly associating with each other. In conversations about celebrity, two quotations often pop up. One is Andy Warhol's: "In the future, everyone will be world-famous for fifteen minutes" (Keyes 2006, 288). The other is Daniel Boorstin's: a celebrity is "someone who is well-known for his well-knownness" (Boorstin 1961, 57). In terms of Rice's application of the celebrity figure to the formerly obscure vampire, we can understand it better if we look at some of the social theory around celebrity. First, celebrity is about status, which reflects the values of the social group. In a culture based on media imagery, for example, people are going to be valued by the qualities that can be conveyed in an image: appearance and sexual attractiveness will be at a premium. In a youth culture, youthfulness will hold value. Immortal creatures that are undead, especially if they are good looking, fit in well into this context. Also, in a culture with fast-moving fashion trends, the ability to keep up with them has value.

Murray Milner uses the term "celebrification" (Milner 2005, 74) referring to both the process of becoming a celebrity and the process of the increasing social value of celebrity status in our culture, compared with other status markers. Modern media not only celebrifies people, but in the broader sense it also increasingly celebrifies society itself. In Todd Gitlin's analysis:

> Media today are occasions for and conduits of a way of life, identified with rationality, technological advancement, and the quest for wealth, but also for something else entirely, something we call fun, comfort, convenience, or pleasure. We have come to care tremendously about how we feel and how readily we can change our feelings. Media are means. (Gitlin 2007, 7)

Gitlin emphasizes that media are not only self-replicating (like vampires?), but also endlessly self-referential. For example, every year thousands of books are published about the media. He also stresses that the emphasis on information—as in the information society—is a smoke screen: "The buzz of the inconsequential is the media's essence" (Gitlin 2007, 8). So, if celebrity is a form of status, it is also a form of content, a commodity. Perhaps it would be appropriate to modify Boorstin's definition of celebrity to "someone who is *paid* for his (or her) well-knownness."

Rice's novels participate in this arena of culture. *Interview with the Vampire* is about the celebrification of a vampire, about the media process of making a celebrity out of a previously unknown person, through what we might now call the charmingly old-fashioned method of the print interview. In *The Vampire Lestat*, we find Lestat doubly celebrified—performing as a rock star in a vampire-themed rock band called "The Vampire Lestat." The fact that we are reading about this in a book, an autobiography with the same title, triples the celebrity. And, of course, the meta-story here is the story of another form of media, the fiction best seller, which brought a previously unknown author into the field of celebrity. Anne Rice is now a carefully self-cultivated media celebrity who keeps in touch with her readers through a website (annerice.com) where she frequently posts messages. Through the web-site, she promotes her books, those of her son, Chris Rice, and those of her late husband, poet Stan Rice. She also endorses various causes, such as the survival of bookstores and gay rights. The site provides access to YouTube videos of Rice being interviewed, doing tours of places mentioned in her books, and much more. Rice not only writes about celebrity, she epitomizes it.

I do not mean to trivialize celebrity culture, although much of it is ephemeral and fluffy. Rice's success alone, her ascendance to celebrity status, points out that celebrity culture is a powerful force in our society. In his analysis of celebrity culture and status, Milner emphasizes:

> My point is not that we should be uncritical of popular culture in general or celebrity culture in particular. Nonetheless, laments that are overly nostalgic about the past are likely to be irrelevant. Effective critique must grapple with the consequences of new patterns of communication, information, and social solidarity. We are unlikely to come to terms with the importance of sheer visibility unless we grasp its sources and its consequences. Allowing visibility to function as a commodity that can be bought and sold to the highest bidder is certainly part of the problem. (Milner 2005, 77)

Since Rice's novels have become popular, the double lens of celebrity-as-vampire and vampire-as-celebrity have become integral to the way we look at vampires, and performing vampirism has developed into something that is not just for Halloween parties, but is actively embraced as a lifestyle. Themes of obscurity versus visibility have become prominent in vampire stories.

Rice has been a canny analyst of celebrity culture in her fictions, and is certainly canny in the way she chooses to use or refuse the various new media. She embraces instant media, such as Facebook, Twitter, and YouTube, while making it clear that fan fiction and mash-ups with her characters will be targeted for litigation. She is outspoken in her opinions and confident enough in her own celebrity status that she is not worried about scaring away her audience by taking on controversial subjects—by reconverting to Catholicism, for example, or by criticizing the Pope. And presenting vampires as celebrities, especially ones as self-serving as Lestat de Lioncourt, offers us another take on the vampire-as-celebrity/celebrity-as-vampire. There is always the question lurking behind the metaphor: To what extent is celebrity culture sucking the life out of us?

CHAPTER 12

Blood Consumers

To the jaded eye, all vampires seem alike, but they are wonderful in their versatility. Some come to life in moonlight, others are killed by the sun, some pierce with their eyes, others with fangs, some are reactionary, others are rebels, but all are disturbingly close to the mortals they prey on. I can think of no other monsters who are so receptive. Vampires are neither inhuman nor nonhuman nor all-too-human, they are simply more alive than they should be.
      —Nina Auerbach, *Our Vampires, Ourselves* (1995, 5–6)

The 1980s saw a revival of the vampire, especially the vampire film, which had a new look, a style influenced by the quick cuts, pounding drum machines, and garish colored lighting of the emerging MTV music video form. Perhaps this vampire craze was another return of the repressed, a rebirth of fascination with monstrosity in an age dominated by Ronald Reagan's vision of "morning in America." Perhaps it was related to the AIDs virus, which was first perceived as a blood-borne illness of outsiders—homosexuals and drug users—but soon found to be a threat to us all. Perhaps it came with a clearer understanding of the dilemma posed by a terminal sexually transmitted disease: as Joni Mitchell's lyric stated, "Sex sells everything, and sex kills." In any case, the vampire returned with a new edge and a new urgency. By the 1980s, vampires had infiltrated even further into the corners of our consumer culture, and they were beginning to get their fangs back. Vampires have always been rich sources for social metaphors, and during the 1980s and 1990s the variety of such metaphors increased.

"Bela Lugosi's Dead" screams the industrial punk band Bauhaus during the opening credits to *The Hunger* (1983). This is a stylish and a star-packed film featuring central performances by David Bowie, Susan Sarandon, and Catherine Deneuve. As the film opens, a youngish John (Bowie) appears at the office of Dr. Sarah Roberts (Sarandon) to consult with her. She puts him off; he waits. By the time a few hours have passed, he leaves. Now he appears to be in his 90s. She tries to get him to return, but now he has no time for her. He returns to the luxurious apartment he shares with Miriam Blaylock (Deneuve) and kills one of her young students. As he withers further, Blaylock brings him to the attic, where a series of coffins hold the shriveled remains of her other lovers. Just like Tithonius in the Greek myth, they are guaranteed eternal life, but not eternal youth. When Dr. Roberts comes looking for John, Blalock seduces her, vampirizing her in her sleep. When she awakens, she is horrified at the prospect of having to drink blood, but is seemingly reconciled when her boyfriend becomes her first victim. When Miriam kisses her, she stabs herself in the throat and forces Miriam to drink her blood. This apparently reinfects Miriam so that she begins aging. Her desiccated former lovers emerge from their coffins and force her to jump off her balcony. Her death causes them to fall to dust, freeing them. The scene then switches to a realtor selling the townhouse. In an ending reportedly tacked on in the postproduction phase, we see Dr. Roberts in a London townhouse with a shriveled Miriam in a coffin in storage.

Here, the vampire can easily be seen as a metaphor for the idle rich. In the opening scene, Miriam and John cruise a club where they take a victim. No one notices in the loud music and flashing lights. They return to the luxurious town house, with its huge spaces, marble floors, and vases of fresh flowers on a grand piano, where Miriam plays classical music. So, the beautiful people live. The film builds itself around such starkly contrasting environments. Their world is cool, spacious, and quiet at home, up high. In the club, and in the clinic there is constant background noise. The shots are dense, close and crowded, suggesting the claustrophobia and confinement in which Dr. Roberts and the rest of mankind live. A shot of an ape in a cage, screaming, reinforces this contrast. If the plot of the film suggests that Miriam, for one, comes to justice for her crimes, its visual language reinforces the fact that Roberts has replaced her in the structure of things, and that structure hasn't changed. Someone is still living up above, looking down on the crowds and the street, living off of them without being part of them. Say hello to the new boss.

Fright Night (1985) is a leadenly plotted teen horror film, whose most redeeming performance is by Roddy McDowall as an aging horror star who hosts a TV show as Vampire Hunter Peter Vincent. The film's protagonist, Charley (William Ragsdale), a teenager who lives with his single mom in an ordinary suburban house, notices some strange things going on in the gothic mansion next door, such as his new neighbors bringing a coffin into the basement. He soon discovers that his suspicions are correct. The new neighbors are a same-sex couple, consisting of a vampire, Jerry (Chris Sarandon), and his assistant Billy (Jonathan Stark). Jerry threatens Charley, but the young man can get no one to believe him except his friend Evil Ed (Stephen Geoffreys) and his girlfriend Amy (Amanda Bearce). The teenagers manage to find Peter Vincent, the TV horror host, and bribe him into helping them. Meanwhile, Jerry meets Amy and we see that she resembles an old portrait that he has—possibly a version of the reincarnation plot—but nothing is made of it. Jerry turns Evil Ed into a vampire, then kidnaps Amy, whom he brings home and bites. This sets up the climactic confrontation. Evil Ed, in wolf form, is staked by Vincent. Charley fights and stakes Billy, turning him into green slime. (It's hard to figure out how this works—he must *not* be a vampire because he is around during the day, but he behaves like one when staked.) Vincent, because he doesn't believe, can't use a cross against Jerry, but Charley can, causing Jerry to fly off as a bat just as the sun comes up. Charley and Vincent chase him to the basement, where they face a vampirized Amy as well. They smash windows so that the sunlight kills Jerry and Amy, luckily, turns back to normal. The final shot shows Charley and Amy turning off Vincent's show to make out. Evil Ed's red eyes appear in the darkness next door—why didn't killing the main vampire return him to normal as well? Sequel time!

This inconsistent and incoherent plot was bolstered by special effects and occasional humor, and turned out to be one of the more successful horror films of the year, coming in second to *Nightmare on Elm Street II: Freddy's Revenge* in box office receipts. Its most egregious message was to code the vampire couple as gay, both in their mannerisms and in the over-the-top furnishings of their mansion. This was not a nod to camp—it just suggests that gay men, like vampires, are evil. Like *Vamp's* treatment of blackness, this was part of the trend in the 1980s to reinforce old stereotypes and prejudices, restoring conservative values after the excesses of the 1960s and 1970s. Vampires are evil because they are outsiders, like people of color, gay people, and so on. Likewise, women in horror would have to wait for a few more years to get beyond the roles of victim or problem (or both).

Lost Boys (1987), directed by Joel Schumacher, started out as a preteen horror/adventure film in the wake of the success of *The Goonies* (1985).

It was based on a Peter-Pan-as-a-vampire concept. Schumacher decided to make the boys teenagers and to go for a cool horror-comedy feel, with a beach town setting and a rock soundtrack. The vampires are a gang of four young men who ride motorcycles, and the plot involves the arrival of a new family in town. Teenage Michael (Jason Patric) and his preteen younger brother Sam (Corey Haim) move to town from Phoenix with their divorced mother Lucy (Dianne Wiest), to live with her father (Barnard Hughes), an aging hippie taxidermist with a sprawling ranch. Driving in, they see a graffito that claims that Santa Clara is the murder capital of the world.

Michael becomes attracted to a girl, Star (Jami Gertz), who introduces him to David (Kiefer Sutherland) and his gang. After a dangerous motorcycle race, they initiate him by having him drink blood—he thinks it is wine. Later that night, the boys, including Michael, all jump from a railroad bridge into a fog bank, and Michael wakes up in bed. Meanwhile, at a comic store, Sam meets two boys his age, the Frog brothers Edgar and Alan (Corey Feldman and Jamison Newlander) who warn him about the vampire threat. They give him comic books to study and learn how to be a vampire fighter like them. The boys are searching for the head vampire, and they decide to test Sam's mother's new boyfriend Max, who comes to dinner and passes all their tests—garlic, a mirror, and so on. Meanwhile, Michael is experiencing bloodlust and other symptoms, such as floating out of his window and fading in the mirror. We find out that he and Star are both half-vampires now until they make their first kill. They team up with the younger boys to kill the vampires in their lair, but only manage to kill one because they discover that vampires hang from the ceiling like bats to sleep, rather than lying conveniently in coffins.

A final battle occurs and the vampire gang is dispensed in various colorful ways; but impaling David doesn't free Star and Michael of symptoms, so he isn't the head vampire. Max and Lucy arrive and Max reveals himself as the vampire leader, after all. He has been courting Lucy so that she can be a mother to his boys. All seems lost when Grandpa arrives and impales Max with a fencepost. He says, "One thing about living in Santa Clara I never could stomach—all the damn vampires."

The film was successful, due to its talented acting and contemporary feel. It manages to play both sides, working with adult anxieties— out-of-control youth, motorcycle gangs, violent crime, disintegrating families—while keeping the teen appeal of sexy young stars playing dangerous characters. The theme of the triumph of innocence is also appealing—the real heroes are the preadolescents. So, representatives of our society's least enfranchised and least powerful groups, children and seniors, basically save the day, while the adults are as bad—or worse— than the out-of-control hormonal teens. Edward Hermann's Max, as the vampire king, is stiff and unctuous and Dianne Wiest, as the gullible, flaky, former hippie mom, is convincingly helpless. But unlike many of the antifeminist backlash films of the 1980s, *Lost Boys* affirms the model of the nontraditional, non-nuclear family. Indeed, it implies through Max's desire to have one that the nuclear family is part of the pathology, not the solution.

Kathryn Bigelow's *Near Dark* (1987) gives us another bad family, in the form of a group of redneck vampires who travel the seedy bars and shabby motels of the modern West, driving stolen junkers and preying on the poor and the dispossessed. Their newest member is an androgynous young woman, Mae (Jenny Wright), who picks up a young cowboy, Caleb (Adrian Pasdar). They spend the night driving around and when he insists that she kiss him, she bites him. As he tries to stagger home, he is grabbed and taken away by her family, who agree to let him try to become one of them; he won't qualify until he kills. They consist of Jesse (Lance Hendrickson) and Diamondback (Jenette Goldstein), the parents, Mae and two brothers, adult Severen (Bill Paxton) and Homer (Joshua Miller), a young boy. Except for Mae, they all behave like psychopaths. With relish and humor, the family slaughters all the people in a small local bar, seeming to get more joy from killing than from actually drinking blood. Caleb pursues a young man, but finally lets him go. Mae feeds him from her wrist until he can learn to kill. After the police track them to a motel room, Caleb manages to save them all by running into the sunlight to retrieve their van, then crashing it into the building. This gains him some degree of respect, along with some gruesome burns.

Caleb escapes from the group when his veterinarian father (Tim Thomerson) finds him and cures him through a transfusion. But there has to be a final showdown. Mae comes to see him and the family kidnaps his little sister Sarah (Marcie Leeds). They square off on the main street of a small town. Severen dies in a fuel truck explosion and Jesse, Diamondback, and Homer get caught out in the just-risen sun, while Mae manages to grab Sarah and get under cover. The film ends with her awakening from a transfusion and embracing Caleb in the sunlight.

The film is obviously a play on the classic Western, complete with an ironic ride into the sunrise for the vampires. The opposing groups, the outstanding moral questions, the general carnage, and the return to order in the conclusion all follow the outlines of this venerable cinematic genre. Even the sheer filthiness of the vampires—they always seem to have either blood or burns on their faces—fits in with more recent, realist Westerns. Nina Auerbach reads the film as a return to patriarchy, with the wayward woman solidly reincorporated into the patriarchal family and the threatening alternative family destroyed:

> The happy ending of *Near Dark* is as checkered as its title. Stereotypes that never existed are restored: crouching daughterly women, innocent children, omnipotent doctors, and benignly caretaking men. If vampirism is a wasting disease like AIDS, its cure is a blessing, but if it contains immortality, secret strength, and forbidden identities, its domestication is a death more painful than Homer's. Bigelow's title carries the same mixed message, for in the sun-struck ending, the cured lovers are nowhere near a dark that in this movie is less assaultive than day. At the end, like vampirism, dark is lost. (Auerbach 1995, 192)

Auerbach also notes that the scale of vampire films in the 1980s tends to be small, centered around the family and not the larger community or political entities. No cosmic horror here. All three of these family films can be seen to reinforce old-fashioned ideas about the value of the traditional nuclear family, but all of them end up with nontraditional, mixed family groups—a mixed message for those who, like Auerbach, want to see in these films a reflection of the reactionary politics of Reaganism. Perhaps we can't go back after all.

There is no family in *Vampire's Kiss* (1989), directed by Robert Bierman. Nicolas Cage plays a vain, superficial literary agent, Peter Loew, who is turned into a vampire, or at least believes he is. He is losing control of his emotions, his mental health, and his life in general, as we find out during his interludes with his therapist (Elizabeth Ashley) that often turn into rants. The film explores and parodies the idea of the yuppie (from YUP, young urban professional), a type that emerged in the Reagan years—privileged young professionals who defined themselves through conspicuous consumption and status competition—and were perceived as vain, self-centered, and narcissistic. This film imagines the yuppie as vampire and presents as Loew's eventual victim a Hispanic immigrant Alva (Maria Conchita Alonso), who works in his office, and whom he browbeats, harasses, stalks, and finally rapes. The film initially brings the viewer along in Peter's belief that he is a vampire, showing him being attacked while having sex with a woman (Jennifer Beals) he meets at a club. By the time he starts eating cockroaches and buys plastic vampire teeth to feed with, we begin to doubt. Because the film makes no clear distinctions between imagined and real episodes, we experience the same confusion that the character does. The final scenes alternate between his fantasy—the therapist introduces him to a perfect woman and forgives him for the rape and murder he confesses to—and his reality, as he walks around on the streets of New York in a blood-stained suit talking to himself. He meets his end at the hands of Alva's brother.

So, the decade of greed ends. This film's stylish contemporary setting and young protagonist might appeal to young urban types, and the vampire metaphor and social message encoded in Loew's harassment of a defenseless member of an oppressed group could be occluded by its surface stylishness. One can almost imagine that a person like Loew could see it as an unfortunate story of someone going insane rather than a piece of social criticism about a society that creates elite vampires to prey on the less privileged. In a way, it brings us full circle back to *The Hunger*, portraying a stylish, urban world where those with wealth prey on those whom they consider to be their inferiors. In *Vampire's Kiss*, Loew's life seems hardly worth living, and the victims do have their revenge. The vampires in *The Hunger*, on the other hand, especially with the added-on ending, just seem to breed more of themselves.

The 1990s give us vampires who keep the vulnerabilities that we saw increasingly during the 1980s, but who develop in several new directions. Francis Ford Coppola (1992) took the reincarnation plot and the title from the 1979 *Bram Stoker's Dracula*, but built it into a high-budget extravaganza, with a variety of contemporary stars. Not to be outdone in star power, Neil Jordan's film version of Rice's *Interview with the Vampire* (1994) sacrificed some of its potential by relying on Tom Cruise and Brad Pitt rather than more skilled and less luminous actors. The *Blade* films (1998, 2002, and 2004) continued this emerging tradition of big-budget vampire films, adding a distinctly technothriller twist.

Coppola's film is a cinematic tour de force, bringing back the swagger of Lugosi and Lee, fleshing out the reincarnation plot, and using a rich color palette and febrile dramatic acting to restore a grand Romantic feel to the vampire genre. As Vincent Canby said in a contemporary review, Coppola presents a "wild dream of a movie . . . with its gorgeous sets and costumes, its hallucinogenic special effects and mad montages . . . this

Dracula transcends camp to become a testimonial to the glories of film making as an end in itself." The film owes much to grand opera in its use of melodramatic set pieces played on extravagant stages with sumptuous costumes. The special effects are all old-school cinema, using lenses, miniatures, makeup, and double exposure rather than relying on postproduction additions and computer-generated imagery. According to Roger Ebert's review, "The one thing the movie lacks is headlong narrative energy and coherence. There is no story we can follow well enough to care about" (Ebert 1992). In like fashion, Canby asks rhetorically, "Shouldn't movies, even Dracula movies, be about something?" (Canby 1992). Instead of a coherent narrative, the film seems to be structured by opposing forces—sexuality, especially female sexuality, is associated with wild animals, as in a scene where Lucy Westenra has sex with Dracula in the form of a Wolf Man in her garden during a thunderstorm. This wanton wildness is contrasted with the very proper behavior of men such as Harker, played by a stiff Keanu Reeves, who seems to be in pain even when he is being seduced by Dracula's vampire brides. Mina, played by Winona Ryder, switches back and forth from a sanctimonious Victorian schoolmistress to a panting adulterous wife seeming to be pushed and pulled by waves of feeling. But the most fluid character is Prince Dracula himself, played by Gary Oldham. Starting as a wrinkled, white-skinned ancient with a double bouffant hairdo and a flowing kimono, he becomes a pointy-eared bat-like creature, a Wolf Man, a serpentine green mist, a pile of rats, and a long-haired Edwardian dandy. While he is in this last form, he introduces himself to Mina as Prince Vlad, and takes her to a cinematograph exhibit of apparently erotic films, where he cannot bring himself to bite her, believing her to be the reincarnation of his wife. Indeed, Coppola has him fail at key moments throughout the film. He tells her, "I am nothing, blackness, soulless, hated, and feared, I am dead. I am the monster that breathing men would kill." Mina effectively seduces *him*, choosing to drink his blood and become unclean. He is masterful and defiant to the men, but helpless in her arms. The final scene has them both alone in his castle, where Mina, at his urging, pushes in the stake. His motivation seems to be to sexually awaken and reclaim her, but only by her free choice. Hers is less clear. She tells him "I love you. Oh God, forgive me I do. I want to be what you are, see what you see, love what you love," but she returns to her old life.

This version of the sensitive vampire as obsessive fits in with the rest of the film, which uses its big budget to give us a series of dramatic, quirky, often emotionally satisfying encounters between the characters. However, it lacks not only narrative continuity, but also thematic consistency. Vampirism is theological: Vlad Dracula curses God and the church after the priest tells him his Elizabeta is damned; vampirism is biological, a blood infection that turns people into lustful animals; vampirism is primitive, a holdover from a less civilized age; vampirism is all about love, but nevertheless the vampire suffers until he is allowed to die. Finally, in this film, vampirism is spectacular and very dramatic. In one of the short documentaries on the DVD, Coppola says that he wants to present Dracula as an actor, someone who changes roles with the circumstances. This seems to contradict the film's presentation of the vampire as an obsessed lover; but perhaps we can find a way to see this figure as a return of the Romantic hero as vampire, a tortured, Byronic character whose drive for love is ultimately a drive toward death.

The vampire Western gets a stylish reboot in the hands of director Robert Rodriguez and screenwriter, producer, and actor Quentin Tarantino in *From Dusk Till Dawn*. This genre-mixing film not only combines the conventions of Western and horror movie, but also adds elements of the crime drama, the road movie, the zombie film, and the B-grade exploitation picture. Two brothers on the run from a badly botched bank robbery abduct a father, his teenage daughter, and his son to get them across the Mexican border in their recreational vehicle. Once they get across, they are to meet their Mexican contact at a stripper bar the next morning. All goes well until it turns out that the bar is full of vampires. A battle ensues, in which the humans get picked off and converted one by one, and vampires get staked, burned, beheaded, disemboweled, and so on. The film is in two distinct parts—getting to the bar, which relies on elements of tension, suspense, and surprise, and once they get there, which is mainly a spectacular series of gory action sequences. Episodes of pathos, humor, and odd characterization alternate with colorful and carefully timed special effects. The film is enhanced by a raucous Tex-Mex rock soundtrack.

Jordan's film of *Interview with the Vampire* works well with Rice's novel (Rice wrote the screenplay) in that it overdetermines the celebrity status of the vampires by having them portrayed by actual celebrities. As Janet Maslin said in a contemporary review, the film provides "an absurdly snobbish, self-important tale that doesn't make great sense and seldom works as metaphor . . . The film never condemns its characters' murderousness nor thinks a thought deeper than 'we must be powerful, beautiful and without regret.' "(Maslin 1994). Like the celebrities they imitate, these vampires don't have to justify themselves. The film is a straight portrayal of the novel, complete with gore, homoerotic sexuality, and a virtuoso performance by Cruise, who leaves behind his usual boyish, playful persona for a more menacing and sophisticated role. Pitt is somewhat less convincing as Louis, and Kirsten Dunst makes a stunning debut, stealing the show as a scheming, preteen Claudia. For a big-budget film, this one takes real risks in its tolerant treatment of alternative sexualities, but any potential advocacy is diluted by its adherence to the codes of celebrity culture.

The *Blade* films are comic book–based technothrillers that have very little to do with race, despite the fact that the main character is black. The films do take us in another direction, as John Jordan points out in his article, "Vampire Cyborgs and Scientific Imperialism." He builds on the ideas of Donna Haraway, a primatologist, who suggests that we adopt the model of the cyborg in order to understand our place in the new systems created by our increasing involvement with technology. Haraway's cyborg is what she calls impure, because it borrows attributes of not just the human and the machine, but also of the animal: it breaks dichotomies. This fits in with some traditional folklore of the vampire, in some cultures seen as a creature with the ability to shape-shift into animal forms; but vampires are also usually seen as belonging to a culture that is associated with much earlier technologies. Since Stoker, vampires are more generally defeated using technology than assisted by it. Jordon argues that the *Blade* series incorporates the figure of the vampire into that of the cyborg:

> In the narrative of *Blade* we find an example of such an attempt to bring mysticism into a scientific worldview. Blade the vampire is made into a cyborg, a creature that seamlessly blends flesh and technology together into an other-worldly being. (Jordon 1999, 9)

He points out that Blade, although he is not physically part machine, relies on biological technology (the serum) in order to keep from turning into a full vampire, and that much of his weaponry is –technologically enhanced, and that technology is necessary to help him find his enemies. Jordon sees the films as examples of scientific imperialism in that they allow science to explain, control and colonize the story of vampires, which had been hitherto the realm of nonscientific metaphysics or superstition:

> The humans in *Blade* recognize that they are imperfect and weak creatures, but instead of turning to an essential humanism for salvation, they look to technology for assistance. *Blade* differs from previous films in the vampire genre in that technology enhances humanity in Blade, making people better humans. Everything from high-tech weapons to the blood in Blade's body is scientized in the film and is positively valued and matched against the nonscientific weakness of the predatory vampires. (Jordon 1999, 10)

This series presents the cyborg in positive terms, unlike other depictions such as the *Terminator* films, which although they feature some good cyborgs, tend to code good and evil in terms of man versus machine. This allows for scientific imperialism to spread its influence, even over the vampire. It also gives us other ways to look at what a vampire is, perhaps the ability to see it as impure like the rest of us.

Haraway herself, in the rather long-titled article "Race: Universal Donors in a Vampire Culture. It's All in the Family: Biological Kinship Categories in the Twentieth Century United States," uses the vampire as a metaphor as she looks at three dominant ways of thinking about race in the 20th century: eugenics, multicultural humanism, and genetics. The first was categorical and hierarchy based; the second was inclusive and diversity based; and the third is schematic and standards based. But Haraway's critique lies in our culture's use of exclusively biological-based (blood-based) models of kinship in all these models. For her, our most important allegiances should be based on affinity, not family, and so:

> Ties through blood—including blood recast in the form of genes and information—have been bloody enough already. I believe that there will be no racial or sexual peace, no livable nature, until we learn to produce humanity through something more and less than kinship. I think I am on the side of the vampires, or at least some of them. (Haraway 2004, 285)

For Haraway, the vampire, like the cyborg, is a monstrous figure that works against the accepted categories by which we understand our world and provides us with a model that feeds off "the always undead corpus of race and sex" (Haraway 2004, 252) but demonstrates how that undead corpus feeds off us. Such a metaphor gives us a clearer understanding of a complicated—and implicated—dynamic.

We have seen how, in these two decades, a variety of filmmakers have used the vampire as a metaphor—for outlaws, outsiders, homosexuals, sexual women, cyborgs, narcissists, the rich, and out-of-control youth. We have seen the figure incorporated into the Western, the crime drama, the romance, comedy, and science fiction. Especially in contrast to the campy, stereotyped figure of previous incarnations, the vampire has proved to be a versatile and dynamic carrier of a daunting variety of cultural messages.

CHAPTER 13

Buffy Rules

I hate it when people talk about Buffy as being campy . . . I hate camp. I don't enjoy dumb TV.

—Joss Whedon, Whedonesque.com

Joss Whedon's *Buffy the Vampire Slayer* series is certainly a cult phenomenon, and one that goes beyond its fan base to provide fodder for an academic industry. It ran for seven seasons, 1997–2003, and is reportedly the most written-about television show to date, especially if one sticks to straight textual analysis (as opposed to audience or fan studies, etc.). As in the case of *Dark Shadows* in the 1960s, the serial form of the weekly show allows for a rich variety of plots. The placement of a small town high school/college community on a Hellmouth, which incidentally needs a Slayer to keep bad things from coming out, would seem to be the perfect combination for a serial drama—when the high school plot gets boring, bring on the monsters! Joss Whedon, the show's creator, states: "The two things that matter the most to me: emotional resonance and rocket launchers. *Party of Five*, a brilliant show, and often made me cry uncontrollably, suffered ultimately from a lack of rocket launchers" (Whedon 2006, DVD Commentary to "Innocence"). The show gives an intriguing mix of the mundane and the supernatural, focusing on a high school student's life, which is also that of a Slayer, the Chosen One. Whedon is a true member of the film school generation for television. He is actually a third-generation television writer, following his father and his grandfather. As such, he brings a high level of cinematic and televisual literacy to his work, as well as a constant stream of rhymes and references to the past. Every once in a while, he sets up a challenge for an episode, such as "Hush" (4.5), in which no one can speak, or "Once More with Feeling" (6.6), which is played as a musical. Such episodes are technical and creative challenges to the actors, writers, and crew. These two serve as tributes both to the silent film era and the musical genre, respectively.

The focus of the series is on Buffy and her gang of "Scoobies" (a reference to the 1970s children's cartoon *Scooby Doo*, which pitted an assortment of young people and a talking dog against various supernatural forces—see Chapter 15). The main narrative is about these characters and their lives, with lots of "rocket-launcher" action added as they battle vampires—not only vampires, but also other types of demons, ghosts, ancient gods, fairy tale monsters, werewolves, and so on. Because the supernatural characters are secondary—by quite a distance—the show encourages its audience to see them metaphorically. Kathleen Tracy, in her book *The Girl's Got Bite: An Unofficial Guide to Buffy's World*, adds a section called "The Real Horror" to each of her episode summaries, emphasizing the real or literal problems dealt with over and above the supernatural ones. A couple of the reoccurring characters, Spike and Angel, are former or (usually) reformed vampires, and Dracula himself, as an ancient master vampire with celebrity status, makes an appearance as well (see below). In the world of *Buffy*, vampires feed on blood, have fangs, are physically strong, but don't (in most cases) have souls, and they usually cannot change form. When they are feeding or attacking, they grow bumpy latex brows like Klingons. Stakes and sunlight are lethal to them. Most, but not all, of the other evil characters are demons of a variety of types, who have glowing eyes and are generally killers of humankind, often hoping for, or working toward, an apocalyptic cataclysm. Demons and vampires are understood to be nonhuman species who have hybridized with humans, losing some of their potency in the process. Vampires are a category of demon who have taken over human bodies, incorporating the memories of the former host, but they lack a soul, and therefore a conscience. Angel is a vampire who has (usually) had his human soul returned to him, and so is (usually) on the side of good. Spike has been similarly reformed by way of having a morality chip implanted in his brain.

I keep putting "usuallys" in the summary above because Buffy's universe (referred to as "the Buffyverse," which is part of the larger "Whedonverse"), like that of comic books and other long-term serial formats, is a rather fluid and changeable place, where, for example, time can be reversed in order to change events, dead characters can be reanimated, and characters from parallel universes can cross over. In true serial form, things change.

Stacey Abbott, in an article entitled "A Little Less Ritual and a Little More Fun: The Modern Vampire in *Buffy the Vampire Slayer*," argues that this fluidity is one of the benchmarks of the show and a central reason why it appeals to its audience. Buffy and the vampires, Abbott argues, start out in a very traditional place: Sunnydale is the contemporary version of the superstitious European village of the traditional vampire tale. Buffy, her mentor Giles, and the Council of Watchers oppose the vampires, who follow a Master and belong to a Brotherhood of Aurelius. So, we have a parallel structure of opposition, with traditional hierarchies representing Good and Evil, respectively. Within the structure, rituals, both Christian and vampiric, reinforce the status quo, and prophecies foretell events to come. But from the opening episode, we find cracks in this simple, symmetrical structure. Each group starts to question and defy its masters—Buffy pushes against Giles's strict rule-based procedures and the Scoobies' allegiance to each other trumps their allegiance to the Council—and eventually Giles and Buffy disobey the Council. Meanwhile, in the episode "School Hard," the young-acting, hip, maverick vampire Spike takes on the Brotherhood. He mocks their Annointed One as the Annoying One, and eventually destroys him with the comment, "From now on, we're going to have a little less ritual and a little more fun around here" (2.3). This introduces Spike's version of a new, less hierarchical vampire mayhem. In her analysis, written after Season 4, Abbott concludes:

> What makes *Buffy the Vampire Slayer* such an effective television program is that the evil that she battles is not a product of an ancient world but the product of the real world itself. *Buffy* has used the past four years to painstakingly dismantle and rebuild the conventions of the vampire genre and work toward gradually disembedding the vampire/slayer dichotomy from religious ritual and superstition. The removal of religious dogma and superstition from the genre and the transformation of the vampire into a physical rather than ethereal being, acknowledges that what we describe as "evil" is a natural product of the modern world. (Abbott 2001, paragraph 19)

The internal tensions within the two groups emphasize the show's other major structuring opposition—that of youth versus established society.

Rhonda Wilcox quotes Whedon in the title to her article, "There Will Never be a 'Very Special' *Buffy*." By this statement, he emphasizes that the show uses metaphor to deal with social problems, so that there won't, as in other teen-based television shows, be special shows dedicated to giving social messages about specific issues. Wilcox argues that the show's use of its own version of teenage language (slayer speak) serves to emphasize the fact that evil (and vampires for that matter) are often coded as adults, so that the Scoobies' solidarity serves to emphasize that teenagers often survive because of the their peer support systems, in spite of the corrupting or clueless influences of the adult world:

> The language of the teens starkly contrasts with that of the adults. This linguistic separateness emphasizes the lack of communication between the generations, as does the series' use of the symbolism of monsters to represent social problems. The parents' inability to deal with real-world horrors is suggested through Buffy's concerned but naive mother, who throughout [the first] two seasons never sees the monsters or knows her daughter is the Slayer. The symbolism re-creates the need to bridge generational division, which is suggested by the language patterns. Viewers must understand both the language and the symbolism to see the reality of teen life. Life and language are not so simple as problem-of-the-week television would suggest, and *Buffy* acknowledges that fact. (Wilcox 1999, 16)

Of course, not all the adults in the show are evil vampires. They are more often clueless, like Buffy's mother. Giles, as the mentor figure, and Angel, as Buffy's older love interest (he is 241 years old), mediate linguistically as well as in other ways, as Buffy and the others grow their way into adulthood:

> Whereas the darkly beautiful Angel (who speaks in neither marked slang nor overly erudite archaisms [like Giles]) suggests the dangerously attractive sexual aspect of adulthood, the Master is associated with work and family. As Buffy moves closer to adulthood in later seasons, the vampire opponents are not just adults but distorted reflections of herself . . . (Wilcox 1999, 22)

As the series progresses through its seven seasons, the high school students go on to college or employment, and much of the action has to do with blurring boundaries between the no-longer separate worlds of adulthood and adolescence, metaphorically coded as creature and human. One of the trajectories of the series as a whole is to complicate the simple us-versus-them oppositions that structure the initial set-up.

In the episode "Buffy vs. Dracula" (5.1), Dracula appears as a vampire with special powers. He can turn into a mist and/or a bat, and he can hypnotize or mesmerize people, including Buffy, into doing what he wants. He can re-form physically after being staked. The episode features many references, both to Stoker's novel and to the Universal *Dracula* films. The character Xander becomes Dracula's lackey and develops, like Renfield, a taste for spiders. Giles, like Jonathan Harker, becomes distracted by Dracula's three vampire brides, but eventually gets free from them. The actor who plays Dracula, Rudolph Martin, had played the part in a film made for the USA network, *Dark Prince: The Untold Story of Dracula* (2000).

The plot of this episode follows the standard plot of a Buffy episode, with Dracula being the threat that is confronted and neutralized. The episode's humor comes from everyone's treatment of Dracula as a star. When he introduces himself to Buffy, she says, "Get out!" in an admiring fashion. When he suggests that she can't resist his will, she quips, "Because you're famous?" The former demon character Anya brags about knowing him in her demon days: "He probably wouldn't remember me." Spike, now implanted with the chip that makes him harmless, calls him a "poncy bugger—owes me eleven pounds," and mocks him for his celebrity lifestyle: "luxury estate, bug-eaters, special dirt." Dracula manages to bite Buffy and get her to drink his blood, first step, as in the novel, to becoming a vampire. He tells her, rather dramatically, "I have searched the world over for you, I have hungered for you: a creature whose darkness matches my own." She eventually breaks free, joking, "the thrall is gone," and she stakes him repeatedly as he re-forms, finally saying to the mist shape, "I'm right here!," so that it disperses away. Although order is restored, it is an oddly incomplete order, and leaves Buffy wondering whether he was right to call her a killer and kindred to him, whether she is beginning to enjoy her role as Slayer too much. In any case, we know that he still exists. In this way, he works as a metaphor for her own doubts about her special status. The episode ends with her asking Giles to come back into his role as Watcher for her, in a way a choice to resubmit to a kind of patriarchal authority, or at least management, after her brush with the patriarch of vampires. She acknowledges that she is becoming an adult, and that requires that she recognize certain monstrous qualities within herself.

This episode demonstrates the effectiveness of the series. Vampires represent evil and the enemy, yes, and Buffy slaughters them by the thousands over the course of seven seasons; but the rules are never hard-and-fast, and boundaries are always blurring. Like their quirky human foes, vampires seem to have a lot of variations, and Dracula, with his ability to shape-shift at will, can represent both the vain, high-maintenance celebrity—the episode actually mentions Lestat at one point—and the ubiquitous evil that lurks under the surface in all of us, even in the Slayer's psyche. Buffy, according to Dracula, is kindred. He defines this in terms of not only her darkness, but also because she is different, and one of the ways that she is different is that she is also, like him, a celebrity of sorts.

At two different points in the show's seven seasons, Buffy dies and is brought back to life. During one of these periods, between Seasons five and six, she remains dead for a few months and is actually buried. Her headstone reads, "She Saved the World—A Lot" after her name and dates. This cutely understated epitaph reveals another of the show's obsessions, millennialism, a theme it shares with much of the cinema of the 1990s. From the second half of the series pilot, "The Harvest," where the Master vampire is thwarted in an attempt to kill off humanity, to the destruction of the high school by the Hellmouth after a plot by the principal and the mayor, Buffy staves off several apocalypses. During the episode "The Gift" (5.22), she asks Giles, "This is how many apocalypses for us now?," and he replies, "Six, at least. Feels like a hundred," a reference to the fact that it is the hundredth episode. The idea of a generational slayer, the Chosen One, is millennial in itself, suggesting that, like the above conversation, the world needs to be routinely saved.

As the series leaves behind its emphasis on ritual and religious paraphernalia, the apocalypse also takes on more physical manifestations. The portal opening at the end of "The Gift" (5.22) is presented as a physical cloud of light from which dragons fly and that Buffy must sacrifice herself, physically, to close. When she is revived, she must physically claw her way out of her coffin. This emphasis on the physical nature of reality serves, like the emphasis on teen melodrama and original language, to ground the supernatural elements of the series in the material world, and to make the millennial threat more believable. It also emphasizes the irony, expressed as far back as the pilot, that this group of mainly normal American teenagers is what stands between order and chaos. Giles expresses this at the end of "The Harvest" (1.2), after Buffy makes a flippant remark about getting kicked out of school. He shakes his head and comments, "The Earth is doomed!"

Despite the fact that there are very real supernatural threats to the world portrayed in the Buffy series, its charm lies in its parallel portrayal of the realities of high school life, and in its refusal to devalue one in favor of the other.

CHAPTER 14

Vampires for Children

A vampire isn't some sort of handsome prince. And a vampire definitely isn't some gloomy teenager who flunked algebra twice and likes to pick on his girlfriend's little brother. A vampire isn't a girl who's read some stupid book seventeen times and thinks she can become one of the characters.

A vampire is a bloodsucking horror who sleeps in a coffin filled with his native soil; lives with bats, rats, and spiders; and carries nothing inside himself but death and disease.

—David Lubar, *Attack of the Vampire* Weenies (2011, 37)

During the 1960s, children were exposed to the Universal monsters on television, as well as to a fair amount of gratuitous violence in cartoons, for which the networks had set aside special children's viewing (and advertising) time, notably on Saturday mornings. By the late 1960s, television programming for children was beginning to change. The adult soap opera *Dark Shadows* was shown daily at 4 P.M. and so, by intention or inadvertently, it attracted a following of young teenagers and children, whom it familiarized with the conventions of the gothic story, sometimes without their parent's knowledge or permission. By the late 1960s, groups of concerned parents were pressuring the networks to provide content that was more wholesome and less violent, as well as to ban or limit advertising to children. The development of PBS, the Public Broadcasting System, which was based on a noncommercial and educational model, was one result of these pressures, as were the development of targeted "after-school specials," programs with positive social messages played in the after-school timeslots by the commercial networks. One result of the attempt to move away from violence led, ironically, to an enduring horror-based cartoon franchise that deliberately used the conventions of the horror film to make it less scary and disturbing to children.

Much of the original cartoon programming on television was developed in the 1930s and 1940s and meant to be shown in movie theaters between features. Much of what we now refer to as classic cartoons come from this era—the early Disney and Warner Brothers short cartoons, for example. The made-for-television cartoons, which were created starting in the 1950s, show a decided decline in quality due to the use of mechanical reproduction technologies, which replaced the hand-drawn figures from the film era. Frenetic cartoon violence had been a hallmark of the animated cartoon from the beginning, the plasticity of the medium allowing for figures to be stretched, distorted, flattened, and so forth, so that shows like Tom and Jerry (originally 1940–1957), Popeye (1933–1957), and the Road Runner series (starting in 1948) developed their plots round the many ways a character could be squashed, burned, blown up, or dropped from a cliff. However, the plasticity of cartoon characters allowed for humorous treatments resulting in quick recoveries, so that the next scene often showed the character back to normal.

The effects of such scenes on the psychological well-being and subsequent behavior of children has been the subject of study and debate from the beginning of targeted children's films. Parents are understandably sensitive to anecdotal stories of children engaging in horrific violence as a result of viewing this kind of content. Studies tend to demonstrate that cartoon shows which present violence as comedic are seen as less violent by adults, while perceptions by children of various ages tend to be more ambiguous. In a review of studies published in 2006, Steven J. Kirsh suggests:

> Although there are theoretical reasons to suggest that comedic elements in cartoons trivialize or camouflage violence depicted within, additional research on youth is necessary to discern whether developmental status influences this process. Similarly, factors that influence the perception of violence in non-comedic cartoons, such as graphicness and perceived reality, appear to be moderated by developmental processes. However, there is limited research in this area. (Kirsh 2006, 555)

Findings seem to suggest that graphicness, meaning representation of blood and gore, is a major factor, and tends to be lacking in children's cartoons, even those from the classic period. In his animated series for adults, *The Simpsons* (starting in 1989), Matt Groening parodies these concerns by having the children watch "The Adventures of Itchy and Scratchy," a cat-and-mouse show dedicated to showing graphic violence and gore—blood spurting, bones sticking out, and so forth.

In the late 1960s and early 1970s, in response to these kinds of concerns by parents, the industry went through a phase of trying to create content that was comedic, but less violent. Out of this context, in 1969, emerged the horror comedy *Scooby Doo, Where Are You?*, the first in a continuing series of Scooby Doo shows, specials, and feature-length films. Originally conceived as a rock group show in imitation of *The Archie Show*, Hanna-Barbera Studios dropped the rock angle and kept the group, developing this show into a mystery/comedy hybrid with a focus on horror-like settings. The character Scooby Doo is a talking dog who is accompanied by four teenagers. They investigate paranormal events, which turn out to be tricks or hoaxes—another version of the explained gothic plot. The explanations, formulaic plots, comedic chase scenes, and the hapless foolishness of the characters serve to make the show nonthreatening, and the violence amounts mainly to pratfalls. In an episode from 1969, for example, "A Gaggle of Galloping Ghosts," the gang travels to Franken castle, where they are chased by a werewolf, a vampire, and a lumbering Frankenstein monster, after being warned off by a gypsy. All the characters turn out to be disguises of Actor Bob, a criminal mastermind, who is brought to judgment. This plot exemplifies the Scooby Doo formula, which was repeated with variations for every show. The gang of teenagers in *Buffy the Vampire Slayer* would give themselves the nickname "Scoobys" in tribute to this show.

The elimination of the more extreme and less realistic cartoon violence found in earlier animated treatments, and its substitution by a sanitized and more realistic comedy, even though it is based in a horror setting, represents a return to the silly, physical comedy of earlier live-action horror parodies like *Abbott and Costello Meet Frankenstein*. The gothic setting and the monsters are the same; it is just that the foolish adult comedy team, Abbott and Costello, have been replaced by a gang of equally foolish teenagers. In hindsight, it is ironic that the Scooby Doo setup—a group of teenagers in a scary place—should become the standard lead-in to the modern slasher film, from *Halloween* through to the self-aware *Scream* films to the recent *Cabin in the Woods*. In a twisted, cannibalistic chronology of genre development, we have gone from exaggerated cartoon violence, to a suppression of violence through cartoon comedy, to an exaggerated realistic violence with comic overtones.

Perhaps because of this process of moving the settings and characters of horror into comedy, the Scooby Doo era of the early 1970s was the time when vampires came to children. The cleaning-up of cartoons, afternoon TV reruns of the old monster films, and comedy/horror sitcoms, such as *The Munsters* and *The Addams Family*, had by this time diffused away horror elements that might have been scary or threatening to children. Vampires had been thoroughly ironized and made into a camp figure in the 1960s, and many children's shows and cartoons had, by this time, incorporated the figure. But we can mark the vampire's complete incorporation into the realm of children's culture by the twin appearance, in 1971 of a breakfast cereal, Count Chocula, and in 1972 of a muppet, Count von Count, on public television's educational *Sesame Street* show. The suddenly harmless vampire had a foot in both of television's fields—the commercial and the educational.

Obviously a version of Dracula with his cape and Central European accent, Sesame Street's Count von Count is also a pun in the form of a puppet. His purpose, taken from his name, is to teach children to count. Like most of the other Muppet characters on this Public Broadcasting System show, he is an animated version of a stuffed doll figure, more cuddly than threatening, although he does have fangs. He first appeared in 1972 in an episode where he counts blocks with the muppet characters Bert and Ernie. Unlike Lugosi's Dracula, he has a goatee and a monocle, and he tends to be accompanied with dramatic movie organ music and thunder and lightning. When he sings, he sings music that is based on Central European folk songs. He lives in a castle where he has pet bats, but he is not apparently able to turn into a bat. In the earlier seasons of the show, the Count had the ability to hypnotize others, usually to facilitate his counting, but this attribute was dropped in later seasons to make him less scary.

He is not very scary, unless you find people with a compulsion to count everything around them scary. Vampires were now teachers as well as product salesmen. Although they still featured scary settings—crumbling castles and dark, stormy nights—the vampire was out of any context that might link him to death or bloodletting. He represents just another fun kind of character within a context that was themed to go along with him. He is based on Lugosi's Dracula—Hungarian accent, evening dress, cape. There is also a female version of the vampire by this time, one who has followed a different lineage. Based on the figure Luna, played by Caroll Borland in Browning's *Mark of the Vampire*, and on subsequent television horror-show hosts Vampira and Elvira, as well as on the mother figures in *The Addams Family* and *The Munsters*, the female vampire is tall, pale, thin, and has long, dark hair. She shares Lugosi's Hungarian accent and penchant for evening clothes, wearing a long, black dress.

By the 1970s, for children, vampires have become one of a set of monsters that are associated with the gothic setting of the haunted house (or castle). The other monsters are versions of other Universal Studio's figures from the 1930s and include the vampire, the wolf man, the mummy, and Frankenstein's monster. Each has been thematically linked to products, such as sugar-filled cereals for children. Along with Count Chocula, General Mills has offered other monster-based cereals— Frankenberry, Boo Berry, Fruit Brute, and Yummy Mummy—some of which are presently marketed seasonally for Halloween.

Children's literature was to be invaded by monsters as well. Following a long tradition of nonhuman creatures that goes back to the German *marchen* or folk tales and their equivalents in cultures all over the world, writers have established a long history of fantasy-based stories for children. As horror themes became sanitized for children through television, monster stories, such as Maurice Sendak's *Where the Wild Things Are* (1963), brought children face to face with threatening, grotesque, but tameable monsters of various sorts. Vampires, maybe because of their bloodletting habits, seem to come late into children's stories, after the cuter monsters have paved the way. By the late 1970s, one of the first children's stories to feature a vampire was *Bunnicula*, a book written by husband and wife team Deborah and James Howe.

Bunnicula begins with a dog bringing a manuscript to an editor. A note explains that the book was written by the dog, a wolfhound mix named Harold, who lives with a family, the Monroes, which consists of himself, two boys, two parents, and a cat named Chester. The story begins one (naturally) dark and stormy night. The human members of the family come in after going to see *Dracula* at the movies, with a box that they found on a seat at the theater. In the box is a baby rabbit, some soil, and a note in a foreign language. Because Harold is part Russian wolfhound, he is able to read the note, which says "Please take care of my baby" in an obscure Carpathian mountain dialect. The family decides that Bunnicula, a combination of bunny with Dracula, is an appropriate name for their new pet because of the circumstances of his discovery. Soon, Chester and Harold begin to notice strange things about the rabbit.

Unlike them, it cannot talk in any language. Instead of regular rabbit teeth, it has two fangs. It sleeps all day, but at night seems to be able to escape its cage at will and get into the refrigerator, where vegetables are found to be drained of their juices, with the result that they turn completely white. Between Harold's naps, he and Chester discuss the rabbit's peculiar behavior. Chester, who is an avid reader and has a vivid imagination, decides that the creature is a vampire and so must be destroyed. He tries to kill it with a stake, but fails because he mistakenly uses a steak. The Monroes come home and find the cat trying to pound a steak into the sleeping rabbit, so they feed the steak to a grateful Harold. Bunnicula doesn't seem to pose a threat to anyone except the vegetables, so Harold loses interest in Chester's attempts to destroy it. Chester manages to keep the rabbit away from any food source for a while, but this eventually backfires, because the Monroes, seeing that Bunnicula is weakening, take him to the vet, who recommends a diet of vegetable juices. This stops the depredations on the vegetables, and results in Chester being sent to a cat psychologist, giving him something else to obsess about—himself.

The story works because it sets up a situation with rules—Chester and Harold can talk, but the humans can't understand them, for instance— that remain consistent. Their characters fit in with our understandings of dogs and cats. Harold can always be distracted by food, for example, and Chester hates to be kissed on the nose. Chester is obsessive and paranoid, whereas Harold is somewhat dim-witted and happy-go-lucky. Chester is the instigator and Harold is the follower. The other characters follow suit—the boys bicker and disagree, the parents act predictably, mediating and intervening when necessary. As in Stoker's *Dracula*, the central character remains a mystery. Bunnicula does seem to be a veggie vampire, but never gets caught and never learns to speak. Once the vegetable juice solution is discovered and Chester's obsession is redirected to himself, the household returns to a state of stability, and it doesn't matter that the bunny is a vampire. If there is a message to the children reading the book, it is that problems can be dealt with best using reason and tolerance rather than violence, and that all questions are not necessarily going to be answered.

This demonstrates that the best children's books are like the best adult books—not rigidly formulaic in their plots or overtly moralistic in their themes. James Howe has gone on to write four sequels to *Bunnicula*, as well as a spin-off series. The most recent one, *Bunnicula Meets Edgar Allan Crow* (2006), makes some postmodern moves, becoming a children's horror novel about a writer of children's horror novels. In it, M. T. Graves, writer of the *FleshCrawlers* series (perhaps a reference to

R. L. Stine, author of the *Goosebumps* series?) visits the Monroes with his pet crow, Edgar Allan. The author turns out to be likeable but neurotic, to have a fear of dogs and to be terribly lonely. After some more of Chester's mistaken speculations, which cause the pets (now joined by Howie, a pun-loving dachshund) to create more problems, everything is resolved, and the writer goes home with Sonnicula, Bunnicula's offspring, and a new girlfriend, Ms. Pickles the librarian. In the course of things, Bunnicula escapes again, and there are more white vegetables found. Again, chaos is followed by a new equilibrium, and some mysteries are still unsolved.

Scary? No, and that is the point. The Count von Count, Count Chocula, Bunnicula—all these 1970s survivors are vampires without the threat. Vampires were somewhat late getting into children's literature, perhaps because it is easy to imagine a sweet monster or a cuddly werewolf, but a dead person with fangs who sucks blood is difficult to make nice with, and the whole point of vampires, even psychic ones, is to drain the life out of others, so it is not easy to make them nonthreatening. Writers of children's books have been wrestling with these issues since the 1970s, with various strategies being used to soften the horror and differing opinions being expressed as to the necessity of such softening. In general, from a beginning point in the early 1970s, the number and intensity of vampires in children's literature have been multiplying, and they vary widely, from truly harmless (at least to humans) to quite dangerous.

For readers in the middle grades, Scholastic publishes a variety of series books, many of which have gothic themes. There doesn't seem to be a house style or specific philosophy to these books, other than providing high-interest materials at an appropriate vocabulary level. On the more harmless side, Daniel Pinkwater has continued with the Bunnicula idea of truly vegetarian vampires with his Henry Count Dorkula, a "fruitpire" with the ability to turn into a fruit bat, who appears in his Werewolf Club Series volume # 3, *The Werewolf Club Meets Dorkula*. It is significant that the story is only one of many in the series, and that the club of preteen monsters it features are werewolves, not vampires. Henry, in true middle school fashion, wants to seem more dangerous than he is, and so the werewolf kids have to out him as a fruitpire.

Another series book in Scholastic's Bailey School Kids series, *Vampires Don't Wear Polka Dots* (1990), centers around a power struggle between a new teacher, Mrs. Jeepers, and Eddie, the class clown. The mischievous third-grade class has driven one teacher out—she reportedly moved to a small town in Alaska. Mrs. Jeepers is from Romania and has a mysterious green stone pendant that matches her eyes. She has moved into an abandoned mansion that everyone thinks is haunted, and she is extremely allergic to garlic. The story occupies a gray area between the explained and the supernatural, because we never actually find out if the teacher is a vampire; but she seems to have mysterious powers. At first, all the students are with Eddie, but he gradually loses their support as they become model students. A pattern emerges: Eddie acts out, she ignores him, then she intervenes in a way that surprises and intimidates his fellow students. She pops Eddie's gum bubble from across the room with a gesture, getting gum all over his face. At one point, she touches her pendant and freezes Eddie, so that he stands in the aisle in a trance for several minutes. Eddie and another student sneak into the basement of her house at night, where they find a coffin-like box. They are trying to open it when a noise scares them away. A spitball incident leads to the final confrontation between them. Mrs. Jeepers takes Eddie out of the room for an extended period of time, and when he returns he is pale and frightened, and never misbehaves again. The story could be about how a clever teacher uses her heritage to ensure good behavior among credulous students, or she could be a vampire, or at least someone with supernatural powers. In any case, she is using her powers for good. As Eddie says before his final reformation, "So far she has made us clean up the room, get our work done, and be quiet in class. Before you know it, she'll have us actually learning!" (Daley and Jones 1990, 70–71).

Similarly, gothic subject matter, but with a higher gross-out factor, characterizes R. L. Stine's vast *Goosebumps* series, also published by Scholastic (149 titles, according to one source). One title, *Vampire Breath*, deals with the subject of vampires. These books were a publishing phenomenon during the 1990s, spawning merchandizing, a television series, video games, and interactive media, all based on a children's horror format that delivers consistent scares and chills, with a fair amount of disgusting detail, but still without violence. These are a step beyond the explained Scooby Doo formula or the completely harmless horror of the Sesame Street/Bunnicula variety, because it has its first-person child protagonists confront actual supernatural threats in settings beyond their control. However, the situations are always resolved back to something like the status quo. In *Vampire Breath*, the narrator Freddy and his friend Cara are roughhousing in Freddy's basement when they discover a hidden doorway. This leads to a tunnel where they find a coffin. In it, they find a glass bottle labeled Vampire Breath. When they open it, they are engulfed in a foul-smelling gas, which disperses to reveal a bald, silver-eyed old vampire. Unable to attack them because he is missing his teeth, the vampire releases more gas, which transports them to a castle full of vampires. Eventually, they find another vial of gas, which brings them home. There they discover that the vampire is Freddy's grandfather, and that his parents and he are vampires. But Freddy doesn't have to deal with being a vampire yet. He is too young to get his fangs—he'll "have to wait at least another hundred years" (Stine 1996, 112). End of story. Everything is almost back to normal, at least for the next 100 years.

A more unusual offering is Laura Marchesani's *Dick and Jane and Vampires* (2010), a mash-up which is targeted at very young readers, or at older readers who grew up with the Dick and Jane series (which is still under copyright to Pearson Education, Inc.). It rewrites the classic primer series of Dick and Jane books, adding a vampire to the wholesome whitebread world of the kids with their nuclear family and their pets. The vampire is sometimes in bat form and sometimes in human form, sometimes scary and sometimes a playmate. The addition of a figure from a very different context—horror movies, gothic novels, haunted houses—serves to highlight the artificiality of the normal world portrayed in the traditional primers.

The vampire serves as a disruptive detail that destabilizes the sanitized, conventional, and standardized world of the book series, at least until the book's end when he is conveniently paired up with a female vampire. The Dick and Jane books, once standard in schools, had been modified in the mid-1960s to include similarly middle-class nuclear family African American characters, but were largely eliminated from use by the 1980s—which brings into question who exactly the audience is for this vampire version. Is it for people in their 40s and older, who remember and feel sentimental about the readers, yet are troubled by their rigid ideology? Is it meant for them to give to their children and grandchildren as an ironic, yet nostalgic, way to remember the past? It certainly demonstrates the ambivalent nature of the vampire figure today: mostly defanged, especially for children, but still with a hint of threat.

A more bizarre vampire story for children is Kirk Scroggs's *Dracula vs. Grampa at the Monster Truck Spectacular*, a story that shamelessly serves up a variety of stereotypes, including old people, vampires, and rednecks. Wiley and his grandfather sneak out of the house, despite warnings of an F5 tornado in the area, so that they can go to the Monster Truck Spectacular, where they meet Colonel Dracula and his Mudsucker, a monster truck that runs on blood. After some scrapes, some narrow escapes, and some naps on Grampa's part, they make it home safely. Delivered in a deadpan, matter-of-fact tone by Wiley, the story's escapades take on the aura of a surrealist painting, or perhaps a Gary Larson cartoon.

In the wake of the Harry Potter phenomenon, there has been an explosion of literature aimed at "tweens," a marketing category for older children who are not quite teenagers, but who are interested in the concerns of adolescence. Many of these are based on vampires. An example of one of many series created for this marketing category is Sienna Mercer's *My Sister the Vampire* series. In the first episode, *Switched*, Mercer introduces us to two contrasting eighth grade girls. Olivia, a cheerleader with a perky, outgoing personality and a preference for pink, starts at the new school Franklin Grove that seems to have a lot of Goths. She meets Ivy, a nerdy pale Goth, who also happens to be a vampire. After a couple of encounters, the girls realize that they have identical rings, which came from their birth parents—both are adopted. They also realize that, under the contrasting styles of clothing and makeup, they are identical twins. They begin switching, changing clothes and using makeup to impersonate each other, so that they can take advantage of each other's skills. Ivy learns to smile and do cheers, while Olivia learns more about Franklin Grove's secret vampire subculture as she helps to plan the All Hallows Ball. The vampires don't attack humans or turn into bats, but get their blood from BloodMart, which is in the basement of the FoodMart. They have a secret community that exists alongside the bunnies, which is what they call non-vampires.

The story ends with a successful Ball, with both girls paired up with the boy of their dreams, and with Olivia making cheerleader. The message about tolerance for differences comes through loud and clear, suggesting that the book could be read as an allegory for accepting people with different sexual preferences—the idea that anyone, even your twin sister, could be a vampire, and that vampires have a secret community suggests such an interpretation. Even the term bunnies for non-vampires suggests a gay term for heterosexuals: breeders—rabbits are famous for their breeding abilities. The heterosexual pairings at the end might be seen as undercutting this idea, but both girls pair up with one of their own kind.

Another series book, *At First Bite* by Ruth Ames, is part of Scholastic's *Poison Apple* series, gothic-themed books by a variety of writers.

Again, a new girl Ashlee arrives at school, but this time she's a recently turned vampire, one of a very small minority, and she's having trouble controlling her bat-shifting ability. Whenever she gets upset, she changes into a bat. The vampires are ruled by a council and drink Sanga!, a synthetic blood drink, for nutrition. They can also feed on animals, but only in bat form. Problems occur when renegade vampires, the Dark Ones, start feeding on humans. Human blood is addictive and they become sick without it. A series of attacks around the school lead Ashlee and her new friends Brendan, another vampire, and his non-vampire sister Sasha, to suspect their English teacher of being a Dark One. They set a trap and manage to catch him. Ashlee abandons her quest to be a popular girl and learns to be happy with her new, somewhat nerdy, friends.

An allegorical reading of this story might see human blood as a stand-in for addictive drugs. One has to be introduced to blood drinking, it is against the Vampire Council's law, and it makes you sick when you don't get enough. Ordinary vampirism is more like methadone maintenance—as long as you get enough Sanga!, you will be fine—once you learn to master the bat shifting.

Like *Buffy the Vampire Slayer*, which serves as an obvious model for their storylines, these series novels focus on the real problems of junior high school—popularity, romance, fashion—with the supernatural parts added on as plot thickening. The protagonists are more concerned with the day-to-day challenges of junior high, and with the problems caused by the supernatural elements—Ashlee experiences a terrible sunburn, for example—than with their exceptional powers. The threats are not particularly scary or deadly, in genre more akin to soap opera than to horror.

Writing horror for this age group, perhaps more aimed at boys, is David Lubar, a writer of Poe-like short stories for juveniles. In his collection, *Attack of the Vampire Weenies* (2011), things often do not go well for the protagonists. In the title story, a young man is disgusted by his older sister's *Twilight* fixation, and so deliberately advertises her vampire party in graveyards and old mansions, places where real vampires might be expected to hang out. He takes precautions against them—holy water, garlic, stakes, crosses—and he is not disappointed. A handsome stranger arrives and asks, "Who gives Count Vranski permission to enter this house?" After he promises not to drink their blood, the sister gives permission. The brother tries the various weapons to no effect—the stranger takes them away. That is when the real vampire arrives:

> Someone old and evil and horribly ugly stepped into the house. His skin was dead white. His teeth were the dull brown color of old blood. A smell of rotten flesh and old clothing drifted from him. White flecks wriggled in his hair and fell to his shoulders. Maggots. (Lubar 2011, 45)

This grisly character is the real Count Vranski, who has been inadvertently invited in by the carefully worded question that his advance team asked. Our narrator, who was perfectly correct in his assessment about the weenie vampires imitated by his sister, is powerless to do anything about it now. Count Vranski and his crew start feeding.

This is true horror, with no holds barred in terms of outcome. The treatment is still appropriate for preteen children, in that Lubar's stories avoid references to sex and do not have graphic descriptions of their often lamentable conclusions. Like Poe's treatment of the horror story, a certain decorous distance is preserved between the audience and the gory details. The young protagonists give readers a point of interest, and the use of slang and appropriate level vocabulary marks it as targeted to preteenagers.

These represent just a sampling of what is available in terms of vampires for children. There are many other vampire-related materials available, including graphic novels. Gary Reed and Becky Cloonan have adapted Stoker's *Dracula* into a graphic version for younger readers, for example. Also, nonfiction treatments produce hybrids, such as Samuel Folly's *Vampireology: The True History of the Fallen Ones*, a scrapbook-formatted treatment that seems to be, like Stoker's novel, based on documentary evidence, telling a story about how vampires descend from three fallen angels—Ba'al, Moloch, and Belial—each of which has fathered a strand of monsters. The book is purported to have been put together around 1920 by a protector, Archibald Brooks, to be passed on to his successor, a Joshua T. Kraik. Readers follow clues found in notes, newspaper clippings, letters, and other documents to put together the story.

This leads us into the realm of literature known as Young Adult, YA for short, which is targeted to teenagers. Because this is the time when young people begin to deal with sexual feelings, with physically changing bodies, with menstruation, as well as with larger questions about life and death, it makes a near-perfect fit with the vampire mythos. It becomes difficult to define what is preteen and what is young adult, the next older category, which blends into adult novels and includes such works, according to some, as the *Twilight* series. One novel series, L. J. Smith's *The Vampire Diaries*, which is now also a television series, will serve to illustrate this category. Originally published as a trilogy in 1991, it is in many ways a model for the *Twilight* books. It involves a love triangle between a mortal (live?) girl and two vampire brothers, one good and one evil. An obvious fact about vampires that has been fairly consistent over time, and that has been kept in the realm of literature for adults, is that they are often about sex. Blood sucking, without going too explicitly into detail, is an exchange of bodily fluids, and so the sexual metaphor is not one that requires much effort to see. It is obvious and not appropriate for children, but much of the young adult market is concerned about sex and sexuality, making jealousy and cheating central themes.

Two writers of YA fiction have engaged in a recent debate about the purposes of horror writing for this age group. In an opinion piece for *The Wall Street Journal*, "Darkness Too Visible," Meghan Cox Gurdon bewails the current offerings of novels for young adults in general and criticizes horror novels in particular. She begins with a story of a mother looking to buy a book for a 13-year-old in a Barnes and Noble store. She can find "nothing; not a thing that I could imagine giving my daughter. It was all vampires and suicide and self-mutilation, this dark, dark stuff" (Gurdon 2011, 1). Gurdon dismisses the idea that these stories might reflect the *sturm und drang* of adolescence. Instead of being "immersed in ugliness," she recommends material that encourages "a child's happiness, moral development and tenderness of heart" (2011, 2). She fears that "books focusing on pathologies normalize them" (2011, 3), and suggests that anyone criticizing content or even "guid[ing] what young people read" is immediately accused of censorship. The result of the permissive attitude of the publishing industry is to "bulldoze coarseness or misery into children's lives" (2011, 5).

Whether one equates vampire stories with descriptions of sexual abuse, self-mutilation, and incest, as Gurden and her informant seem to, is an important question. Do teenagers not have the ability to distinguish fantasy from realism? But on a more fundamental level, horror is horror, so perhaps we can concede that point. One of the authors she quotes, Sherman Alexie, who is the author of a YA novel, entitled *The Absolutely True Diary of a Part-Time Indian* (2007), takes issue with Gurden's whole premise. In his reply, "Why the Best Kid's Books Are Written in Blood," he describes Gurdon's position as condescending and patronizing to a group who are already knowledgeable about the topics discussed, many of whom are already traumatized by poverty and abuse. He cites his own experience as a teenager with saviors who were trying to protect him: "Wow. You are way, way too late" (Alexie 2011, 2). "As a child, I read," he says, "because books—violent and not, blasphemous and not, terrifying and not—were the most loving and trustworthy things in my life" (2011, 4).

Horror for children is problematic. Vampires are scary, problematic creatures that don't fit the rules, and can be very threatening. Children and young adults today have a huge variety of monsters to choose from—some they can laugh at, some can give them a thrill of fear, and some are utterly, horribly scary. Perhaps the best parents can do is to keep close watch, to explain and comfort, and to always be ready to sympathize. We have seen that monsters for children can be sanitized, comedified, defanged, and made educational. But one of the things horror stands for is that extra presence beyond the door, the thing that we don't yet know about. Alexie, who writes about real life not fantasy horror, claims:

> I don't write to protect them. It's far too late for that. I write to give them weapons—in the form of words and ideas—that will help them fight their monsters. I write in blood because I remember what it felt like to bleed. (Alexie 2011, 4)

Are sheltered children happier? Perhaps. But the kind of ignorance of anything bad that Gurdon—and maybe, ideally, all of us—wishes for the young isn't going to last. What parents and adult writers can hope to do is to participate in the learning, to provide skills for dealing with what is to come. Maybe monsters and vampires and horror—those things that don't fit.

CHAPTER 15

White Trash and Teen Melodrama

Vampires belong to a modern popular folklore that few will admit
to believing but that has become part of a way of thinking about
and ordering our vision of the world around us.
> —Mary Hallab, *Vampire God*, (2009) 9.

The decade after 2000 brought a variety of new vampires. In this
chapter, I focus on the vampire lite series of novels and films known
collectively as the *Twilight* saga, in contrast with the HBO television
series *True Blood*. The primary result of the proliferation of series
fictions in the 1990s was an enormous stretch in the possibilities of
what a vampire could be. The series form makes possible an embrace of
both the endless stories that series provide and the addition of fantastic
elements from folklore and genre fictions. Has vampire fiction become
a genre in itself? It depends, of course, on how one chooses to define
genre. The term, used in publishing, refers to established forms with
established conventions, such as science fiction, horror, fantasy, and
romance, all distinguished from nongeneric serious or literary fiction,
which is not only traditionally expected to be fairly narrowly realistic
in terms of subject matter, but also to use experimental and fantastic formal variations, such as stream-of-consciousness (at least in its
modernist phase). For an example from movies, film noir has elements
of realism in its focus on gritty cityscapes, monetary desperation, and
sexual obsession, but is modernist in its expressionistic use of lighting
and camera angles.

The postmodern era in fiction is generally accepted as beginning about
mid-century, after World War II, and understood to signal a break with
the established conventions of the modernist fiction that dominated the

literary field in the first half of the 20th century. Postmodernism, like its predecessor modernism, is a broad field, finding expression in many areas other than literature and film, including the arts, philosophy, and religion. In general, the change is seen to be a breaking down of coherent grand narratives in favor of smaller, fragmented, more local, and more contingent stories. Postmodern expression is often described as playful rather than serious, ironic or cool, and rich in recycling and quotation from a variety of source materials. Categories tend to be broken down, especially categories that support traditional truths. We can see that these attributes—questioning eternal verities, focusing on local examples, an ironic attitude—would explain why postmodernism is also seen as concerned more with surfaces or styles rather than with deep meanings. Indeed, it brings into question both the value and the concept of depth.

So, the vampire as a superhero or romantic lead rather than a tortured Romantic at odds with his own nature makes sense in a postmodern context, as does the vampire as a role to play, either as part of a game or as a serious lifestyle. In the decade 2000–2010, the various vampires that emerged in the 1990s—both those represented in fiction and those embodied in role playing and subcultures—have invaded a wider cultural space, as they did in the more innocent 1960s, including not only in the world of teen melodrama in the *Twilight* material and the world of adult drama in the *True Blood* series, but also spawning other post-Buffy TV series, such as *Forever Knight* and *The Vampire Diaries*, and finding their way into classic literature in mash-up novels, such as *Jane Slayre* and *Little Vampire Women*. The postmodern view of a vampire seems to be more of a pastiche or collection of vampires past, combining our attitudes toward superheroes, animals, the dead, and zombies with hotness, which can be seen as a postmodern take on sexual attractiveness, based on a combination of physical looks and hipness.

Postmodern vampires bring their attractiveness from the styles of the past as well as those of the present. So, when Sookie Stackhouse (Anna Paquin), a waitress at Merlotte's Bar in Bon Temps, Louisiana, meets her first vampire, Bill Compton (Steven Moyer), a Civil War veteran who has come home to his ancestral house, she is as attracted to his old-fashioned manners as to his seductive vampire sexuality.

The *True Blood* series, which has, as of this writing, concluded its fourth season, is based on a series of novels by Charlaine Harris, written as horror/mystery hybrids. As a premier cable series, the show makes liberal use of nudity, sexuality, and bloody violence. The protagonist, Sookie, is a psychic who can hear other people's thoughts, who works as a waitress in a respectable redneck bar. Her ability—she refers to it in the novels as a disability—has proved to be a problem for her romantically, so her inability to read Bill's mind adds to his attractiveness to her. In the first season, vampires have just come out of the coffin and revealed themselves publicly, as the result of the availability of TruBlood, a Japanese product that provides them with nutrition, so that they no longer have to feed on humans. There are obvious parallels to the Civil Rights movement of the 1960s and to the present movement for lesbian, gay, bisexual and transgender (LGBT) rights—the opening title sequence features an illuminated sign stating that "GOD HATES FANGS" (a play on the GOD HATES FAGS signs at antigay protests) and shows children in Ku Klux Klan regalia. Alan Ball, the creator of the TV series, and an out-of-the-closet gay man, suggests that such an interpretation is simplistic. "To look at these vampires on the show as metaphors for gays and lesbians is so simple and so easy, that it's kind of lazy," Ball told the *New York Post* ("Flesh & Blood" 2009). Still, a different kind of people who practice a different kind of sex and pose a threat to conservative, especially religious, values, people who have concealed themselves within the human population for thousands of years—the parallels are there. Ball's series complicates the mix by foregrounding other codes of difference as well, primarily those of race and social class.

The most obvious way that the show has deviated from its source in the novels is in its treatment of African Americans. Ball changed Sookie's white best friend Tara Thornton into an African American (Rutina Wesley), brought her in earlier in the plot, gave her a righteous attitude, and made her into a central character. Tara's introduction in the first episode is a scene where she is working as a retail clerk. She is reading *The Shock Doctrine*. She insults a condescending white woman, accuses her boss of sexual harassment, and quits her job, neatly playing on both white characters' fears of black stereotypes, then calling them on it: "Oh My God! I'm not serious, you pathetic racist. I don't have a baby. I know y'all have to be stupid, but do you have to be that stupid?" Ball has also capitalized on Harris's existing black characters, expanding the role of Lafayette Reynolds (Nelsan Ellis), Tara's cousin, who is an effeminate troubled gay man in the novel, but whom Ball developed into a much stronger character. As Ball describes this:

> Lafayette is more overtly feminine in the books, and I . . . I didn't really want to do that. I wanted him to be strong, because I feel that if you are gay, and black, in a small town, in Louisiana, you

are either . . . not going to live to see twenty or you are going to be strong enough to kick some serious ass. (Ball, DVD audio commentary, *True Blood* 1.1)

He also states that he is not in favor of improvisation, but that in the case of Nelsan Ellis, who plays Lafayette, he wants to "just get out of this guy's way, because he is so gifted" (Commentary 1.1).

Overall, Harris's novels work in the tradition of Southern fiction that follows the conventions of realism without disturbing the sensibilities of Southern middle-class readers. Like Sookie, her characters tend to be witty and perceptive, unpretentious and eccentric, but in introducing a South teeming with vampires, shape-shifters, and a variety of other supernatural types, she chooses to place them in a context that doesn't break the established class boundaries of the traditional South. In this world, "bed" becomes an active verb referring to sex, vampire kings and queens have huge plantation houses, werewolves congregate in red-neck bars, and waitresses (other than Sookie) tend to be slutty single mothers. Harris's South is equivalent to the Regency period for writers of romances—a recognizable world with a framework of established social mores. For her readers, the novels provide a familiar, comfortable world with clear rules of behavior, into which Harris can then bring the monsters.

Sympathetically portrayed, in-your-face black characters don't fit into this comfortable context. In this way, Ball's vision of the South has more in common with the Southern Gothic literary tradition, which presents a land of contradiction and conflict, a setting that could break into violent chaos at any moment, peopled with characters who are often grotesque—physically and emotionally deformed. This is the South of early William Faulkner, of Erskine Caldwell, Tennessee Williams, Truman Capote, and Flannery O'Connor, and of later writers like Cormac McCarthy, Larry Brown, and—not coincidentally—Chris Offutt, a Kentucky writer whom Ball hired as story editor for the first season. Although Alan Ball has followed Harris's plots faithfully, we know from the opening credits of *True Blood* which South the series inhabits. The opening credits, a brilliant montage sequence by Digital Kitchen, contrasts decaying architecture, decaying animal corpses, blood, and shots of swampland with frenetic scenes of religious frenzy, lovemaking in a bar, and children in KKK regalia, against the soundtrack of Jace Everett's "Bad Things," with the growling chorus, "I want to do bad things to you." In Ball's words, he is working for a contrast with the "highly polished and mechanical" world of most recent vampire movies, lit by a "cold, metallic, silver-blue light." According to Ball, the world of *True Blood* "is wet and dirty, and sticky, and it smells, and it's loud with bugs and creepy stuff" (Ball 2009, Commentary 1.1). For him, vampires are about sex: "To me, vampires are sex," Ball told *Rolling Stone*. "I don't get a vampire story about abstinence. I'm 53. I don't care about high school students. I find them irritating and uninformed" (Grigoriadis 2010, 56).

The series gives us a wide variety of characters that include vampires, shape-shifters, evangelical fanatics, and many small town Southern eccentrics. There is no simple moral dichotomy between good guys and bad guys—everyone is a mixture, often surprising or disappointing the audience. Sookie is a virgin when the series starts and retains a kind of innocence, but she relishes sex, as do most of the other characters—it is a hormonal swamp as well as a literal one.

Ball's comment about high school students and abstinence, of course, invokes a very different world, the world of the *Twilight* novels and films. Stephenie Meyer, targeting teenagers, has made her vampire hero old-fashioned as well, but she frames it in terms of the debate over abstinence. Edward Cullen will not "bed" Bella until they are married, and once this happens, the result is—even against the way that the vampires understand their own biology—pregnancy. But given this difference, the similarities between the vampires in these two series are striking. In both cases, vampires are hard and cold, beautiful, sexy, immortal, and practically indestructible—Meyer's vampires can even endure sunlight, although it can identify them to humans because their skin sparkles. This idiosyncrasy explains the setting in the Pacific Northwest—they prefer areas with a lot of cloud cover.

In both cases, vampires have formed their own culture alongside humans, but Meyer's group is still closeted, so the minority metaphor is less prominent. In terms of character, Meyer is not burdened by the Southern literary tradition of lively and eccentric characterization, so her Bella has few distinguishing features, except a tendency to depression and physical clumsiness. The vampire family, the Cullens, tend to fall easily into stereotypes—the altruistic doctor father, the sweet nurturing mother, the ethereal psychic daughter, and so forth. All are fairly predictable. What unites Bella with Sookie is the way that both have an apparently irresistible smell to vampires. All human prey smells good, of course, but these girls have a special odor. One of the traits that has become fairly commonplace in vampire stories is the claim that vampirism provides a boost to one's consciousness. As in Rice's stories, being turned sharpens the senses of the victim. This makes sense by way of the animal analogy—if vampirism brings us closer to our animal natures, especially as predators, one would expect that enhanced senses, especially smell, would come with the transformation. In both the world of *Twilight* and the world of *True Blood*, the human protagonist has a special appeal signaled by her scent, not only to the love interests Edward and Bill, but also to other vampires. This fits in with popular beliefs about pheromones, odors that supposedly signal or trigger sexual response in insects and in animals. Whether such triggers exist for humans is debated, but a phenomenon such as the way that women living together start to menstruate according to the same schedule has been proven by researchers to relate to unconscious responses to changes in body chemistry signaled by smell. So, we have a contemporary folkloric understanding of vague, unconscious hormonal responses that result in attraction. Past ages might have construed romantic attraction as a kind of spiritual affinity, but we tend to materialize such claims into equally vague scientific explanations.

Apparently, both Bella and Sookie have special pheromones that trigger predatory and sexual attraction in vampires. During Sookie's first encounters with Bill, he asks her more than once, "What are you?" The answer, we find out later in the series, is that she has fairy blood, which also accounts for her psychic disability. Bella is apparently just uniquely fertile; the first time that she and Edward have sex, finally, after they are married, she conceives a fast-growing and maternally destructive vampire child. This is the first time this has happened, in anyone's knowledge—the vampires had believed that their undead state made them sterile.

The other folkloric trait that vampires seem to share in these two interpretations is a pack hierarchy based on age. *True Blood*'s vampires are divided into kingdoms which are subdivided into districts ruled by sheriffs, a hierarchy based on their increasing strength which they gain as they age. In *Twilight*, vampires live in similarly hierarchical covens dominated by the older members. Even though Carlisle, the doctor/father, is a vegetarian and dedicated to helping humans rather than preying on them, the Cullens are a patriarchal family who follow his leadership. Edward, although frozen in a 17-year-old body, is almost a century older than Bella, and therefore plays the role of father as well as love interest. He always seems to know what is best for her, and it is by his insistence that they refrain from sex until after marriage. The *Twilight* vampires' supernatural rivals are a pack of werewolves, one of whom, Jacob, is also Edward's rival for Bella's affections. These shape-shifters, stereotypically defined as a Native American tribe, share thoughts when in animal form and are compelled to follow their Alpha, a hereditarily determined leader. *True Blood* also has werewolves, who tend to exhibit pack behaviors, follow their Alphas, and meet in redneck bars.

Some of the most alarming aspects of the relationship between Bella and Edward, especially for adult members of the audience, have to do with his cool dominance of every aspect of her life. As one blogger opines:

> The things that upset me the most about this series are, I think, the things that upset most women who believe that their existence constitutes more than window dressing. I tend to concur with various critics who claim that the series promotes a not so implicit valorization of abuse (he leaves, he comes back, he lies, he causes her much emotional and physical pain), that it works to undermine female agency and independence (Bella is always rescued by Edward, Bella is always put in harm's way by him as well, and she continually enables this scenario to remain manifest), and that it reinforces dangerous and, I'd like to believe outdated, Victorian era notions of male and female sexuality: he's a beast who must learn to control his baser lusts, and she, simply by virtue of the fact that she's female, is responsible for inciting those lusts. And despite the fact that Bella wants sex, he just can't defile her (t'would be so wrong), unless they get married. (LW 2011)

The vampires in *Twilight* resemble comic book superheroes—they are faster, smarter, harder (rock-hard and sparkly skin), stronger, and better looking than ordinary humans. They are also richer, having apparently unlimited disposable income. They are creatures of a kind of sanitized fantasy, where the goal is getting to a very low-threshold version of normal—marriage, parenthood—that has a potential to last forever. Even though she is accepted to Dartmouth, Bella doesn't need (or apparently want) to go to college. All that Bella and her new family have to do is avoid the notice of humans and keep from depleting the food supply. In the words of Anna Silver:

> While she is not the heroine that I would choose as a model for my female students—marriage and motherhood at age nineteen and the curtailing of her education are irresponsible advice for today's girls—the book demands a detailed analysis of how Meyer

depicts motherhood as a means of personal fulfillment and, more generally, underscores the series' persistent theme that identity comes from affiliation rather than individual accomplishment. (Silver 2010, 138)

Much has been made of the conservative values expressed in the *Twilight* stories, but, as Silver points out, its ultimate values reflect a kind of communitarianism that also goes against the ideology of American individualism. What is most conservative about Meyer's fantasy, as Emily Wilkinson points out in her investigation of the ethics of the *Twilight* world, is that this world is presented in essentially black and white terms—the evil predatory vampires against the good ones who don't feed on people:

In order to enjoy the *Twilight* novels, you have to be willing to enter into an intense emotional and hormonal fundamentalism, the twin of the moral fundamentalism apparent in Meyer's refusal of nuance and ambivalence in favor of an either/or approach to good and evil. (Wilkinson 2011, II)

By definition, fundamentalisms tend to be simplifications, a boiling down of conflict and complexity into simple, rule-based methods of living. Despite the formulaic plotting of Harris's *Southern Vampire Series* novels—each follows a murder mystery to its solution—the world she imagines is provocative and exciting, in part because of its moral complexity. What is missing in the world of *Twilight* comes into focus by contrast. In Wilkinson's words, its identity as fantasy is "total—as much a fantasy about human nature and love as it is a generic fantasy" (Wilkinson 2011, II).

True Blood's world is, in the description of its creator, Alan Ball, "cluttered and messy" (Ball 2009, Commentary 1.1). Although these vampires have the option to really be vegetarian, thanks to TruBlood which provides them with cruelty-free nutrition, many of them choose to drink the old-fashioned way, while having sex with a human. Reverse vampirism is also taking place, now that humans have discovered that vampire blood is a potent recreational drug and nutritional supplement. Harris's vampires are not only fast and strong, and can glamor most humans, but are also nocturnal and are much more vulnerable than those in Meyer's world. And there are a wide variety of other superhuman forms around, including werewolves, shape-shifters, maenads, and fairies, making Ball's version of Harris's South cluttered indeed. The innocent but strong Sookie becomes a valuable asset in the power struggle of vampire politics because of her mind-reading ability, but contact with Bill and drinking his blood (to save her life) changes her, making her more aware of the contradictory forces within her as well. No one is particularly innocent or completely evil here, and there is a lot of using going on. This is a world wary, indeed critical of "fixed, inflexible human characters and easy moral absolutes" (Wilkinson 2011, II), as exemplified in the fundamentalist hate church, the Brotherhood of the Sun, on the one hand and the libidinous, human-sacrificing maenad Marianne on the other.

If Nina Auerbach is correct in suggesting that we get the vampires we deserve, perhaps the best way to understand these two worlds is through the lens of contemporary politics. Harris's and Ball's combined perspective gives us a fairly liberal and inclusive big tent, where a variety of groups try to work out solutions that will benefit them while recognizing the rights of others. Meyer gives us a simpler world where right and wrong are clear-cut, where a small group holds most of the cards—wealth, beauty, power, eternal life—and where the rest are safest when they stay in their places and are grateful for the altruism of the shadowy elite. We can easily imagine an ideological stalemate between these two perspectives, because we see something very similar playing out in our political system.

CHAPTER 16

Vampire Comedy

> Hollywood's stock-in-trade is the romantic combination of genres, not the classical practice of generic purity. In one sense, this is hardly surprising; by definition, genres are broad public categories shared across the entire industry, and Hollywood studios have little interest in anything that must be shared with their competitors. On the contrary, they are primarily concerned to create cycles of films that will be identified with a single studio. [. . .] studios prefer to establish cycles (which are proprietary), rather than genres (which are sharable).
>
> —Rick Altman, *Film/Genre* (1999, 59)

To look at vampire comedies in film, we must first take on the question of genres. Genres date back to the Greek and Roman classical period when conceptions of literary categories, which were still associated with the oral tradition, tended to be based on content. These were comedy, tragedy, lyric, and epic categories, terms that still carry meanings for us today, although we tend to see them as subcategories of the major distinctions that we use to categorize written literature, such as fiction, nonfiction, poetry, and drama. These categories are based on written form rather than on content, and demonstrate that our understanding of literature tends to be about written (and printed) texts rather than about oral or performed ones. The resurgence of the performed and visual text through film, television, and internet, as well as the survival of older performative forms, such as live drama and opera, tend to complicate our understanding of genres further.

For film, genres (or subgenres) have continued to evolve, creating new hybrids such as screwball comedy and film noir, as well as genre mixtures such as the subject of this chapter, the horror comedy. As the opening quotation by Altman suggests, genre issues in film also have to do with the proprietary nature of film as a commercial product. To apply this to *Abbott and Costello Meet Frankenstein*, for example, neither horror nor comedy are proprietary to Universal Studios, but the specific monsters featured (Frankenstein's monster, Dracula, the Wolf Man), as well as Abbott and Costello and the "Abbott and Costello Meets . . ." series are properties, and the studio has a clear profit motive in promoting any and all of these features. Genre studies suggest that audiences use genres both to choose ("I love chick flicks") and to refuse ("I can't stand superhero movies") films by category. So, genre can be a double-edged sword for a film's producers. If possible, they want a generic classification to have a positive value for the audience, who will then be further drawn in by elements that are proprietary, such as series branding or the popularity of a certain star.

Why, starting with *Abbott and Costello Meet Frankenstein*, do we have an established tradition of vampire comedies? One obvious answer is that humor serves to defuse or subvert fear, to render it acceptable and harmless. This is, as we have seen, the direction of camp. If we turn the vampire into a mannered buffoon, a predictable stock figure, he ceases to be threatening. However, this isn't always what happens. I want to look at a series of vampire comedy films from the 1940s to the 2000s to demonstrate the different ways in which writers and directors have tried to make vampires funny, or at least to insert vampires into a plot that is essentially comic. In this look at vampire comedy, I am excluding serious films with comedic episodes—which most of them have—as well as comedic films that have brief appearances of vampires, but whose emphasis is elsewhere. In generic terms, I want to look at horror comedies—films that seek to balance these two contradictory or at least contrasting emphases.

Genre blending can have a huge payoff, because it has the possibility of drawing two or more audiences in while weakening the refusal factor and providing a sense of novelty. A good example of this is Joss Whedon's television series, *Buffy the Vampire Slayer*, a teen melodrama crossed with horror and action genres. He followed *Buffy* with *Angel*, which combined a young adult drama with film noir and horror, and *Firefly*, which combined science fiction with the Western. To return to an example of a vampire-based horror/comedy hybrid, I discussed Wes Craven's *Vampire in Brooklyn* (1995) in Chapter 9 in terms of its treatment of race, but it is a good example of a generic hybrid. Although it stars a comic actor, Eddie Murphy, and contains many comic sequences, the overall plot takes its premises seriously, and both Murphy and Angela Bassett treat their roles as romantic leads and vampires (or potential vampires) seriously. Such a treatment inverts the model set by its predecessor *Abbott and Costello Meet Frankenstein* by foregrounding the serious (horror/romance) plot while providing humorous characters and sequences in a secondary fashion.

In its simplest sense, comedy wants to make us laugh, to demonstrate human foibles, to show us the absurdity of the human condition. According to traditional practice, a comic plot introduces some kind of chaos and concludes with a restoration of order, often in the form of a wedding or other public ceremonial ritual. Although there are certainly a wide variety of comedies, the comic hero tends to be an ordinary person, and the wishes, desires, and motivations that compel her or him tend to be those that most people share in common. According to literary genre critic Northrop Frye, "The theme of the comic is the integration of society, which usually takes the form of incorporating a central character into it" (Frye 1957, 43). Ultimately, comedies reinforce such communal social values as generosity, altruism, cooperation, and collaboration, in general recognizing that the common good is, or should be, the dominant goal for human interaction. To quote Frye again, "Comedy is a vision of *dianoia,* a significance which is ultimately a social significance, the establishment of a desirable society" (Frye 1971, 286).

You can see where I'm going with this. Comedy is not only in opposition to tragedy, with its serious emphasis on the extraordinary individual in a sacrificial situation that is not resolved satisfactorily, but also to the gothic and its various generic stepchildren like horror and film noir, which tend to emphasize the power of chaos and violence, and the inability of social norms or conventions to deal with these forces. Vampires, being rather predatory and monstrous, are usually linked with generic categories that are not comic. Comedy and horror share some attributes. Both go for a physical response, as the title to one study suggests: William Paul's *Laughing Screaming: Modern Hollywood Horror and Comedy* (1994). Both are, as Paul points out, lower class genres that go, increasingly in the 1970s and 1980s, for the gross-out, a response that aims to push beyond the audience's comfort level. Referring to literary theorist Mikhail Bakhtin's idea of the grotesque, Paul asserts:

> Official culture sees the high, the "noblest" aspects of experience (mind and spirit) as superior to the low, the body in its most grossly

physical terms (the mouth, the genitals, the anus). But Bakhtin
believes that it is precisely the point of grotesque art . . . to level this
hierarchy by reversing it, by elevating the "material bodily lower
stratum." (Paul 1994, 46)

This lower level is the realm of most comedy and horror—the humor of
the pratfall as well as sexual and scatological jokes, the revulsion at the
body reduced to vulnerable meat. But with vampires, for all their sexual
allure and animal ferocity, we still associate a certain level of class or
aristocratic behavior, which explains why vampire horror/comedy is
usually not as deliberately aimed at the gross-out as that involving other
kinds of monsters.

Noel Carroll, in an article entitled "Horror and Humor," uses *Abbott
and Costello Meet Frankenstein* as an example to set up a contrast
between the functions of monsters in horror and in comedy. He
sees both genres as operating as "jammers" of existing "categories,
concepts, norms, and commonplace expectations" (Carroll 1999, 154).
Horror does this through the fear we share with the protagonists and
humor does it based on incongruity without the edge of threat. He
states, "Horror equals categorical transgression or jamming plus fear;
incongruity humor equals, in part, categorical transgression or jamming minus fear" (Carroll 1999, 157). So, such monsters as Dracula or
the Frankenstein monster can be exactly the same, even played by the
same actors in the same way, but because we have no real fear that Bud
Costello will come to harm, we see these category-jamming creatures
(dead/alive, human/inhuman, human/animal) as sources of amusement.
My terror at the film, as a child, might have had to do with the fact
that I didn't yet have an understanding of the way that comic actors are
invulnerable.

We return again to *Abbott and Costello Meet Frankenstein*, generally
considered to be the last of the classic Universal monster movies, often
seen as a blatant attempt to squeeze a last few dollars out of a declining
franchise (the Universal monster film) by combining it with one that
was a box office guarantee (the Abbott and Costello comedy team). The
film was the fourth monster mash-up to combine monsters, following
Frankenstein Meets the Wolf Man (1944), *House of Frankenstein*
(1944), and *House of Dracula* (1945), but the first to combine all three
monsters—the Wolf Man, Frankenstein's monster, and Dracula—
and the first of these to use a comedy format. In terms of Abbott and
Costello's career trajectory, it is part of a series of "Abbott and Costello
Meet . . ." films that exploited the star team's name recognition, after

they became established in the early 1940s by the success of such films as *Buck Privates* (1941). Jeffrey Miller points out that *Abbott and Costello Meet Frankenstein* was not the first horror comedy hybrid, as there was already an established genre known as "old dark house comedies," where comic actors were placed in a horror setting, typically the gothic house or castle, with a plot that involved comic interludes punctuated by scares. Miller distinguishes between parodies and spoofs. The parody:

> is a ridiculous imitation of another work or style that strives for a comic effect. A horror parody mocks all the conventions of the horror genre. There is nothing scary or frightening about this type of film; it is played strictly for laughs all around. (Miller 2000, 2)

In contrast, a

> horror spoof treats the genre with respect. A spoof is a light, humorous imitation that makes good-natured fun of its target. It is deceptive in that it can be mistaken for the real thing until closer examination reveals the intended humor. Horror spoofs are films meant as comedies but containing horror sequences played straight. (Miller 2000, 2)

In this case, some of film's humor comes from the contrast between the horror elements and the comedy ones. The three monsters are not ridiculous, not parodies of themselves, but are played as real monsters.

The film follows two plots. In one, Dracula and his accomplice Dr. Sandra Mornay plan to replace the Frankenstein monster's brain with Wilbur's (Costello's) in order to make it more controllable. She uses her sex appeal and Dracula uses his hypnotic abilities to manipulate others, especially Wilbur. Lugosi plays Dracula straight as the horror villain. The Wolf Man character (Lon Chaney, Jr.) is also played straight, as a tortured man unable to control his transformations. In the comic counterplot, Chick (Abbott) is jealous of Wilbur's apparent success with the ladies and refuses to believe him about the monsters, whom he somehow avoids seeing until the film's final episodes. As usual, he plays the adult, rational, and masculine figure in contrast to Costello's childlike, emotional, and (occasionally) feminine one. Miller has pointed out that the film follows a schema where the sexually (or romantically) active characters, including Costello, are associated with the monsters and can see them, whereas the ones excluded from the romantic plot, including

Abbott, do not see or believe in the monsters until near the end. This can be seen as a precursor to the familiar plot device from later horror films, where the characters who have sex tend to get killed off first.

After *Abbott and Costello Meet Frankenstein*, Abbot and Costello continued the "Abbot and Costello Meet . . ." series with *Abbott and Costello Meet the Killer, Boris Karloff* (1949), *Abbott and Costello Meet the Invisible Man* (1951), *Abbott and Costello Meet Dr. Jekyll and Mr. Hyde* (1953), and *Abbott and Costello Meet the Mummy* (1955). These films followed a similar formula, playing the monsters straight against the comedians. *Abbott and Costello Meet Frankenstein* is considered the best of the series. By the early 1960s, horror comedies had migrated to the small screen in the two series of *The Munsters* and *The Addams Family*, but these shows were more like the scary old house films in that they borrowed the trappings of horror, in a camp-based self-aware fashion, to do comedy. Although the characters of Grandpa Munster and Morticia Addams, for example, embodied the visual characteristic and mannerisms of vampires, there was no attempt to have them behave like vampires—no victims, no sucking of blood. In the spirit of camp, they were more like an in-joke or quotation, recognized as figures out of horror, but not presented as scary, much like the gothic house settings of these shows. The audience for the television shows was primarily children, whereas the film aimed to target a broader audience. In the television comedies, unlike in *Abbott and Costello Meet Frankenstein* and their other monster films, the monsters were not presented seriously.

Roman Polanski's *The Fearless Vampire Killers* (1967) is a horror comedy that shows the influence of the Abbott and Costello films, although it is weighted toward the comedy end of the scale. It pits an incompetent duo, an old professor and a young student, against a vampire threat. Polanski was not happy with the final release version of this film, which starred Sharon Tate, Jack MacGowran, and himself. "I wanted to make a poetic fairy tale for kids, not the vulgar burlesque he turned it into," Polanski complained, referring to the producer who made the final cuts (Heffernan 2004, 189). His first big-budget film, it features lush color in the Hammer tradition, with beautiful Central European winter landscapes. The vampire killers of the title are Professor Abronsius (MacGowran) and his apprentice Alfred (Polanski), who bumble their way through the film in a series of hapless adventures somewhat reminiscent of Abbott and Costello's, and who do display a kind of childlike innocence. The film's conclusion mimics the ending of *Abbott and Costello Meet Frankenstein*, where the heroes have escaped only to find themselves in a boat with the invisible man. The vampire killers escape, to find that Sarah (Tate), the woman they rescued, has been turned into a vampire. She bites Alfred as the film ends.

In this film, the hunters are innocent, if inept and clumsy fools, but the vampires are played straight in the Hammer style. Count Von Krolock, the head of the vampires, played by Ferdy Mayne, very much resembles Christopher Lee's imperious Dracula. The line that Polanski claimed was crossed in changing the film from fairy-tale to burlesque is primarily a question of editing and pacing. One can still see, in some of the longer scenes, how the film might have played as more fantastical and dream-like. The contrast between the two styles is a bit confusing to the audience, and may have led to the film's lukewarm reception. In any case, the film was a box office failure and was soon overshadowed by the director's next film, *Rosemary's Baby*, which was both a popular and a critical success, and helped to redefine the horror field.

Vampira, renamed *Old Dracula* (1974) in order to capitalize on the success of Mel Brooks's *Young Frankenstein* (1974), stars aging British comic actor David Niven as an aging Dracula. It is also a somewhat self-conscious spoof of the Blaxploitation vampire films *Blacula* (1972) and *Scream, Blacula, Scream* (1973). Dracula is renting out rooms in his castle to tourists, who provide financial support. But he also drugs them and transfuses their blood. After four Playboy playmates stay over and unknowingly contribute their blood, he uses it to revive his bride, Vampira (Teresa Graves), who has been frozen for 50 years. When he does so, she unexpectedly wakes up transformed into a black woman. This leads to the major action of the film. Dracula, Vampira, and Dracula's servant Maltravers (Peter Bayliss) travel to London, where they attempt to get more samples from the women, while their chaperone Angela and her boyfriend Marc attempt to protect them. Since Niven plays Dracula as a perfect gentleman and everybody else just seems to want to enjoy the late-mod London scene, the audience is not particularly drawn to see one side succeed. Marc alternately resists and succumbs to Dracula's hypnotic control and various mishaps occur. Finally, all is resolved when Vampira bites Dracula. The last scene shows a bootblacked Niven, fairly unconvincing as a black man, boarding a plane to go home. Although the film can be seen as offensive in all kinds of ways, especially in the light of the minstrel show tradition, it doesn't really cooperate with either racist stereotypes or Blaxploitation's in-your-face attitude. It ends up with the sort of bland, feel-good take on racial difference that we would interpret today as denial, but is interesting as a product of the time in which it was made in its refusal to push racial buttons. As a comedy/horror hybrid, it fails to deliver the horror while at the same time taking the monster's plight (if one can see the suave, courtly Niven as a monster at all) seriously. One way to read it is as a metaphor that emphasizes the problems involved in intergenerational relationships, since the much younger Graves's Vampira is portrayed as wanting to go out and have a good time dancing in the discotheques, while Niven's Dracula seems to want a much quieter life, strolling around London with his walking stick.

In 1979, George Hamilton starred in *Love at First Bite*, a comedy treatment that focused on social commentary over horror. Hamilton's Dracula is kicked out of his castle by the Romanian Communist government so that they can use it for a training facility for gymnasts. He and Renfield (Artie Shaw) go to New York, where he seeks out a model, Cindy Sondheim (Susan Saint-James), whom he believes to be a reincarnation of his former love. Her psychiatrist, Jeffery Rosenberg (Richard Bemjamin), turns out to be a descendant of Van Helsing, who attempts to destroy Dracula in a variety of ways. He is institutionalized as insane, but rescued by a police lieutenant who believes him. As the pursuit heats up, Dracula and Cindy flee the country as bats, heading for Jamaica, where his coffin has been mistakenly sent. Hamilton plays the part seriously, and the film stresses the incongruity of having an old style aristocrat negotiating the grime and glitter of 1970s New York.

The horror comedies that followed tend to skew in one direction or the other, either doing pure comedy with horror themes or pure horror with comic moments. A failed example of the first, from 1985, is *Transylvania 6–5000*, a film full of talented actors (Jeff Goldblum, Ed Begely, Carol Kane, Michael Richards, and Geena Davis) that just doesn't work. Like *Abbott and Costello Meet Frankenstein*, it involves a comic presentation of many standard movie monsters, including a vampire, a hunchback, Frankenstein's monster, a wolf man, a mummy, a mad scientist, and so on, in a plot about two tabloid reporters sent to Transylvania to investigate a mysterious videotape. A simple plot goes wrong into a complex mess, and the film never really finds its feet. The plot concludes with a classic comic ending, as all is explained in the context of a public celebration, a wine festival that threatens to turn into a mob scene. It is basically an explained gothic plot, with the vampire (Davis) being a shy woman with no self-esteem, the wolf man (Donald Gibb) being the victim of a medical disorder, the monster being a patched-up victim of a car accident, and so forth.

A more modest and yet more successful pure comedy about vampires is *My Best Friend Is a Vampire* from 1988. In it, a teenage boy, Jeremy (Robert Sean Leonard), is turned into a vampire through a sexual encounter with a mysterious older woman. They are interrupted and attacked by a fanatic professor, Dr. McCarthy (David Warner). Jeremy escapes and later finds out that the woman's house has been burned down. This sets up the plot of the film: Jeremy must learn to deal with his new vampirism, while he and his best friend are being pursued by McCarthy. He is also dealing with a typical teenage problem—he is attracted to a girl and wants a relationship with her, but his vampire traits keep getting in the way. A vampire mentor Modoc (Rene Auberjonois) appears and helps Jeremy to adjust to his new lifestyle, which includes obtaining pig's blood from a local butcher. Meanwhile, Jeremy's parents know that he is concealing something from them, and conclude that he is gay. In a final confrontation, Modoc and his fellow vampires turn McCarthy into a vampire, and Jeremy introduces his new girlfriend to his parents, after they tell him that they know about and support his lifestyle.

There are no horror elements to this comedy. No one dies or is even very seriously scared, and it concludes with a return to order, if a somewhat changed one. It reverses the traditional vampire/hunter opposition to make the hunter the bad guy. In its explicit coding of vampirism as alternate lifestyle, it shows a surprisingly liberal perspective for the 1980s (see my discussion of *Vamp* and *Fright Night* in Chapter 11). The vampire as homosexual metaphor had been an implied one in the past—in Nina Auerbach's reading of the Romantics and of Browning's original *Dracula* film, for instance—but this film's treatment brings it out into the open, with a young man being initiated by an older man, with the use of the term lifestyle, and so forth, even though it is finally presented as a parental misinterpretation.

John Landis's *Innocent Blood* (1992) blends horror and comedy with the gangster film. Marie (Anne Parillaud) is a vampire living in Pittsburgh, Pennsylvania. She preserves a moral code by only feeding on bad people, killers, and would-be rapists. When she makes a mistake by not killing a crime boss, Salvadore "The Shark" Macelli (Robert Loggia), he adjusts rather well to being a vampire and starts converting his henchmen. Marie teams up with a sympathetic detective, Joseph Gennaro, to deal with the situation. This is a true horror comedy, providing a serious villain who is quite terrifying, along with an interesting take on vampire identity.

Buffy the Vampire Slayer (1992), the film, is somewhat different from the long-running TV series. Although the script is by Joss Whedon, the creator of the TV show, direction was taken out of his hands. The result is, especially for fans of the series, a fairly thin teen comedy. As in many quest narratives, Buffy resists taking her assignment seriously at first, but is drawn into the role. Donald Sutherland plays her mentor, Merrick Jamison-Smythe, and some of the film's humor comes from the ironic contrast between her Southern California casualness and his stiff British formality. This film lacks the edge of much of Whedon's series. It focuses on Buffy's transformation from vapid Valley Girl cheerleader to athletic vampire fighter. The film version lacks the Scoobies, the team of misfits who support Buffy in the series, substituting instead a romantic plot where Pike (Luke Perry), a local mechanic, falls for Buffy and has to be repeatedly saved by her.

The film's comedy comes from the ironic contrast between the superficial, spoiled teenagers and Buffy's life-or-death struggles with some fairly nasty vampires. It is certainly augmented by an over-the-top performance by Paul Reubens as Amilyn, the vampire leader's wild-haired sidekick, who loses an arm early on and, when Buffy finally stakes him, puts in a long, rather coy, melodramatic death scene. As the vampire leader himself, Rutger Hauer is icily threatening but a bit too precious. Being a vampire in this film seems to require lots of hysterical laughter, which allows Buffy plenty of staking time, but tends to cut down on the horror potential. The film comes off finally as more of a romantic comedy with horror sequences than a horror/comedy hybrid. At the time, its girl-power message and deliberate role reversal—the girl repeatedly saving the guy—made it stand out more than it would, perhaps, 20 years later. It certainly gave birth to an interesting franchise, which preserved the light tone and verbal cleverness, while expanding on other aspects of the plot and characters.

Dracula: Dead and Loving It (1995) represents Mel Brooks's attempt to do with Dracula's legacy what his *Young Frankenstein* (1974) did to the legacy of the Frankenstein films. It is generally seen as a failure, a parody that falls short in terms of humor. Its general flatness is further exacerbated by poor casting and an unimaginative script. Using Leslie Nielsen, a prominent comic actor at this time, following his success in farces such as *Airplane!*, goes in the face of the emerging romantic treatment of the vampire figure, turning him into an aging buffoon. The plot follows Browning's original *Dracula* pretty closely, with a few pratfalls and comic routines added in, including one sequence parodying Coppola's film. In terms of acting, Peter McNichols is a standout as

Renfield, playing the role of a madman with zest. Brooks himself plays Van Helsing, hamming up the Austrian accent, and Harvey Korman does a very straight Dr. Seward. The younger actors playing Mina, Lucy and Harker put in fairly thin performances. In comparison to the over-the-top, gleeful sending-up of an established series of films that we find in Brooks's earlier comic masterpiece, *Young Frankenstein, Dracula: Dead and Loving It* looks even worse.

Since the mid-1990s, there has been a general decline in horror comedies, at least where vampire films are concerned, in the United States. A well-funded exploitation film like *Bordello of Blood* (1996) can give us some insight into why there has been such a decline. The film, which is part of a *Tales from the Crypt* series based on the series of comic books of the same name, combined nudity, splatter, and half-hearted social satire with a detective plot. It stars Dennis Miller as a wise-cracking, down-at-the–heels detective who is out to find the missing brother of a woman (Erika Eleniak) who works as a televangelist's (Chris Sarandon) publicist. It turns out that the televangelist is in cahoots with a gangster who is helping to run a whorehouse disguised as a funeral home, where all the whores are vampires. The film ends with a gory slaughter of the vampire prostitutes, followed by an equally gory confrontation with the queen vampire Lilith (Angie Everhart). It is as if the creators of this film watched *From Dusk till Dawn* and tried to incorporate all the elements of that film without its style, pacing, or humor. In this case, the horror outweighs the humor partly because the humor is not very funny. Of course, over-the-top splatter shots lose their potential as horror with overuse, so that aspect of the film lacks effectiveness as well. Did this film kill vampire comedy?

There is a recent saying that suggests that zombies are the new vampires, and this seems to be true for the last decade or so in the United States, at least when it comes to comic treatments. Where we have seen some good comic treatments of the zombie figure in such films as *Zombieland* (2009) and the British film *Shaun of the Dead* (2004), there have not been equivalent comic treatments of vampires, discounting such direct take-offs as *Vampires Suck* (2010), a fairly labored attempt to parody the *Twilight* films, and *Stan Helsing* (2009), which does the same with *Van Helsing* (2004).

If we look at the general evolution of the vampire figure, we could say that camp defanged the vampire in the 1960s, which led to a spate of comic treatments, including figures in *The Munsters* and *The Addams Family* television shows, comic treatments for children, and a number of comic films in the 1970s, including *Old Dracula* and *Love at First Bite*.

These treatments continued into the 1980s, although the vampires were beginning to regain their threatening potential in films, such as *My Best Friend Is a Vampire*. By the 1990s, younger, sexier, and more Romantic vampires were emerging, and although we have vampire comedies like *Vampire in Brooklyn*, the vampire figure is not presented as comic. In the ineffective *Dracula: Dead and Loving It*, although the Dracula figure is not primarily a comic figure, it may be that an old, funny Dracula was out of step with the times, and that may have compounded its other failings.

In *Buffy the Vampire Slayer*, film and series, the *Blade* series, the *Underworld* series, the *True Blood* series, and the *Twilight* series, vampires are presented quite seriously. In the last decade of the 20th century and the first of the 21st century, we have rehabilitated the vampire as a young, sexually alluring, charismatic, Byronic, and threatening figure, with perhaps less of the beast in him (or her) than in past incarnations. My introduction is entitled "Taking Vampires Seriously," and we have been, perhaps to an extreme—perhaps it is time to get away from the terrible earnestness of contemporary vampires, to start laughing at them again.

Where Do We Go from Here?

All the vampires walking through the valley
Move west down Ventura Boulevard
And all the bad boys are standing in the shadows
All the good girls are home with broken hearts.
—Tom Petty, "Free Fallin" (1989)

If there is a recent trend in the vampire story, it is in serialization.
Whether it is a television series, such as the *Vampire Diaries* or *True
Blood*, a book and film series, such as the *Twilight* saga, or a series of
books around a central character, such as Laurell V. Hamilton's or Jim
Butcher's book series, audiences seem to want these stories to continue
beyond a single volume or film. Is this because vampires are immortal?
Serialization is not new—*Varney the Vampire* ran to 220 episodes in
1847, and there is some evidence that Stoker planned to bring Dracula
back. In today's multiplatform publishing environment, a successful
series can cross over seamlessly from book, to film, to TV series, to
graphic novel, to video game. So, a potential writer of vampire stories
might be advised to plan ahead, to choose the vampire's traits carefully,
because there may be a long series of plots to follow. How vulnerable
or invincible the vampires are will play an important part in those plots.
Too vulnerable, or vulnerable to too-common items, and there's little
threat or conflict—this can be a problem, for example, with light sensitivity. Of course, if they are too invincible, they could become boring
(and sparkly).

Mixing genres always seems to work. *Buffy the Vampire Slayer*
combined horror/vampire film elements with a teen melodrama to good

effect. Charlaine Harris's Southern vampire series, on which Alan Ball's *True Blood* is based, neatly incorporates a murder mystery into each of the novels. In like fashion, Laurell K. Hamilton's Anita Blake series, now at 20 novels, uses the first-person perspective, the seedy urban setting, and other conventions of the hard-boiled detective story to create hybrid vampire novels. A trend that is appearing in various series is the supernatural melange, which includes a variety of supernatural creatures in the fictional world. Harris's Southern Vampire novels include werewolves, shape-shifters, fairies, and maenads along with vampires. Butcher's series, in like fashion, includes a variety of different magical and supernatural creatures. This is a good way to thicken a wide variety of plots, and to keep them coming.

Another always effective strategy is to go back to the roots. A recent example of this is Guillermo del Toro and Chuck Hogan's recently completed trilogy, which includes *The Strain* (2009), *The Fall* (2010), and *The Night Eternal* (2011). Del Toro (the writer and director of *Pan's Labyrinth*) and Hogan (a writer of thrillers, such as *The Blood Artists*) resurrect the Central European folk vampire who has a special desire for family members as victims, but they add more recent components, resulting in a creature that blends the old and the new. Their vampires use a stinging appendage that shoots out from under the tongue, and is susceptible to light and silver. But del Toro and Hogan also incorporate the more popular recent concept of vampirism as a disease, positing infection that travels through blood-borne worms. And they include a master vampire, who emerges into the modern world, appropriately, from the death camps of the Second World War.

The Strain begins in New York City with a modern version of Dracula's arrival in England. A jetliner manages to land, but contains no survivors, everyone aboard having fallen victim to an epidemic. The novel's main character, Ephraim Goodweather, is an epidemiologist brought in to solve this mystery. As he investigates, and as the corpses from the airplane start to come back to life, we are introduced to a shadowy corporate CEO, Eldrich Palmer, and a conspiracy to conceal information about the incident. Things escalate, the vampire plague spreads, and we end up with a small band of vampire fighters resisting the plague of vampires, who are quickly becoming the majority of the population. They include Goodweather, his assistant Nora Martinez, Vasily Fet, an exterminator, and the Van Helsing figure for this story, Professor Abraham Setrakian, a Romanian Jew who has spent his life preparing for a conflict with the vampires, ever since he escaped from the Trebliinka death camp. They discover that the vampires share a kind of hive mind and are dominated by the Master, who travels from one human host to another. The story blends an apocalyptic scenario—the vampire plague spreading across North America—with a conspiracy on the part of collaborationist humans who are setting up breeding centers for uninfected humans. Throughout *The Fall* and *The Night Eternal*, the band of resistors fight against overwhelming odds to try to destroy the Master, who kidnaps and starts to turn Goodweather's teenage son.

These vampires are more like a hybrid with the conventional zombie, shambling around clumsily and fairly easily dispatched with silver or UV light. They are vaguely drawn to their former family members and tend to blindly obey the Master's will. The real threat is from the cunning intelligence of the Master and from the schemes of his human allies. The vampire/zombie takeover also leads to environmental devastation—a cloud cover envelops the earth, so as to keep out the burning rays of sunlight. The trilogy concludes rather dramatically, and an origin story is provided that goes back to the Old Testament and a trio of angelic beings. But del Toro and Hogan manage to balance this cosmic plot with close attention to the lives of the protagonists, focusing on their changing psychological and personal interactions.

The combination of shambling, deadly masses and vicious behind-the-scenes conspiracies plays to the fears of a public influenced by the financial downturn. The financial disaster was created by the practices of a relative few to the detriment of much of the population, resulting in the financial ruin of some. The results were similar: large number of victims and a small number of perpetrators who managed to conceal what they were doing until it was too late. The group of resistors that Hogan and del Toro have chosen are, like Stoker's Band of Light, representatives from a variety of professional and social classes, whose skills begin with scientific research and analysis, but develop into fighting and survival skills. Unlike Stoker's crew, however, they do not broadly represent their society. Ultimately, the group consists of two scientists and two immigrants. The bad guys, who choose to collaborate with the Master, include a Marilyn Manson style rock star, a scientific bureaucrat, and a secretive CEO. Once social structures collapse, self-reliance and loyalty to the group become paramount, and those who try to adjust to the new order find that it has little benefit to them.

By splitting the Master from his minions, Hogan and del Toro manage to provide their audience with both a Dracula-like antagonist and a plague-borne world disaster with environmental consequences.

The challenges are split in like ways—finding food and water and weapons to deal with immediate survival threats while attempting to map out a strategy for overcoming the source of the disaster.

Since Matheson's *I Am Legend*, the infection scenario has been popular. Indeed, forensic scientist Katherine Ramsland has speculated on the various ways that such an infection might actually work in her nonfiction book, *The Science of Vampires* (2002). She points out that viruses can change the genetic programming of a cell by replacing DNA. If a virus could manage to get past the body's defenses and replicate fast enough, the circulatory system would be an effective way to distribute it widely enough throughout the body so that it could, in theory, take over a living organism. This is the scenario in many vampire stories, although Stoker's is based more on his contemporary understandings of germ infection, especially Koch's *Postulates* (1890), which demonstrated how to diagnose disease by effectively isolating a disease pathogen.

Many recent treatments of vampirism have imagined it as a blood-borne viral pathogen. Justin Cronin's *The Passage* (2009) follows this pattern, starting off as a kind of medical thriller, with the U.S. government setting up a secret laboratory to develop a viral weapon isolated from South American monkeys. Convicts are brought in to serve as incubators in a compound located in an isolated part of the Rocky Mountains. Unsurprisingly, the plague gets out. The story then jumps 60 years into the future, to deal with a new culture of humans raised in a walled community that has protected them from the infected creatures living outside. The novel ends with enough unresolved questions to make a sequel or sequels inevitable.

Another form of the return to roots is to keep the vampire, who has been so much in the spotlight, as a figure in the background, as Stoker did. Elizabeth Kostova's *The Historian* provides readers with a Stoker-like investigation into a young woman's family history. Her quest eventually leads to a shadowy vampire figure, made more so because he is able to erase memories.

Vampires may have become rather mundane, but they still have the ability to surprise us. A recent example is the excellent Swedish film *Lat den Ratte Komme In* (*Let the Right One In*, 2008). Directed by Tomas Alfredson and based on a novel by John Ajvide Lindqvist, it is a touching story of an adolescent friendship between a lonely adolescent boy and a girl, apparently his own age, who turns out to be a vampire. It catches the tender awkwardness and fierce loyalty of young teenagers, making the vampire story secondary. The film has been remade in an

English language version, *Let Me In* (2011), an unnecessary decision that has produced a very similar film, predictably, but one without dubbing or subtitles. In the way that Hollywood now routinely reproduces foreign films into English-language versions, it is almost as if we are going back to the 1930s, where Universal used the script, sets, costumes, and equipment of the English-language film to produce the weirdly similar, Spanish-language version of *Dracula*, filmed entirely at night.

Another recent international film is the Korean film *Bakjwi* (*Thirst*, 2008), by the brilliant director Chan-Wook Park, about a priest who becomes a vampire by mistake, being transfused with vampire blood. As a priest, he has ethical issues with being a predator. Because he is opposed to killing, he survives by drinking blood in small quantities from terminal, comatose patients in a hospital. The ethical dilemma that the priest faces in this story brings to mind a recurring theme in recent vampire treatments—that of the vegetarian vampire. The Cullens, the good vampires in the *Twilight* series, are often called so inaccurately, because they choose to eat large animals instead of humans. They are vegetarian only by metaphor. The out vampires in the *True Blood*/Southern Vampire Series, who don't feed on humans but drink synthetic TruBlood, could actually be vegetarian, provided that the product is synthesized from vegetable sources. Similarly, in *Buffy*, vampires like Angel with his soul and Spike with his microchip, much like Blade with his serum, are defanged, so to speak, by the fact that they don't victimize humans.

In any case, whatever we call them, we see a spate of vampires who don't kill humans. Is this an attempt to make them into a more acceptable life-form, less dangerous, more like us? But isn't the point of being a vampire to be a predator? So, aren't these wimpy vampires somehow superfluous? This might explain why writers, like Cronin, Kostova, and del Toro and Hogan, are looking to the past to find vampire figures with, if you will forgive me, more bite. Perhaps this will be the new trend. Vampire writers of the future, it is in your hands.

Selected Chronological Filmography

A Fool There Was (1915). Dir. Frank Powell. With Theda Bara, Edward Jose. Fox Studios. A silent classic, one of the few surviving films starring Theda Bara. Listed as "the vampire" in the credits, Bara plays an adventuress who seduces a married diplomat and metaphorically sucks the life out of him. It launched Bara's career and popularized the term vamp. See Bram Dijkstra's *Evil Sisters* for an extended cultural analysis.

Nosferatu (1922). Dir. F. W. Murnau. With Max Schreck and Greta Schroeder. Prana Film Productions. Names and locations were changed because the film was not authorized by Stoker's estate. A German Expressionist treatment of Dracula as Count Orlock, a bald, fanged, ratlike monster who is tricked by Ellen (who sacrifices herself) into being exposed to a beam of sunlight, which destroys him. This is the first use of this method of vampire destruction, one that will gain popularity in later films. Murnau and his production company were successfully sued for copyright infringement by Stoker's estate, which required that all copies be destroyed. Some survived and were revived in the 1960s, after the copyright expired.

Dracula (1931). Dir. Tod Browning. With Bela Lugosi and Helen Chandler. Universal Pictures. The first in the series of "classic" horror films that Universal produced in the 1930s. This performance by Lugosi defined the role of vampire for years to come. Lugosi plays a well-dressed, impeccably well-behaved aristocrat with hypnotic eyes. Edward Sloan plays Van Helsing as an elderly, thoughtful, and deliberate scientist. Dwight Frye plays Renfield as an over-the-top, bug-eating madman.

Dracula (1931). Dir. George Melford. With Carlos Villarias and Lupita Tovar. Universal Pictures. A Spanish-language version of Browning's film, filmed simultaneously, at night, on the same sets. With noticeably more lively performances, this version is considered by some to be superior to the Browning film, possibly because Melford may have had the advantage of seeing the dailies for the English-language version.

Mark of the Vampire (1935). Dir. Tod Browning. With Bela Lugosi, Carroll Borland, and Lionel Barrymore. Metro-Goldwyn-Mayer. The second and final pairing of director Tod Browning with Bela Lugosi after 1931's *Dracula*, this film fits into the cinematic equivalent of the "explained gothic" genre. After a murder that seems to be a vampire killing, suspicion falls on Count Mora (Lugosi) and his daughter Luna (Morland). At the film's end, they are revealed to be actors hired to help identify the real killer. This type of plot harkens back to the 1920s and films, such as Browning's (lost) *London After Midnight* (1927), which starred Lon Cheney as a detective disguised as a vampire. Gives us the iconic image of the female vampire that would be imitated by such figures as Vampira, Elvira, and Morticia Addams.

Dracula's Daughter (1936). Dir. Lambert Hillyer. With Gloria Holden and Otto Kruger. In a realistic London setting, Countess Zaleska, the daughter of the title, preys on a bohemian young woman in a lesbian-implied scene. She hates her vampire nature and goes to a psychologist, Dr. Jeffrey Garth (Kruger), for help. The portrait of a conflicted vampire would be very influential, as would be the implied vampire-as-homosexual metaphor.

Son of Dracula (1943). Dir. Robert Siodnak. With Lon Chaney, Jr. and Louise Allbritten. Set in the American South, this atmospheric film seems to be trying to capitalize on the success of *Gone with the Wind*, as well as present a different take on Dracula from Lugosi's. The plot is somewhat incoherent and so not entirely successful, but has some beautifully filmed sequences; for example, one where the vampire's coffin rises out of a swamp and he rides it like a surfboard.

House of Dracula (1945). Dir. Erie C. Kenton. With Lon Chaney, Jr., Glenn Strange, and John Carradine. Universal Pictures. This was the third monster combination film from Universal, following *Frankenstein Meets the Wolf Man* (1943) and *House of Frankenstein* (1944). Carradine plays Dracula in this one, as a tall thin man with a top hat and a pencil-thin moustache.

Abbott and Costello Meet Frankenstein (1948). Dir. Charles Barton. With Bud Abbott and Lou Costello. Universal International Pictures. This film followed *House of Dracula* and was the last in a series of monster mash-ups, where Universal combined their famous monsters, in this case, the Wolfman, Dracula, and Frankenstein's monster. Instead of straight dramatic horror, the decision to market the established Universal monsters in a comedy is a new direction, brought on by changing audience tastes and a move in the industry toward more psychological horror. Here, the monsters are further combined with the comedy team Abbott and Costello. Bela Lugosi reprised his Dracula role and Lon Chaney, Jr. reprised his role as the Wolfman.

The Thing from Another World (1951). Dir. Christian Nyby. With Robert Cornthwaite, Kenneth Tobey, and Margaret Sheridan. RKO Radio Pictures. A vampire-like alien is discovered in a flying saucer that crashed in the Arctic. It is actually a vegetable life-form that needs blood and lumbers around in the shape of a man. The plot involves a disagreement between an idealistic scientist and a practical Air Force pilot. "The thing" is eventually destroyed by electrocution. A good example of the sci-fi horror genre popular in the 1950s.

Dracula (1958). (American title: *Horror of Dracula*) Dir. Terence Fisher. With Christopher Lee and Peter Cushing. Hammer Studios. The first in the Hammer series of horror films, with colorful understated costume dramas. Lee is a feral, sexy Dracula pursued by a cool, rational Cushing as Van Helsing.

Curse of the Undead (1959). Dir. Edward Dein. With Don Hoyt and Michael Pate. Universal. Possibly the first vampire Western, this film owes its vampire theme to Spanish rather than Transylvanian folklore. It is typically Western, with a vampire villain.

The Last Man on Earth (1964). Dir. Ubaldo Ragona. With Vincent Price and Franca Bettona. API Films. First film adaptation of Richard Matheson's *I Am Legend* and the one truest to the novel's plot. Neville, the protagonist, is killed on an altar after taking refuge in a church—fairly heavy-handed symbolism.

The Munsters (1964–1966). Television series. Prod. Joe Connoly and Bob Mosher. With Fred Gwynne and Yvonne DeCarlo. Columbia Broadcasting System (CBS). Kayro-Vue Productions. A situation comedy with a family of monster characters based loosely on the Universal monsters. Al Lewis played Grandpa, who was an elderly Lugosi-type, albeit working-class, vampire.

Billy the Kid vs. Dracula (1966). Dir. William Beaudine. With John Carradine and Chuck Courtney. Embassy Pictures. A low-budget and predictable Western that pits Billy the Kid against Dracula in a contest over Dracula's attempt to vampirize Billy's fiancée. Significant because it is an early vampire Western, paving the way for such later films as *Near Dark* and *From Dusk till Dawn.*

Batman (1966–1968). Television series. Prod William Dozier. With Adam West and Burt Ward. Television drama/sitcom, American Broadcasting Company (ABC). Greenway Productions/Twentieth Century Fox. Bland, campy television comedy with self-consciously comic book features, such as cliché-ridden dialogue and sound-effects intertitles (BAM!) during fight sequences. The show recruited a wide variety of Hollywood personalities who appeared as guest stars, usually villains, and in cameos. Not about vampires, but significant to our understanding of camp.

Dracula: Prince of Darkness (1966). Dir. Terence Fisher. With Christopher Lee and Barbara Shelley. Hammer Studios. The sequel to the 1958 Hammer *Dracula.* A couple, coincidentally named Charles and Diana, manage to defeat Dracula by drowning.

Dark Shadows (1966–1971). Television series Dir. Dan Curtis. With Alexandra Moltke and Jonathan Frid. American Broadcasting Company (ABC). Dan Curtis Productions. Gothic afternoon soap opera that came to feature Barnabas Collins (Frid) as a vampire living in an ancestral house in Maine. May be the first to use the reincarnation plot, where the vampire is seeking a reincarnated version of his lost love. Barnabas is unsatisfied with being a vampire and seeks to return to mortal status.

The Girl with the Hungry Eyes (1967). Dir. William Rotsler. With Adele Rein and Cathy Crowfoot. Something Weird Productions. A low-budget sexploitation film about lesbian obsession, with little resemblance to Leiber's story of the same name.

Dracula Has Risen from the Grave (1968). Dir. Freddie Francis. With Christopher Lee, Rupert Davies, and Veronica Carlson. Hammer Studios. Blood from an injured priest revives Dracula from his watery grave. A young man, Paul, manages to stake Dracula, but it is ineffective because he is an atheist. In a final confrontation, Dracula falls on a cross and is staked, but does not die until a priest recites the Lord's Prayer.

Scars of Dracula (1970). Dir. Roy Ward Baker. With Christopher Lee and Patrick Troughton. Hammer Studios. Once again resurrected by blood, this time with a bat's help, Dracula slaughters all the women in a village in revenge after the villagers burn his castle down. A young man, Simon, is imprisoned in the castle ruins. Assisted by Dracula's assistant Klove, he manages to stake Dracula with an iron stake, but Dracula removes it, only to be struck by lightening and destroyed.

Taste the Blood of Dracula (1970). Dir. Peter Sasdy. With Christopher Lee, Geoffrey Keen, and Gwen Watford. Hammer Studios. A dissipated young man resurrects Dracula in a satanic ritual with three men who he met in a brothel. When he falls unconscious, they beat and abandon him. His corpse turns into Dracula, who then enacts vengeance against the three. He is killed in the reconsecrated church, through the Lord's Prayer being recited.

The Vampire Lovers (1970). Dir. Roy Ward Baker. With Ingrid Pitt, George Cole, and Peter Cushing. Hammer Studios. First in the Karstein trilogy, loosely adapted from Sheridan LeFanu's *Carmilla*.

Lust of a Vampire (**American title:** *Love for a Vampire*) (1971). Dir. Jimmy Sangster. With Ralph Bates, Barbara Jefford, and Susanna Leigh. Hammer Studios. Second installment in the Karstein trilogy.

The Omega Man (1971). Dir. Boris Sagal. With Charlton Heston, Anthony Zerbe, and Rosilind Cash. Warner Brothers Pictures. Second film adaptation of Richard Matheson's *I Am Legend*, with a decidedly more science-fiction style.

"The Girl with the Hungry Eyes" (1972). TV episode of Rod Sterling's *Night Gallery*, directed by John Badham. This follows the plot of the 1945 Fritz Leiber story, but as a color update set in the 1960s, loses its noir flavor.

Twins of Evil (1972). Dir. John Hough. With Peter Cushing, Madeleine Collinson, and Mary Collinson. Hammer Studios. Third installment in the Karstein trilogy features twins—one good, one evil—and Peter Cushing as a Puritanical witch hunter.

Dracula A.D. 1972 (1972). Dir. Alan Gibson. With Christopher Lee, Stephanie Beacham, and Peter Cushing. Hammer Studios. A declining Hammer Studios attempts to appeal to the youth market with a group of hippies who conjure up Dracula from his ashes.

Blacula (1972). Dir. William Crain. With William Marshall and Vonetta McGee. American International Pictures. Shakespearian actor Marshall brings gravitas to a Blaxploitation horror role. The main character is an African prince, Mamouwalde who went to the original Count Dracula in the 18th century to try to end the slave trade. Instead, Dracula turned him and boxed him away until the present, when he arrives in Los Angeles. He falls for a woman whom he believes is his reincarnated wife. When she is killed, he commits suicide by exposing himself to sunlight.

Scream, Blacula, Scream (1973). Dir. Bob Kelljan. With William Marshall and Pam Grier. American International Pictures. Sequel that incorporates a somewhat more Afrocentric perspective. Prince Mamouwalde is resurrected by a voodoo practitioner in a power struggle. Pam Grier is a voodoo priestess who tries to help free him from the vampire curse, but ends up destroying him instead.

The Satanic Rites of Dracula (1973). (American title: *Dracula and his Vampire Bride*). Dir. Alan Gibson. With Christopher Lee, Joanna Lumley, and Peter Cushing. Hammer Studios. A James Bond-influenced plot about Dracula as a CEO who wants to kill off humanity with a viral plague. The next to last Hammer vampire film, before the vampire/ martial arts hybrid *The Legend of the 7 Golden Vampires*.

Ganja and Hess (1973). (Alternate/edited version: *Blood Couple*). Dir. Bill Gunn. With Duane Jones and Marlene Clark. Kelly/Jordan Enterprises. A difficult-to-classify film that was often mistakenly included in the category Blaxploitation because of when it was released. Actually a poetic treatment of the vampire theme. The main character, Dr. Hess, is a Black archaeologist who becomes infected by an ancient African dagger, turning him into a blood drinker. He infects his wife-to-be, Ganja, but they ultimately choose different paths. Vampirism is a link to an African tribe, the Myrthians, and has none of the European folkloric elements, beyond blood drinking and opposition to Christianity.

Bram Stoker's Dracula (1974). Dir. Dan Curtis. With Jack Palance, Simon Ward, and Nigel Davenport. Latglen, Ltd. TV movie version, with a very Hammer-like style. Does follow the plot of Stoker's novel fairly faithfully, with fewer characters. Like Curtis's *Dark Shadows* series, uses the reincarnation plot as a motivator for Dracula's pursuit of Lucy.

The Legend of the 7 Golden Vampires (1974). Dirs. Roy Ward Baker and Chang Cheh. With Peter Cushing and David Chiang. Hammer

Film Productions/Shaw Brothers Studios. The last vampire film made by Hammer Studios, this is an odd collaboration between Hammer and Shaw Brothers, a Hong Kong studio known for its martial arts action films. Peter Cushing plays Van Helsing again, in a story where he takes on Dracula and his Chinese disciples during a visit to China in 1904.

Vampira (1975). (American title: *Old Dracula*). Dir. Clive Donner. With David Niven and Teresa Graves. World Film Services. Niven plays a down-on-his-luck Count Dracula, who must host vampire tours at his castle. After reviving his bride and inadvertently turning her into a black woman, he goes to London to try to solve this problem. Eventually, he is turned black by her bite.

Martin (1977). Dir. George Romero. With Jon Amplas, Elyane Nadeau, Tom Savini. Libra Films International. A well-crafted low-budget film about a young man with vampiric habits, set in a rusty industrial suburb of Pittsburgh, Pennsylvania. Living with his uncle, who knows he is a vampire, Martin seduces and drugs women, then slits their wrists to drink their blood. He becomes a local celebrity through a call-in radio show. Amplas plays Martin as an innocent, and the film leaves the vampire question open. The uncle and Martin both believe in his vampirism, and black-and-white flashback sequences seem to justify this, but they are so formulaic that they could easily be fantasies generated by the movies.

Nosferatu the Vampyre (1979). Dir. Werner Herzog. With Klaus Kinski, Isabelle Adjani, and Bruno Ganz. Werner Herzog Films. A remake of F. W. Murnau's 1922 silent classic, but using the original names from Stoker's novel. Herzog changed the ending of Murnau's film somewhat, with Jonathan Harker ultimately escaping as a vampire.

Dracula (1979). Dir. John Badham. With Frank Langella and Laurence Olivier. Based, like Browning's 1931 Dracula, on the Deane and Balderson play version, which had been revived successfully on Broadway with Langella and a black-and-white Edward Gorey set. Mina's and Lucy's original roles are reversed; Mina dies. A final confrontation at sea finds Van Helsing dead, Lucy restored, and Dracula's cape floating mysteriously away.

Love at First Bite (1979). Dir. Stan Dragoti. With George Hamilton, Susan Saint-James, Arte Johnson, and Richard Benjamin. American International Pictures. A comedy where Dracula comes to New York to find the reincarnation of his lost love in a fashion model. Her psychiatrist, who happens to be a descendant of Van Helsing, tries unsuccessfully to destroy him. Eventually, the couple leaves for a new life in Jamaica. A nicely paced social comedy with some dated material.

The Thing (1982). Dir. John Carpenter. With Kurt Russell and Wilford Brimley. Universal Studios. Carpenter's remake of *The Thing from Another World* (1951). A blood-eating, shape-shifting alien works its way through the crew at a U.S. Antarctic base. Two alternate ambiguous endings suggest it may have survived. The Thing is not a vampire per se, but it shares many vampiric qualities.

Vamp (1986). Dir. Richard Wenk. With Grace Jones and Chris Makepeace. Balcor Films. Frat boys meet the Vampire Queen, who runs a sleazy bar. Unfortunately, Jones's nonverbal, animalistic vampire only reinforces stereotypes about African Americans. Includes an interesting MTV-influenced dance sequence with Jones in whiteface.

Near Dark (1987). Dir. Kathryn Bigelow. With Adrian Pasdar and Jenny Wright. F/M Near Dark Joint Ventures. A modern-day vampire Western. A young man is attracted to a mysterious young woman, who bites him and introduces him to her family, who turn out to be rampaging vampire serial killers. Fortunately, before they are too far gone, they can be cured by transfusion.

Vampire's Kiss (1989). Dir. Robert Bierman. With Nicolas Cage and Maria Conchita Alonzo. Herndale Film Corporation. A point-of-view psychological drama that follows a vain yuppie literary agent as he becomes convinced that he is turning into a vampire. He rapes a co-worker and is killed by her brother.

Buffy the Vampire Slayer (1992). Dir. Fran Rubel Kuzui. With Kristie Swanton, Luke Perry, and Donald Sutherland. Twentieth Century Fox. Although this film was written by Joss Whedon, the creator of the subsequent TV series, it was not directed by him and exists in a kind of parallel universe to the later work. It is a light comedy about a cheerleader who is designated the Chosen One, a unique individual selected each generation to do battle against evil.

Innocent Blood (1992). Dir. John Landis. With Anne Parillaud, Anthony LaPaglia, and Robert Loggia. Warner Brothers. This film blends the horror genre with comedy with the gangster film. Set in Pittsburg's Little Italy, it involves an ethical vampire (Parillaud) who only kills criminals. She mistakenly turns a mob boss (Loggia), who then begins to create a vampire mafia. With the help of a sympathetic detective (LaPaglia), she works to make things right.

Bram Stoker's Dracula (**1992**). Dir. Francis Ford Coppola. With Gary Oldham, Winona Ryder, and Anthony Hopkins. American Zoetrope. Coppola's operatic take on the Dracula story, filmed without postproduction or computer-generated special effects. Oldham's conflicted Count pursues Ryder's conflicted Mina in a series of epic set pieces. The film contains brilliant performances by Anthony Hopkins as a manic Van Helsing and Tom Waits as a strangely sympathetic Renfield.

Chronos (**1993**). Dir. Guillermo del Toro. With Federico Luppi and Ron Perlman. October Films. A bug-like antique device created by an alchemist comes to life in present-day Mexico City. Its bite has many vampire-like qualities, causing the bitten one to feel younger and stronger, but to thirst for blood.

The Girl with the Hungry Eyes (**1995**). Dir. Jon Jacobs. With Christina Fulton and Isaac Turner. Columbia Pictures. Set in Miami, this is the story of a hotel that wants blood, so it reanimates a former owner who committed suicide. In her quest for blood, she meets a down-at-the-heels photographer, who does a photo session with her, creating great demand among his clients. The third film version of Leiber's story of the same name, it provides a gothic backstory for the photographer/model plot from the original short story.

Vampire in Brooklyn (**1995**). Dir. Wes Craven. With Eddie Murphy and Angela Bassett. Paramount Pictures. Murphy plays a vampire/ shape-shifter who is looking for a lost relative, who turns out to be a New York police detective (Bassett). Murphy becomes various characters, including a preacher and a mafia wannabe. His lackey, played by Kadeem Harrison, keeps losing body parts. Runs a balance between serious drama and comedy, playing most of the film seriously, with the comedy reserved for the secondary characters.

Dracula: Dead and Loving It (**1995**). Dir. Mel Brooks. With Leslie Nielsen and Peter MacNichol. Castle Rock, Gaumont and Brooksfilms. Not one of Brooks's most successful films, it failed to deliver on the promise of *Young Frankenstein* (1974), his earlier horror spoof. A seemingly half-hearted attempt to do a comic parody of *Dracula*, primarily based on the 1931 film. Peter MacNichol does a good job as Renfield and Nielsen plays the title role seriously, with a few pratfalls.

But in an era when the vampire is experiencing a rebirth in a younger, sexier, more romantic form, this presentation just seems thin, lame, and anachronistic.

From Dusk till Dawn (1996). Dir. Robert Rodriguez. With George Clooney and Quentin Tarantino. Dimension Films. Campy Western vampire crime drama hybrid. Two brothers on the lam from a bank robbery gone bad, kidnap a family in an RV to get them across the Mexican border. Once there, they hole up at a stripper bar that turns out to be infested with vampires. Mayhem ensues. The script by Tarantino blends the genres of crime caper, horror, Western, and action film, adding quirky, demented characters, and snappy dialogue. Rodriguez contributes complexly choreographed, over-the-top bloody action sequences, which rely more on latex than CGI.

Bordello of Blood (1996). Dir. Gilbet Adler. With Dennis Miller, Erika Eleniak, and Chris Sarandon. Universal Pictures. A film with many of the same elements as *From Dusk till Dawn*. A comparison of the two demonstrates how films with similar material can succeed, or, in this case, fail miserably. Poorly written, weakly characterized, unevenly paced story about a bordello of vampires which is hidden behind the façade of a funeral home. Miller, as an inept detective, finds links between this business and that of a televangelist (Sarandon). It all ends up in a splatter-filled slaughter of the vampire women, followed by a fairly predictable surprise ending.

Vampires (1998). Dir. John Carpenter. With James Woods and Daniel Baldwin. Columbia Pictures. A vampire Western/action film that ends with a showdown on the main street of a small town between Woods's character, the leader of a team of vampire hunters, and the king vampire (Thomas Ian Griffith), who is trying to get an artifact that will allow them to come out during the day.

Buffy the Vampire Slayer (1997–2003). Television series. Dir. Joss Whedon. With Sarah Michelle Gellar, Nicholas Brendan, and Alyson Hannigan. Mutant Enemy Productions. Twentieth Century Fox TV. Ground-breaking TV series about high school students battling the woes of adolescence and the fate of the world simultaneously. A generic blend between the horror film tradition and that of the teen melodrama.

Angel (1999–2004). Television series. Dir. Joss Whedon. Mutant Enemy Productions. Twentieth Century Fox TV. With Jason Borentz and Charsima Carpenter. This series is a spin-off from *Buffy the Vampire Slayer*, featuring Borentz as Angel, a vampire who has been cursed by gypsies so that he retains his soul. This time, Whedon used the conventions of urban film noir and the hard-boiled detective story, blended with a young adult supernatural drama. Set in Los Angeles.

Shadow of the Vampire (2000). Dir. E. Elias Merhige. With Willem Dafoe, John Malkovich, and Udo Kier. Saturn Films/Long Shot Pictures/BBC. A retelling of the making of *Nosferatu*, with Malkovich as director Murnau, who knows that the actor Schrek (Dafoe) is really a vampire.

Dracula: Pages from a Virgin's Diary (2002). Dir. Guy Madden. With Zhang-Wei Qiang and Tara Birtwhistle. CBC Television. A silent film version of a ballet of the Dracula story originally presented at the Royal Winnipeg Ballet. From that description, one might not expect this film to work, but it does. Using all the conventions of the silent film—whiteface makeup, intertitles, exaggerated action—combined with a monochrome palette with color highlights—blood, for example—and a frenetic musical score, Madden's film brings passion, grace, and an infusion of new energy to the Dracula story.

Underworld (2003). Dir. Len Wiseman. With Kate Beckinsale and Scott Speedman. Screen Gems. A stylishly rendered action film that pits aristocratic vampires against commoner Werewolves (Lycans) in an urban setting. It is filmed in a palette of blues that emphasizes its setting and tone. The vampires are hierarchical and tradition bound, and concerned about a Lycan plot to mix the blood of the two species.

Underworld: Evolution (2006). Dir. Len Wiseman. With Kate Beckinsale and Scott Speedman. Screen Gems. The second film in the underworld series. Conflicts exacerbate within the vampire ranks over the emergence of vampire/Lycan hybrids.

Thirty Days of Night (2007). Dir. David Slade. With Josh Harnett and Melissa George. During the annual 30-day dark of winter in Barrow, Alaska, the town is invaded by vampires under a master named Barlow (after King's master vampire in *'Salem's Lot*). The townsfolk dwindle as a beleaguered few fights back, using some ingenious methods to kill the vampires.

I Am Legend (2007). Dir. Francis Lawrence. With Will Smith and Alice Braga. Warner Brothers. Contemporizes and softens Matheson's story *I Am Legend*. Smith plays Robert Neville, a plague survivor and scientist. He is trying to cure a vampire plague which was caused by a cancer cure gone bad. As far as he knows, the virus has taken over the world, turning its victims into zombie-like vampires who only come out at night and are sensitive to garlic and silver. Neville is conducting research into a possible cure. As in the original, he does not survive, but in this version he succeeds in creating a serum and getting it out to a band of other survivors.

Bakjwi (**English language title:** *Thirst*) (2008). Dir. Chan-Wook Park. With Kang-ho Song and Ok-bin Kim. Moho Films. A priest is accidentally turned into a vampire by a blood transfusion. This raises difficult ethical questions for him, which he solves then by drinking donated blood in a hospital.

Lat den Ratte Komme In (**English language title:** *Let the Right One In*) (2008). Dir. Tomas Alfredson. With Kare Hedebrant, Lina Leandersson, and Sandrew Metronome. Based on a novel by John Ajvide Lindqvist, this is a lyrical treatment of a touching preadolescent relationship that happens to involve a vampire.

Twilight (2008). Dir. Katherine Hardwicke. With Kristen Stewart, Robert Pattinson, and Taylor Lautner. Summit Entertainment. A faithful adaptation of the book, following it in a workmanlike manner. Kristen Stewart brings an understated charm to a bland character, and Taylor Lautner's charisma (or is it his chest?) makes Robert Pattinson's character seem, well, pale.

Underworld: Evolution (2009). Dir. Patrick Tatopoulos. With Bill Nighy and Michael Sheen. Screen Gems. The third *Underworld* film, this is a prequel to the first two. It tells the story of the first Lycans and their rebellion against the vampire overlords.

The Vampire Diaries (2009–2012, continuing). TV Series. Creators: Kevin Williamson and Julie Plec. Outerbanks Entertainment/Alloy Entertainment/CBS/Warner Brothers. CW Channel. Based on an adolescent novel series by L. J Smith, the series pits two brothers against each other in a high school context. One, Stephan, is a vegetarian (in the sense that he won't feed on humans) and scrupulous; the other, Damon, is not, and so is stronger. Stephan is in love with a high school girl, Elena, who resembles his long-dead lover.

The Twilight Saga: New Moon (2009). Dir. Chris Weitz. With Kristen Stewart, Robert Pattinson, and Taylor Lautner. Summit Entertainment. This sequel follows the book.

The Twilight Saga: Eclipse (2010). Dir. David Slade. With Kristen Stewart, Robert Pattinson, and Taylor Lautner. Summit Entertainment. Close to the written text, as far as the plot goes.

Let Me In (2010). Dir. Matt Reeves. With Kodi Smit-McFee and Chloe Grace Moretz. EFTI/Hammer Films. This is an English-language remake of the Swedish film *Lat den Ratte Komme In* (*Let the Right One In*, 2008—see above), about a bullied teenage boy and his vampire friend. Very faithful adaptation of the original, but set in Los Alamos, New Mexico.

Vampires Suck (2010). Dirs. Jason Freidberg and Aaron Seltzer. With Jenn Proske, Matt Lander, and Deidrich Bader. Regency Enterprises/ Twentieth Century Fox. A weak parody of the Twilight films, with an occasional reference to other cinematic vampires.

The Twilight Saga: Breaking Dawn, Part 1 (2011). Dir. Bill Condon. With Kristen Stewart, Robert Pattinson, and Taylor Lautner. Summit Entertainment. As in the Harry Potter series, the studio decided to get two films out of the last book in the series. It is still faithful to the story as written.

Underworld: Awakening (2012). Dir. Mans Marlind and Bjorn Stein. Filmed in 3D. With Kate Beckinsale and Sandrine Holt. Screen Gems. The fourth installment in the Underworld Series, this takes place after *Underworld: Evolution* (2006). Previous events have led to an outing of vampires and Lycans, and a widespread human attempt to eliminate both groups. Selene (Beckinsale) is awakened after 12 years in suspended animation, escapes, and attempts to reunite the few surviving vampires and hybrids.

Bibliography

Abbott, Stacey. " 'A Little Less Ritual and a Little More Fun': The Modern Vampire in *Buffy the Vampire Slayer.*" *Slayage* 1.3. Online International Journal of Buffy Studies. June 2001. Web. 21 August 2011.

Alcott, Louisa May and Lynn Messina. *Little Vampire Women.* New York: HarperTeen, 2010. Print.

Alexie, Sherman. "Why the Best Kid's Books Are Written in Blood." *Wall Street Journal.* 9 June 2011. www.wallstreetjournal.com. Web. 20 April 2011.

Altman, Rick. *Film/Genre.* London: British Film Institute, 1999. Print.

Aubry, Kim, Prod. and Dir. *The Blood Is the Life—The Making of Dracula.* Zoetrope Aubry Productions. Sony Pictures, 2006. DVD.

Aubry, Kim, Prod. and Dir. *In-Camera—The Naïve Visual Effects of Dracula.* Zoetrope Aubry Productions. Sony Pictures, 2006. DVD.

Auerbach, Nina. *Our Vampires, Ourselves.* Chicago: University of Chicago Press, 1995. Print.

Ball, Alan. *True Blood.* "Audio Commentary" to Season 1, Episode 1. "Strange Love." Home Box Office, 2009. DVD.

Barber, Paul. *Vampires, Burial and Death: Folklore and Reality.* New Haven, Connecticut: Yale University Press, 2010.

Bell, Michael. *Food for the Dead: On the Trail of New England's Vampires.* New York: Carroll & Graf, 2001. Print.

Benefiel, Candace. "Blood Relations: The Gothic Perversion of the Nuclear Family in Anne Rice's *Interview with the Vampire.*" *Journal of Popular Culture* 38.2 (2004): 261–273.

Boorstin, Daniel Joseph (1961). *The Image: A Guide to Pseudo-Events in America.* New York: Vintage, 1992. Print.

Borde, Raymond and Etienne Chaumeton (1955). *A Panorama of American Film Noir, 1941–1953.* Trans. Paul Hammond. San Francisco: City Lights Books, 2002. Print.

Bronte, Charlotte and Sherri Browning Erwin. *Jane Slayre.* New York: Gallery Books, 2010. Print.

Butler, Octavia. *Fledgling*. New York: Seven Stories Press, 2005. Print.

Canby, Vincent. "Coppola's Dizzying Vision of Dracula." Review of *Bram Stoker's Dracula*. *New York Times*. Web. nytimes.com. 13 November 1992. Web. 22 August 2011.

Carroll, Noel. "Horror and Humor." *Journal of Aesthetics and Art Criticism* 57.2 (1999): 145–160. Print.

Castle, Gregory. "Ambivalence and Ascendancy in Bram Stoker's *Dracula*." *Dracula*. Ed. J. P. Riquelme. 518–537. Print.

Dadey, Debbie and Marcia Thornton Jones. *Vampires Don't Wear Polka Dots*. The Adventures of the Bailey School Kids Series. Illustrated by John Steven Gurney. New York: Scholastic, 1990. Print.

Davis, Blair. "Horror Meets Noir: The Evolution of Cinematic Style, 1931–1958." *Horror Film: Creating and Marketing Fear*. Ed. Steffen Hantke. Jackson: University Press of Mississippi, 2004. 191–212. Print.

Deresiewicz, William. "The End of Solitude." *The Chronicle of Higher Education* 55.21 (2009). *Academic OneFile*. Web. 18 Aug. 2011.

Dijkstra, Bram. *Evil Sisters: The Threat of Female Sexuality and the Cult of Manhood*. New York: Knopf, 1996. Print.

Du Bois, W.E.B. *Souls of Black Folk* (1904). Ed. David W. Blight and Robert Gooding Williams. New York: Bedford, 1997. Print.

Ebert, Roger. "Bram Stoker's Dracula." Review. *Chicago Sun-Times*. 13 November 1992. Rogerebert.com. Web. 20 March 2010.

Ellis, Bill. "The Highgate Cemetery Vampire Hunt: The Anglo-American Connection in Satanic Cult Lore." *Folklore* 103 (1993): 13–39. Print.

Folley, Samuel. *Vampireology: The True History of the Fallen Ones*. Somerville, MA: Candlewick Press, 2010. Print.

"Flesh & Blood: How HBO series has turned hot vampires into gay rights analogy." *New York Post*. 23 June 2009. Web. 24 August 2011.

Freeman, Mary Wilkins. "Louella Miller." *Vampires: Encounters with the Undead*. Ed. David J. Skal. New York: Black Dog and Leventhal, 2001. 261–271. Print.

Freud, Sigmund. "The Uncanny." Trans. James Strachey. *The Standard Edition*, vol. XVII. London: Hogarth Press, 1955. 217–256. Print.

Frye, Northrop. *Anatomy of Criticism*. Princeton, NJ: Princeton University Press, 1957. Print.

Gates, R. Ruggles. "Heredity and Eugenics," *Eugenics Review* 12 (1) April 1920. Available: http://www.ncbi.nlm.nih.gov/pmc/issues/190027/. Web. 27 June 2011.

Gelder, Ken. *Reading the Vampire*. New York: Routledge, 1994. Print.

Gitlin, Todd. *Media Unlimited, Revised Edition: How the Torrent of Images and Sounds Overwhelms Our Lives*. New York: Picador, 2007. Print.

Gordon, Joan and Veronica Hollinger, Eds. *Blood Read: The Vampire as Metaphor in Contemporary Culture*. Philadelphia: University of Pennsylvania Press, 1997. Print.

Grigoriadis, Vanessa. "The Joy of Vampire Sex." *Rolling Stone* 1112 (2010): 54–59. Print.

Gunn, Bill. "To Be a Black Artist." Letter. *New York Times.*13 May 1973: 7, 30. nyt.com. Web. 15 August 2011.

Gurdon, Meghan Cox. "Darkness Too Visible." *The Wall Street Journal.* Bookshelf section. 4 June 2011.www.wallstreetjournal.com. Web. 20 April 2012.

Hallab, Mary Y. *Vampire God: The Allure of the Undead in Western Culture.* Albany, NY: State University of New York Press, 2009. Print.

Haraway, Donna. "Race: Universal Donors in a Vampire Culture. It's All in the Family: Biological Kinship Categories in the Twentieth Century United States." *The Haraway Reader.* Ed. Donna Haraway. New York: Routledge, 2004. 251–293. Print.

Heffernan, Kevin. *Ghouls, Gimmicks, and Gold: Horror Films and the American Movie Business, 1953–1968.* Durham, NC: Duke University Press, 2004. Print.

Howe, James. *The Celery Stalks at Midnight.* Illustrated by Leslie H. Morrill. New York: Atheneum Books for Young Readers, 1983. Print.

Howe, James and Deborah Howe. *Bunnicula: A Rabbit-Tale of Mystery.* Illustrated by Alan Daniel. New York: Aladdin Paperbacks, 1979. Print.

Howe, James. *Bunnicula Meets Edgar Allan Crow.* Illustrated by Eric Fortune. New York: Atheneum Books for Young Readers, 2006. Print.

James, Henry. *The Altar of the Dead; The Beast in the Jungle; The Birthplace, and Other Tales.* London: Macmillan, 1992.

Jaynes, Julian. *The Origin of Consciousness in the Breakdown of the Bicameral Mind* (1976). New York: Mariner Books, 2000. Print.

Johnson, James Weldon. "The White Witch." *The Book of American Negro Poetry.* Ed. James Weldon Johnson. New York: Harcourt, Brace, 1922. 42. Print.

Jordan, John J. "Vampire Cyborgs and Scientific Imperialism: A Reading of the Science-Mysticism Polemic in *Blade.*" *Journal of Popular Film & Television* 27 (1999): 5–15. Print.

Keyes, Ralph. *The Quote Verifier: Who Said What, Where, and When.* New York: St. Martin's Griffin, 2006. 288. Print.

King, Stephen. *Danse Macabre.* New York: Berkley Books, 1981. Print.

King, Stephen. *Salem's Lot.* New York: Pocket Books, 1975. Print.

Kipling, Rudyard. "The Vampire." *The Works of Rudyard Kipling.* Teddington, UK: Echo Library, 2008. Print.

Kirsh, Steven J. "Cartoon Violence and Aggression in Youth." *Aggression and Violent Behavior* 11 (2006): 546–557. Print.

Kleinhans, Chuck. "Taking Out the Trash." *The Politics and Poetics of Camp.* Ed. Moe Meyer. New York: Routledge, 1994. 161–162. Print.

Kramer, Heinrich and James Sprenger. *Malleus Maleficarum.* Trans. Montague Summers. New York: Dover, 1971. Print.

Leatherdale, Clive. *Dracula: The Novel and the Legend.* Westcliff-on-Sea, UK: Desert Island Books, 2001. Print.

Leiber, Fritz. "The Girl with the Hungry Eyes." *Vampires: Encounters with the Undead.* Ed. David Skal. New York: Black Dog and Leventhal, 2001. 417–428. Print.

Lovecraft, H. P. "Supernatural Horror in Literature." Included in *At The Mountains of Madness.* New York: Modern Library, 2005. Print.

Lovecraft, H. P. "The Hound" (Originally published February 1924 in *Weird Tales*, Vol. 3, No. 2, p. 50–52, 78). *The Call of Cthulhu and Other Stories.* Ed. William Roberts. New York: Penguin, 2005. 81–88. Print.

Lubar, David. *Attack of the Vampire Weenies and Other Warped and Creepy Tales.* New York: Starscape/Tom Doherty Associates, 2011. Print.

LW. *The Vegan Body Project. Post:* 2/27/2011. http://veganbodyproject. blogspot.com/2011/02/vegan-and-vegetarian-vampires.html. Web. 20 August 2011.

Marchesani, Laura. *Dick and Jane and Vampires.* New York: Grosset & Dunlop, 2010. Print.

Marling, William. *The Detective Novel: An Overview.* Available: detnovel.com. 4 December 2009. Web. 27 June 2011.

Marx, Karl. *Capital: A Critique of Political Economy.* Volume 1. (1867) Trans. Ben Fowkes. New York: Penguin, 1976. Print.

Maslin, Janet. "*Interview with the Vampire*: Rapture and Terror, Bound By Blood." *New York Times.* nytimes.com. 11 November 1994. Web. 22 August 2011.

Matheson, Richard. *I Am Legend* (1954). New York: Orb, 1995. Print.

McNally, Raymond T. and Radu Florescu. *In Search of Dracula: The History of Dracula and Vampires.* Boston: Houghton Mifflin, 1994. Print.

Menand, Louis. *The Metaphysical Club: A Story of Ideas in America.* New York: Farrar, Straus, and Giroux, 2001. Print.

Mercer, Sienna. *Switched.* My Sister the Vampire Series # 1. New York: Harper Trophy, 2007. Print.

Miéville, China. "Introduction. H.P. Lovecraft." *At The Mountains of Madness.* Ed. China Miéville. New York: Modern Library, 2005: v-vii. Print.

Miller, Elizabeth. *Dracula's Homepage.* "Historiae Personae" from Stoker's notes for Dracula. Web. Available: http://www.ucs.mun.ca/~emiller/ NotesDescrip. htm. 2005. Web. 21 February 2011.

Miller, Jeffrey S. *The Horror Spoofs of Abbott and Costello: A Critical Assessment of the Comedy Team's Monster Films.* Jefferson, NC: McFarland and Company, 2000. Print.

Milner, Murray, Jr. "Celebrity Culture as a Status System." *The Hedgehog Review* 7.1(2005): 66+. *Academic OneFile.* Web. 18 August 2011.

Mitchell, Joni. "Sex Kills." *Dog Eat Dog.* Atlantic Records, 1988. Audio CD.

Moretti, Franco. *Signs Taken for Wonders* (1983). New York: Verso, 1988. Print.

Newland, Paul. "The Grateful Un-Dead: Count Dracula and the Transnational Counterculture in *Dracula A.D. 1972.*" *Draculas, Vampires, and Other Undead Forms: Essays on Gender, Race, and Culture.* Ed. John Edgar Browning and Joan (Kay) Picart. Lanthan, MD: The Scarecrow Press, 2009. 135–151. Print.

Paul, William. *Laughing Screaming: Modern Hollywood Horror and Comedy.* New York: Columbia Unversity Press, 1994. Print.

Petty, Tom. "Free Fallin'." *Full Moon Fever.* MCA Records, 1989. Audio CD.

Pinkwater, Daniel. *The Werewolf Club Meets Dorkula.* Werewolf Club Series #3. Illustrated by Jill Pinkwater. New York: Aladdin Paperbacks, 2001. Print.

Penzler, Otto. *The Best American Noir of the Century.* Ed. James Elroy and Otto Penzler. Boston: Houghton Mifflin Harcourt, 2010. Print.

Ramsland, Katherine. *The Science of Vampires.* New York: Berkley Boulevard Books, 2002. Print.

Reed, Gary and Becky Cloonan. *Bram Stoker's Dracula: The Graphic Novel.* New York: Puffin, 2006. Print.

Rice, Anne. *Anne Rice website.* www.annerice.com. Web. 19 August 2011. Rice, Anne. *Interview With the Vampire.* New York: Knopf, 1976. Print.

Rice, Anne. *The Vampire Lestat.* New York: Knopf, 1984. Print.

Roosevelt, Theodore. *Letters and Speeches.* New York: Library of America, 2007. Print.

Roszak, Theodore. *The Making of a Counter-Culture.* Berkeley: University of California Press, 1968. Print.

Roszak, Theodore. *Where the Wasteland Ends.* New York: Bantam, 1972. Print.

Scroggs, Kirk. *Dracula vs. Grampa at the Monster Truck Spectacular.* New York: Little, Brown Books for Young Readers, 2006. Print.

Silver, Alain and James Ursini. *The Vampire Film: From Nosferatu to Bram Stoker's Dracula.* Revised Edn. New York: Limelight Editons, 1993. Print.

Silver, Anna. "Twilight" Is Not Good for Maidens: Gender, Sexuality, and the Family in Stephenie Meyer's *Twilight* Series." *Studies in the Novel* 42.1/2 (2010): 121–138. Academic Search Premier. Web. 20 Nov. 2011.

Skal, David, Ed. *Vampires: Encounters with the Undead.* New York: Black Dog and Leventhal, 2001. Print.

Skal, David. *Hollywood Gothic: The Tangled Web of Dracula From Novel to Stage to Screen.* New York: Faber & Faber, 2004. Print.

Skal, David. *Romancing the Vampire: From Past to Present.* Atlanta, Georgia: Whitman Publishing, 2009. Print.

Skal, David. *The Monster Show: A Cultural History of Horror* (1993). Rev Edn. New York: Faber & Faber, 2010. Print.

Skal, David and Elias Savada. *Dark Carnival: The Secret World of Tod Browning.* New York: Doubleday Anchor, 1995. Print.

Sontag, Susan. "Notes on 'Camp.'" (1964). *Camp: Queer Aesthetics and the Performing Subject: A Reader.* Ed. Fabio Cleto. Ann Arbor, MI: University of Michigan Press, 1999. 53–65. Print.

Spadoni, Robert. *Uncanny Bodies: The Coming of Sound Films and the Origins or the Horror Genre.* Berkeley: University of California Press, 2007. Print.

Stine, R.L. *Vampire Breath.* Goosebumps Series. New York: Scholastic, 1996. Print.

Stoker, Bram. *Dracula* (1897). Ed. John Paul Riquelme. New York: Bedford Case Studies in Contemporary Criticism, 2002. Print.

Stoker, Bram. *Personal Reminiscences of Henry Irving.* 2 Vols. (London: Heinenan, 1906). Westport, CT: Greenwood, 1970. Print.

Telotte, J.P. *Voices in the Dark: The Narrative Patterns of Film Noir.* Urbana: University of Illinois Press, 1989. Print.

Tracy, Kathleen. *The Girl's Got Bite: An Unofficial Guide to Buffy's World.* Los Angeles, CA: Renaissance Books, 1998. Print.

Twitchell, James. *The Living Dead: A Study of the Vampire in Romantic Literature.* Durham, NC: Duke University Press, 1981. Print.

Walpole, Horace. Introduction to *The Castle of Otranto.* In *The Castle of Otranto, by Horace Walpole. Vathek, by William Beckford. The Vampyre, by John Polidori. Three Gothic novels, and a fragment of a novel by Lord Byron.* Ed. E.F. Bleiler. New York, Dover: 1966. Print.

Warren, Louis. "Buffalo Bill Meets Dracula: William F. Cody, Bram Stoker, and the Borders of Racial Decay." *The American Historical Review* 107.4 (2002): 1124–1157. Print.

Whedon, Joss. DVD Commentary to "Innocence." *Buffy The Vampire Slayer, Season 1.* WB Television, 2006.

Wilcox, Rhonda V. "'There Will Never Be a 'Very Special' Buffy." *Journal of Popular Film & Television* 2 (1999): 16-23. Print.

Wilkinson, Emily Colette. "Ethical Vampires, Part I: April 9, 2010; Ethical Vampires, Part II: April 14, 2010." *The Millions.* Online journal. Available: http://www.themillions.com/2010/ 04/ethical-vampires-part-i.html. Web. 18 August 2011.

Williamson, Milly. *The Lure of the Vampire: Gender, Fiction and Fandom from Bram Stoker to Buffy the Vampire Slayer.* New York: Wallflower Press, 2005. Print.

Index

Abbott and Costello Meet Dr. Jekyll and Mr. Hyde, 136
Abbott and Costello Meet Frankenstein, 46, 65, 132–38
Abbott and Costello Meet the Invisible Man, 136
Abbott and Costello Meet the Killer, Boris Karloff, 136
Abbott and Costello Meet the Mummy, 136
Absolutely True Diary of a Part-Time Indian, 119–20
The Addams Family, 110–11, 136, 141, 150
"The Adventures of Itchy and Scratchy," 109
Afrocentric vampire tale, 73–74
"After-school specials," programs, 107
Alienation, 51
Altman, Rick, 131
American Amateur Press Association, 34
Andy Warhol's Dracula, 67
Angel, 132
The Archie Show, 109
Art of black-and-white film-making, 46

Attack of the Vampire Weenies, 107, 117–18
Auerbach, Nina, 3, 4, 56, 87, 92

Bakjwi, 147
Batman, 64–65
Bell, Michael, 17
Benefiel, Candace, 77
Biological plague model of vampirism, 53
Birth of a Nation, 28
Black Power nationalists, 69
Black vampires: Afrocentric vampire tale, 73–74; Blacula figure, 71–72; Blaxploitation, 69; (reversal of roles in, 71); imagery from vigilante terror practices, 70–71; racism and white culture traditions, 69; racist stereotypes, 74; science fiction with racial issues, 76; semi-vampirism, 75; vegetarian vampires, 76; whiteness, academic work in, 70; witch/vampire figure as white, 71
Blacula, 67, 70, 71–73, 137
Blade: comic book–based technothrillers, 96; series, 96, 142; trilogy, 75, 144

"Blaxploitation," 69

Blood and pulp: cosmic horror, Lovecraft's, 37–39; Cowboy stories, 34; Eugenics movement, 35; fear of gender difference, 37; genetic experiments of Mendel, 35; "Jukes," 36; literary writers in pulp, 34; Lovecraft, Howard Phillips, 33; Oedipus complex (Freud), 34–35; pulp fiction, 33; "pulps," 34; racial swarming, 36; sociological scholarly narratives, 36

Blood consumers: *Blade* films, comic book–based technothrillers, 96; *Fright Night*, 88–89; *The Hunger*, 87–88; *Lost Boys*, 89–91; revival of the vampire in 1980s, 87; sensitive vampire, 94; *Terminator* films, 97; vampire as a metaphor, 97–98

Blood Couple, 73

Blood Read, 1–3

Bordello of Blood, 141

Boss Nigger, 70

Bram Stoker's Dracula, 66, 93

Brides of Dracula, 57, 60

Browning, Tod, 5, 33, 41–47, 59, 65, 111, 139–40

Buck Privates, 135

Buffy rules: *Buffy the Vampire Slayer* series, 99; (characters and their lives, 100); us-versus-them oppositions, 103; vampire, hierarchy, 100; vampires, characteristics, 100

Buffy series, 6–7, 105

Buffy the Vampire Slayer, 99, 101, 109, 117, 132, 140, 142–44

Bunnicula, 111–14

Bunnicula Meets Edgar Allan Crow, 112

The Cabinet of Dr. Caligari, 41

Cabin in the Woods, 109

Carmilla, 3, 57

Cartoon: programming on television, 108; violence, 109–10

"Celebrification," 83–84

Celebrity biographies, 82

Children, vampires for, 107–20; *Attack of the Vampire Weenies*, 117–18; *Buffy the Vampire Slayer*, 117; *Bunnicula*, 111, 113; *Bunnicula Meets Edgar Allan Crow*, 112; cartoon programming on television, 108; cartoon violence, 109–10; Chester and Harold, 112; *Dick and Jane and Vampires*, 115; *Dracula vs. Grampa at the Monster Truck Spectacular*, 115–16; *At First Bite*, 116–17; *FleshCrawlers* series, 112–13; *Goosebumps* series, 114; Harry Potter phenomenon, 116; horror for children, 120; horror into comedy, 110; Monroes, 112; monsters, 111; scary settings, 110–11; *Scooby Doo, Where Are You?*, 109; self-aware *Scream* films, 109–10; *The Simpsons*, 109; Sonnicula, 113; "The Adventures of Itchy and Scratchy," 109; *Vampire Breath*, 114–15; *Vampireology: The True History of the Fallen Ones*, 118; *Vampires Don't Wear Polka Dots*, 113–14; version of Dracula, 110; *The Werewolf Club Meets Dorkula*, 113; Young Adult, YA, 118–19

Christian religious orthodoxy, 62

Civil Rights movement, 69

Classic horror: art of black-and-white film-making, 46; conflict between social classes, 44; Hollywood adaptations, 42; homosexuality, 47; Jazz Age, 44; lesbian interpretation, 47; "medium sensitivity," 43; Motion Picture Code, 44; New Deal, 44–45; *Nosferatu*,

41–42; production values, 46; suspense, 42; transition to sound, 43
Coffy, 70
Comedy, vampire, 131–42; *Abbott and Costello Meet Frankenstein,* 132–33; *Bordello of Blood,* 141; *Buffy the Vampire Slayer,* 132, 140; chaos and violence, 133; comic treatments, 141–42; decline in horror comedies, 141; *Dracula: Dead and Loving It,* 141; *From Dusk till Dawn,* 141; evolution of the vampire figure, 141–42; fairly nasty vampires, 140; *Fearless Vampire Killers,* 136–37; film noir and horror, 132–33; genres (subgenres), 131–32; Hammer style, 137; horror and fear, 132, 134–35, 138; idea of grotesque (Mikhail Bakhtin), 133–34; influence of Abbott and Costello films, 136–37; *Innocent Blood,* 139; *Laughing Screaming: Modern Hollywood Horror and Comedy* (1994), 133; legacy of the Frankenstein films, 140–41; literary genre critic Northrop Frye, 133; *Love at First Bite,* 138; *My Best Friend is a Vampire,* 139; Salvadore "The Shark" Macelli (Robert Loggia), 139; sexual and scatological jokes, 134; social commentary over horror, 138; success of Mel Brooks's *Young Frankenstein,* 137–38; *Tales from the Crypt* series, 141; television comedies, 136; tradition of, 132; Universal monster movies, 134–35, 138; *Vampira (Old Dracula),* 137–38; *Vampire in Brooklyn* (Wes Craven's), 132; wedding or public ceremonial ritual, 133; zombies, 141
Comic book–based technothrillers, 96

Comic treatments, 141–42
Conservative, family-oriented messages, 59
Cosmic horror (Lovecraft), 37–39
Countering vampire culture: comforting figure in 1970s, 67; dilemmas faced by televised vampires, 66; domestication of the vampire figure, 65; funny monsters, 65; mass-media audience and camp, 63; 1960s eclecticism, 66; 1960s fashions, 63; short subjects and cartoons, 63; soap operas, 67; subcultural materials and styles, 63
Cowboy stories, 34
Cult-associated activities, 60

Dark Carnival, 5
Dark Changeling, 7
Dark Prince: The Untold Story of Dracula, 103–5
Dark Shadows, 66–67, 72, 99, 107
Degeneration, 10–11, 15, 30, 32
Dick and Jane and Vampires, 115
Different Blood: The Vampire as Alien, 7
Dijkstra, Bram, 27
Dracula A. D. 1972, 57
Dracula (British play), 2, 17; Browning's, 41–47, 65; end of, 3; first in Universal's series of classic horror films, 46; German version, 28; influence of, 25; Lee's, 58, 60–61; Lugosi's, 3, 42, 65, 67, 110; Spanish-language version, 147; Stoker's, 2–3, 5, 7, 9–10, 18–19, 27, 41, 60, 66, 93, 112, 118; success of, 5; vampire capital, 4; Van Helsing, 44
Dracula: Dead and Loving It, 140–42
Dracula Has Risen from the Grave, 57

Dracula: Prince of Darkness, 57
Dracula's American: Anglo-Saxon
  race, 14–15; Band of Light, group
  of vampire fighters, 10; charac-
  teristic of Ascendency writers,
  11; Irish issues, 11–12; literary
  criticism, 10; Mina's comments,
  11; Morris: (character of, 13–14;
  incompetence of, 15)
Dracula's Daughter, 46, 66
Dracula's Dog, 67
Dracula Sucks, 67
*Dracula: The Vampire and the
  Critics,* 2
*Dracula vs. Grampa at the Monster
  Truck Spectacular,* 115–16
Dreams, 50

Early new world vampires: female-
  centered lives and communities,
  23; in fictional accounts, 20–23;
  folklore vampire of New England,
  26; folkloric and the literary, combination of, 25; "Louella Miller,"
  (story), 23–24; New England vampire, 18; regionalist writers, 23;
  skeptical perspective, 20; superstition (or magic) and medicine, 19;
  vampire- related events or practices across New England, 19
Ethan Frome, 25
Eugenics movement, 35
Evangelical fanatics, 125

Fearless Vampire Killers, 136–37
Film noir, 50
At First Bite, 116–17
Fledgling, 75–76
FleshCrawlers series, 112–13
Folklore vampire of New England,
  26
Food for the Dead, 17
A Fool There Was, 28–31, 70
Frankenstein, 41, 46, 65, 67

Frankenstein Meets the Wolf Man,
  46, 134
Frankenstein monster, 65, 109,
  134–35
Freaks, 5, 46
Freud, Sigmund, 4, 34–35, 43–44,
  50, 58
Fright Night, 88–89
*From Demons to Dracula: The
  Creation of the Modern Vampire
  Myth,* 7
From Dusk till Dawn, 95, 141
Frye, Northrop, 133

"A Gaggle of Galloping Ghosts," 109
Ganja and Hess, 70, 73
Gelder, Ken, 57
Genetic experiments of Mendel, 35
Genres, 49; mixing, 143–44
*The Girl's Got Bite: An Unofficial
  Guide to Buffy's World,* 100
Girl with the Hungry Eyes, 49,
  52–53
"The Girl with the Hungry Eyes,"
  (Fritz Leiber's story), 52–53
A Glimpse of America, 13
"GOD HATES FANGS," 123
Goosebumps series, 113–14
Gordon, Joan, 1–2
Great Depression, 42, 44

Hallab, Mary *(Vampire God),* 8,
  121
Halloween, 84, 109, 111
Hammer horror films, 57; opening
  sequences, 58; signature style of
  Hammer studio, 57–58; simplicity
  of the Hammer formula, 62
Harry Potter phenomenon, 116
The Historian, 146
History of Consciousness program,
  80
Hollinger, Veronica, 1, 2
Hollywood adaptations, 42

Hollywood Gothic, 5
Hollywood, vamps in: conventional histories in early films, 28; early cinema, 27; female vampires or vamps, 28; (Dijkstra's study, 28–32); female vampirism, 30–31; sexuality, 31
Homosexuality, 47
Horror, 132, 138; for children, 120; into comedy, 110
"Horror and Humor," 134
The Hound (tales), 37–39
House of Dracula (1945), 46, 134
House of Frankenstein, 46, 134
Hunchback, 138
The Hunger, 87–88

I Am Legend, 49, 53–55, 146
Innocent Blood, 139
Interview with the Vampire, 77, 81–82, 84, 93, 95
Investigation plots, 51
The Invisible Man, 46, 136–37

Jazz Age, 44
"Jukes," 36

Kiss of the Vampire, 61
Ku Klux Klan regalia, 123–24

The Last Man on Earth, 55
Lat den Ratte Komme In, 146
Laughing Screaming: Modern Hollywood Horror and Comedy, 133
Legend of the Seven Golden Vampires, 62
Lesbian interpretation, 47
Let Me In, 147
Little Caesar, 44
The Living Dead, 6
London after Midnight, 5, 43, 46, 150
The Lost Boys, 3, 89–91
"Louella Miller," (story), 23–24

Love at First Bite, 138, 141
Lovecraft, H. P., 33
Lubar, David, 107
Lure of the Vampire, 6
Lust of a Vampire, 57

The Making of a Counter-Culture, 79
Malleus Maleficarum, 1
Mandingo, 70
Mark of the Vampire, 46, 111
Medical thriller, 146
"Medium sensitivity," 43
Monsters, 6, 41, 46, 58, 65, 77, 87, 99–100, 102, 107, 109, 111, 118, 120, 124, 132, 134–36
The Monster Show, 4–5
Morrison, Toni, 69
Motion Picture Code, 44
The Mummy, 46
The Munsters, 65, 110–11, 136, 141
Murphy, Eddie, 74–75, 132–33
My Best Friend Is a Vampire, 139, 142
My Sister the Vampire series, 116

Near Dark, 3, 91–92
New Deal, 44–45
New England vampire, 18
Night of the Living Dead, 62
Noir-inflected stories, 56
Nosferatu, 5, 28, 41–42
Nosferatu the Vampyre, 28

Oedipus complex (Freud), 34–35
"Old dark house comedies," 135
Old Dracula, 67, 74, 137, 141
The Omega Man, 55
The Origin of Consciousness in the Breakdown of the Bicameral Mind, 80

Our Vampires, Ourselves, 3
Outside the Law, 43

Panorama of American Film Noir, 50
The Passage, 146
PBS (Public Broadcasting System), 107, 110
Penzler, Otto, 49
Personal Reminiscences of Henry Irving, 13
Popeye, 108
Professor Van Helsing, 9
Psycho, 62
"Pulps," 34

Racial swarming, 36
Reading the Vampire, 4
Regionalist writers, 23
Rice, Anne, works of, 77–85
Road Runner series, 108
Romancing the Vampire: From Past to Present, 5–6
Rosemary's Baby, 62, 137

Salem's Lot, 77–79; drug experience, 79; focus on vampire *consciousness,* 80; trio of vampires, 77–78
Salvadore "The Shark" Macelli (Robert Loggia), 139
The Satanic Rites of Dracula, 57, 60–61
Scars of Dracula, 57
Scholarship, vampire: American culture's fascination with horror, 5; ESP and hypnotism, 8; European folk beliefs, 2; features of vampires in books, 3; forensic crime procedural on television, 7; physical, sexual, and behavioral symptoms, 8; religion, 8; Romantic and Victorian sources, 2; vampire as mythic figures of the Romantic

era, 6; vampires as aliens, 7; vampire texts with specific locales, 4
Science-fiction threats, 58
The Science of Vampires, 7, 146
Scooby Doo, Where Are You?, 109
Scrapbook-style picture book, 5
Scream, Blacula, Scream, 70, 73, 137
The Seduction of the Innocent, 65
Self-aware *Scream* films, 109–10
Semi-vampirism, 75
Sensitive vampire, 94
Serialization, 143
Sesame Street show, 110
Shadow of the Vampire, 28
Shaft, 70
Shape-shifters, 124–26, 128, 144
Shaun of the Dead, 141
The Shock Doctrine, 123
Signs Taken for Wonders, 4
Silent era, 41–43, 50
The Simpsons, 109
Sincerity/authenticity/connectivity, 82–83
Skeptical perspective, 20
Sociological scholarly narratives, 36
Sonnicula, 113
Souls of Black Folk, 72
Southern Vampire Series (Harris), 128
Stan Helsing, 141
The Strain, 144–45
Summer, 25
Superstition (or magic) and medicine, 19
Surprise, 146–47
Suspense, 42
Sweet Sweetback's Baadasssss Song, 70

Tales from the Crypt series, 141
Taste the Blood of Dracula, 57, 61
Teen melodrama, 121–29; "GOD HATES FANGS," 123; Harris's *Southern Vampire Series* novels,

128; in-your-face black characters, 124; KKK regalia, 124; post-modern era in fiction, 121–22; tradition of Southern fiction, 124; *True Blood* series, 122–23; *True Blood*'s vampires, 126–27; *Twilight* novels and films, 125, 127–28; *Twilight* saga (vampire lite series of novels and films), 121; vampire as a superhero or romantic lead, 122

Terminator films, 97

Theatrical Touring Party, 13

Tom and Jerry, 108

True Blood series, 121–28, 142–44, 147

Twilight, 119, 125, 127–28, 141–42, 147

Twilight saga, 121, 143

Twins of Evil, 57

"The Uncanny" (Freud's essay), 4, 35, 44

Underworld series, 142

The Unholy Three, 5, 43

United Amateur Press Association, 34

The Unknown, 43

Uptown Saturday Night, 70

Urban legends: alienation, 51; 'ambivalent,' 51; biological plague model of vampirism, 53; 'cruel,' 51; dreams, 50; 'erotic,' 51; *film noir*, 50; genres, 49; "The Girl with the Hungry Eyes," (Fritz Leiber's story), 52–53; *I Am Legend* (Matheson), 53–55; investigation plots, 51; noir-inflected stories, 56; 'oneiric,' 50; 'strange,' 51

Vamp, 74, 139

Vampira (Old Dracula), 67, 111, 137–38

Vampire as a metaphor, 97–98

The Vampire as Metaphor in Contemporary Culture, 2

Vampire Breath, 114–15

Vampire celebrities: "celebrification," 83–84; celebrity biographies, 82; *Interview with the Vampire*, 81–82; Rice, Anne, works of, 77–85; *Salem's Lot*, 77–79; "drug experience, 79; focus on vampire *consciousness*, 80; trio of vampires, 77–78"; *sincerity/authenticity/connectivity*, 82–83

The Vampire Diaries, 119, 122, 143

The Vampire Film, 67

Vampire Forensics, 8

The Vampire God, 8, 121

Vampire in Brooklyn, 74, 132, 142

The Vampire in Europe, 1

The Vampire Lestat, 81

Vampire Lovers, 57

Vampireology: The True History of the Fallen Ones, 118

Vampires, Burial and Death, 19

Vampires Don't Wear Polka Dots, 113–14

Vampire's Kiss, 92–93

Vampires Suck, 141

Vampires: Their Kith and Kin, 1

Van Helsing, 141

Varney the Vampire, 34, 47, 143

Vegetarian vampires, 76

Version of Dracula, 66, 110, 144

The Wall Street Journal, "Darkness Too Visible," 119

The War of the Worlds, 7

The Werewolf Club Meets Dorkula, 113

Wes Craven's *Vampire in Brooklyn*, 132

Whedon, Joss, 99
Where the Wasteland Ends, 79
Where the Wild Things Are,
  111
Wilson, Woodrow, 27–28
The Winning of the West, 14
Witch/vampire figure as white, 71
Wolf Man, 46, 134

Young Adult, YA, 118–19
Young Frankenstein, 67, 137, 141
Youth culture: threat of youth cults,
  61; and vampirism, 60; and youth
  cult connection, 60

Zombieland, 141
Zombies, 53, 122, 141, 145

About the Author

LOUIS H. PALMER is an Associate Professor in the English Department at Castleton State College in Castleton, VT. He holds a PhD from Syracuse University, Syracuse, NY, an MA from Appalachian State University in Boone, NC, an MEd from Converse College in Spartanbutg, SC, and a BA from Williams College in Williamstown, MA. He is Gothic Area Chair for the Popular Culture Association and a member of the editorial board of the *Journal of Popular Culture*. He has published articles on Southern and Appalachian literature and on William Faulkner. This is his first book.